Outsider in the House

To: Brian

Best Wish

Bernie Sanders

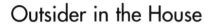

V

OUTSIDER IN THE HOUSE

Bernie Sanders
with Huck Gutman

VERSO
London · New York

The publishers wish to acknowledge the following photographers whose picturesappear in this book: Heather Driscoll, Graig Line, Glenn Russell, Toby Talbot, and Vyto Starinskas.

First published by Verso 1997
© Bernie Sanders 1997
All rights reserved

Verso
UK: 6 Meard Street, London W1V 3HR
USA: 180 Varick Street, New York, NY 10014

Verso is the imprint of New Left Books

ISBN: 1-85984-871-0

British Library Cataloguing in Publication Data
A catalogue record of this book is available from the British Library

U.S. Library of Congress Cataloguing-in-Publication Data
A catalogue record of this book is available from the Library of Congress

Design by POLLEN
Printed in the USA by R.R. Donnelley and Sons

For my Parents
Eli and Dorothy Sanders

Acknowledgments

I want to thank the people of Burlington, Vermont, and the people of the state of Vermont for their support over the years. In going outside of the two-party system and electing an Independent mayor for four terms, and an Independent congressman for four terms, you have done what no other community or state has done in modern American history.

Thank you very much for giving me the opportunity to serve.

Thank you, Jane. Without your love and support as my wife, much of what is described in this book would not have occurred.

Thank you, Levi. You have traveled the state with me to political meetings since you were a year old. Your love, loyalty, and friendship have always sustained me.

Thank you, Heather, Carina, and Dave. You have let me into your lives and, in doing that, have helped show me the meaning of family.

Thank you, Larry. As my older brother, you opened my eyes to a world of ideas that I otherwise would never have seen.

Thank you, Huck. Without your help and tenacity, this book would not have been written.

Thank you, Colin Robinson, for Verso's strong support for this project.

ACKNOWLEDGMENTS

No member of Congress achieves much without the support of a strong and dedicated staff. In that respect, I have been extremely fortunate in having so many wonderful and hard-working co-workers. The following people have served on my congressional staff since 1991, and I thank all of them for their efforts: Paul Anderson, Mark Anderson, Lisa Barrett, Dan Barry, Stacey Blue, Debbie Bookchin, Doug Boucher, Steve Bressler, Mike Brown, Katie Clarke, Greg Coburn, Mike Cohen, Steve Crowley, Clarence Davis, Jim DeFilippis, Don Edwards, Christine Eldred, Molly Farrell, Phil Fiermonte, John Franco, Mark Galligan, Liz Gibbs-West, Dennis Gilbert, Bill Goold, Huck Gutman, Theresa Hamilton, Katharine Hanley, Adlai Hardin, Millie Hollis, Lisa Jacobson, Carolyn Kazdin, Nichole LaBrecque, Megan Lambert, Rachel Levin, Sascha Mayer, Florence McCloud-Thomas, Ginny McGrath, Chris Miller, Elizabeth Mundinger, Laura O'Brien, Eric Olson, Kirsa Phillips, Anthony Pollina, Jim Rader, Tyler Resch, Mary Richards, Jane Sanders, Jim Schumacher, Brendan Smith, Tom Smith, Sarah Swider, Doug Taylor, Eleanor Thompson, Jeff Weaver, Cynthia Weglarz, David Weinstein, Ruthan Wirman, Whitney Wirman, Tina Wisell.

Huck Gutman wishes to thank his wife, Buff Lindau, for her unstinting love and her endlessly generous support. He also wishes to thank Bernie Sanders for showing Vermont, and the nation, what a progressive politics looks like when it works, successfully, in the real world.

Contents

Introduction

November 5, 1996. We won. Blowout. By 7:30 pm, only half an hour after the polls close, the Associated Press, based on exit polls, says that we will win, and win big.

The town-by-town election results are coming in by phone and over the radio. In Burlington, my home town where we always do well, we are running much stronger than usual. We even win the conservative ward in the new north end. We win Shelburne, a wealthy town usually not supportive. Winooski. Landslide. We win Essex, my opponent's home town. We're now getting calls in from the southern part of the state. Brattleboro. We're winning there almost three to one. Incredible. We're even winning in Rutland County, traditionally the most Republican county in the state. We're also winning in Bennington County, where I often lose.

By ten o'clock, Jane and I and the kids are down at Mona's restaurant where we're holding our election night gathering. The crowd is large and boisterous. When our victory celebration appears on the TV monitor, the crowd becomes very loud. I can hardly hear myself speak into the microphones. The noise is deafening. The next day the *Rutland Herald* describes my remarks as "vintage Sanders": "We know that there is something wrong in this country when you have one percent of the population owning more wealth than the bottom ninety percent." I said a few other things as well. I was very happy.

My Republican opponent, Susan Sweetser, calls to concede and we chat for a few minutes. She then goes on television to thank her supporters and wish me well. Jack Long, the Democratic candidate, drops by to offer congratulations.

The extent of our victory becomes clear the next morning when the newspapers publish the town-by-town, county-by-county breakdown of election results: 55 percent of the vote to Sanders, 32 percent to Sweetser, 9 percent to Long. We won in every county in the state and nearly every town. Who could have imagined it? An Independent victory—much less a sweep—is rare. So rare that when *USA Today* published the nationwide tallies for congressional races, the copy under Vermont read: "At Large—56%, Democrat Jack Long—9%, Republican Susan Sweetser—33%." Apparently, "Independent" is not a category in the paper's database.

The newspaper in front of me says that "Sanders is the longest-serving Independent ever elected to Congress, according to Garrison Nelson, a political science professor and an expert on Congressional history." Gary, who teaches at the University of Vermont, knows about these things. That's what he studies. Who would have believed it? Thank you, Vermont.

But this had been a tough race, far more difficult than the final election results indicate. Newt Gingrich and the House Republican Leadership had "targeted" this election, and spent a huge sum of money trying to defeat me. Some of the most powerful Republicans in the country came to Vermont to campaign for Sweetser, including Majority Leader Dick Armey, Republican national chairman Haley Barbour, presidential candidate Steve Forbes, House Budget chairman John Kasich, and Republican convention keynote speaker Susan Molinari. As chairman of the House Progressive Caucus, a democratic socialist, and a leading opponent of their "Contract with America," I've been a thorn in their side for some time. They wanted me out—badly.

My campaign was also targeted by corporate America. A group of major corporations organized by the U.S. Chamber of Commerce, the National Association of Manufacturers, and the National Federation of Independent Businesses put me at the top of their "hit list" and poured tens of thousands of dollars into the state to sponsor negative and dishonest TV ads, as well as a statewide mailing. By the end of the campaign Vermonters were watching four different TV ads attacking me.

The wealthiest people in Vermont went deep into their pockets for my Republican opponent. They wrote out dozens of $1,000 checks (the legal maximum) and attended $500-a-plate functions. We also took on the National Rifle Association (NRA), the National Right to Work Organization, and other right-wing and big money organizations. Never before had the ruling class of Vermont and the nation paid quite so much attention to a congressional race in the small state of Vermont—a state with just one representative.

By contrast, as an Independent, my campaign ran without the support or infrastructure of a major political party. There were no campaign contributions from our "central office" in Washington, no "coordinated campaigns" with other candidates, no photo-ops with a presidential candidate at the local headquarters, no votes from families with a long and proud record of commitment to our party's ideals. We had to fight for every vote that we got. And that's what we did.

We rose to the occasion and ran the best campaign that we had for many years—perhaps ever. Our coalition—of unions, women's organizations, environmental groups, senior citizens, and low-income people—had done a terrific job. We raised close to a million dollars, and over 20,000 individual contributions, distributed by hand over 100,000 pieces of literature, made tens of thousands of phone calls, and sent out over 130,000 pieces of mail. The campaign staff was fantastic, our volunteers dedicated—and it all came together on Election Day.

Obviously, this book is more than a manual on running a successful congressional campaign. It is a political biography. It talks about some of the victories that I and my co-workers in Vermont have had, but also about a lot of *unsuccessful* campaigns and derailed ventures. (Given the state of the left in America, how could it be otherwise?)

This is a book about hopes and dreams that will not be realized in our lifetimes. It is about the fragility of democracy in America, a nation in which the majority of people do not know the name of their congressional representative and over half the people no longer vote. It is about a political system in which a tiny elite dominates both parties—and much of what goes on in Washington—through financial largesse.

Here is a story of corporate greed and contempt for working people, of private agendas masquerading as the public good and corporate America's betrayal of workers in its drive for galactic profits. It describes a national media, owned by large corporations, which increasingly regards news as entertainment, insults the intelligence of American citizens daily, and is even further removed from the reality of everyday life than the average politician.

And Vermont. This is a book about the great state of Vermont—my favorite place in the world—and about our "big city" Burlington, with 40,000 people. It visits our small towns where most Vermonters live, and drops by our county fairs and our parades to look at the kind of special relationship that exists between people in this small state.

It is about my eight years as mayor of Burlington, and how the progressive movement there helped make that city one of the most exciting, democratic, and politically conscious cities in America. Yes! Democracy can work. It is about the United States Congress, the good members and the not so good. It examines the two major political parties—neither of which comes close to representing the needs of working people—and the frustrations and successes of helping to create an independent progressive political movement. It reviews some of the battles in which I've participated—for sane priorities in our federal budget, for a national health care system guaranteeing health care for all, for a trade policy that represents the needs of working people rather than multinational corporations, for an end to corporate welfare, and for the protection of programs which sustain the weakest and most vulnerable among us.

Most of all, this book is about the struggle to maintain a vision of economic and social justice, and the optimism necessary to keep that vision alive.

It goes without saying that I never would have become mayor of Burlington, Vermont, or a U.S. congressman without the help of dozens of close friends and co-workers who have worked at my side for many, many years. They have energized me and sustained me. Thanks to all of them.

You Have to Begin Somewhere

May 20, 1996. I'm tired. It was too hot last night and I didn't sleep well. All night a raccoon chattered in the attic of the house, finally waking me up for good at 6:30 a.m., after only four hours sleep. All night I worried about the impact of Dick Armey's visit to the state of Vermont.

Armey, Newt Gingrich's number-two man and the type of reactionary who makes even Gingrich look like a liberal, came to Vermont to endorse Susan Sweetser, my opponent in the upcoming congressional election. More importantly, he came to raise money for her. Sweetser probably made a big mistake by inviting him, since Armey, the majority leader in the House, epitomizes the congressional right wing which is every day sinking lower in the public's estimation. About thirty Vermonters demonstrated at the hotel where Armey was speaking at a $500-a-plate dinner. They are not great fans of the Gingrich-Armey "Contract with America."

The article in the *Burlington Free Press*, the largest paper in the state, gave decent coverage to the demonstrators' protest against the savagery of the Republican cuts in Congress. The press coverage raised important issues about the Republican agenda, with its attacks on the poor, the elderly, and women, and in doing so tied Sweetser to that unpopular agenda. It even quoted someone from the local chapter of the National Organization of Women (NOW), a definite plus. Still, Sweetser ended up raising $30,000 in one night, which is a helluva lot of money, especially in a small state like Vermont.

Sweetser had advertised the Armey event as a "private briefing by the Majority Leader." I wondered if Armey was going to share his wisdom with rich Vermont Republicans about how we should eliminate Social Security, Medicare, Medicaid, and the concept of the minimum wage, ideas he had voiced in the past. Or maybe he was just going to talk about the "Republican Revolution." In any case, in Vermont $500 is a lot of money for dinner. I hope these rich folks enjoyed themselves.

I feel in my gut that this is going to be a very, very tough campaign. I won the last election by only three points, and Sweetser is much better organized than my previous opponent. She has started her campaign much earlier and is going to raise a lot more money than he did. I also fear that it will be a nasty campaign, with personal attacks that will become increasingly ugly. It's going to be a brutal six months, and frankly I'm not looking forward to it.

What is really distressing is not only the negative campaigning—the lies and distortions that have already begun—but the enormous amount of time I am going to have to spend raising money and dealing with campaign operations, rather than doing the work I was elected to do in Congress. Sweetser began her campaign in *November*—less than halfway into my two-year term. That's crazy. That means that I have to keep my mind on an election for twelve months, rather than focusing on my real work.

The last couple of weeks I played a leading role in opposing the Republican Defense Authorization Bill, which supplied $13 billion *more* for defense than Clinton's budget had allocated. And Clinton's budget was already way too high. But now, instead of concentrating on the important issues facing Vermont and America, I will have to devote more and more energy to the campaign. I am going to have to start getting on the phone and raising money.

I'm going to have to think about polling, and TV ads, and a campaign staff. I'm going to have to make sure that we don't repeat the many mistakes that we made in the last campaign. Basically, I'm going to have to be more *political*. It's too early for that, and I don't like it.

Most people don't realize how far Newt Gingrich, Rush Limbaugh, and their friends have shifted the debate about where the country should be moving. In terms of the defense budget, 75 House Democrats—out of 197—supported the outrageous boost in military expenditures. Of course, almost all of the Republicans (including those fierce "deficit hawks") backed the increase. The Cold War is over, we spend many times more than all of our "enemies" combined and, with very little fanfare, the defense budget is significantly raised.

In the Armed Forces Committee, the vote for increased military spending was almost unanimous. Only two members, Ron Dellums and Lane Evans, out of the 55 members of the committee, voted against it. That's pathetic. A little pork for my district, a little pork for yours—and taxpayers end up spending tens of billions more than is needed.

Ditto for the intelligence budget. Major Owens of New York, Barney Frank of Massachusetts, and I have been trying to cut the CIA and other intelligence agency budgets for the last five years. This year, while introducing an amendment to trim their budget by 10 percent, I read into the record a *New York Times* article which described how the National Reconnaissance Office, one of the larger intelligence agencies, had *lost* $4 billion. That's right. They lost the money. They simply could not account for $4 billion, and their financial records were a complete shambles. No problem. The intelligence agencies got their increase anyhow.

Meanwhile, the Republican Congress, with many Democrats in agreement, are cutting back on every social program that people need—for the elderly, for children, for the sick and disabled, for the homeless, for the poor. That's called "getting our priorities straight."

I always feel anxious at the beginning of a campaign, but I feel more so this time. It's bad enough to be on the hit list of Gingrich and Armey, and to have the chairman of the Republican National Committee come to Vermont to announce he will give Sweetser the maximum allowable under the law, $153,000. What is most worrying, however, is that we progressives are not generating the excitement and support we need. That's the situation even in Vermont, where independent progressive politics is as advanced as any place in the country.

I have no illusions. This is my fifth race for Congress. I lost in 1988, won in 1990, '92, '94. People are not as excited as they were when I first ran. "Reelect Bernie—Again" is not an especially stirring slogan. And there simply aren't enough progressives committed to *making* the electoral struggle. The activities of most progressives revolve around specific issues and action groups. Many are not really in touch with their communities, nor do they appreciate the hard work involved in winning a congressional seat, a governorship, or even a mayoralty. Theory and ideas are exciting, but the practical work of capturing and holding public office—that's another story. So I'm concerned about running into the same problem we saw two years ago: lack of motivation among our core supporters.

One difficulty we're up against is that, to a large degree, modern American politics is about image and technique. In case you haven't noticed, elections do not have much to do with the burning issues facing our society. Ideas. Vision. Analysis. Give me a break! Most campaigns are about thirty-second TV ads, getting out the vote, polling, and reaching undecided voters.

It is six months before the election, and the Republicans have already done their focus groups. How do I know? I can hear it in their "message," which they repeat over and over again like a mantra: "Bernie Sanders is ineffective. Bernie Sanders is out of touch. Bernie Sanders is a left-wing extremist. Bernie Sanders rants and raves on the House floor and still no one listens to him. Susan Sweetser, on the other hand, is a sensible moderate who can work with everyone." They think that's how they can beat me. Maybe.

It is very frustrating that, because modern electoral politics is driven by technique, one needs more and more sophisticated "experts" in order to compete in the big league of congressional campaigns. But how far does one go in this direction? Was I elected to Congress as the first Independent in forty years so that I could hire a slick Washington insider consultant who will tell me what to say and do? Not very likely. Am I going to be shaped and molded by a Washington insider? Not while I have a breath in my body.

On the other hand, is it against some law of nature for a progressive and democratic socialist to present effective television ads, or is that just something that Republicans and Democrats are allowed to do? No. In my view we should do our TV well. Shouldn't we be prepared to respond immediately to TV ads from my opponent which distort my record? Yes. Are we betraying the cause of socialism because we don't communicate with mimeographed leaflets and pictures of Depression-era workers in overalls and caps? No. The world has changed, and it's appropriate to use the tools that are available.

Still, I have reservations. From my first day in Vermont politics, I prided myself on never once having gone to an outside consultant. We did everything within the state of Vermont, everything "in-house," usually in *my* house. You should have seen how we wrote the radio ads—around my kitchen table. John Franco, a former Assistant City Attorney in Burlington, loud, brilliant, occasionally vulgar. George Thabault—my assistant when I was mayor, imaginative, funny. David Clavelle, a local printer who had also worked in my administration. Huck Gutman and Richard Sugarman—college professors. Jane and me. Quite a crew. A helluva way to write a radio ad.

As for our television ads, we always went with my close friends and wonderful Burlington filmmakers, Jimmy Taylor and Barbara Potter. They were always good, sometimes brilliant, and they knew Vermont. My wife Jane, who is the most visual person that I know, was also in the middle of things. In 1990, when I won my first congressional race, Jimmy, Barbara and Jane produced an ad that received rave reviews. It was taped in Jimmy and Barbara's living room in Burlington. For two hours, with the camera pointed straight at my face, Barbara and I chatted informally about why I was involved in politics and what issues were of greatest concern to me. Jimmy and Barbara then edited the content down, and we aired a five-minute spot.

At a time when the vast majority of TV commercials were thirty seconds or less, this ad was not only well received for its straightforward focus on the issues, but for the novelty of its length. Later, we cut the ad into one-minute and thirty-second sections, reinforcing what the voters had already learned from the original.

In 1990, local talent was enough. It helped us win an election that most people thought we would lose. And it was more than effective in 1992 and '94. But now, in 1996, we are taking on the Republican National Committee, probably the most sophisticated political organization in the world, with money to burn. I know that we are not as prepared for the Republican assault as we should be, that we are facing the fight of our lives and we need all the help we can get.

So, for the first time, I went out of state to a real, grown-up "consultant." I figured that we really didn't have to do what they said, but that it wouldn't hurt to listen. But more on that later.

Plainfield, Vermont, fall 1971. I had just moved from Stannard, a tiny town in that remote section of Vermont we call the Northeast Kingdom, and was living in Burlington which, with less than 40,000 inhabitants, is the state's largest city. I had originally come to Vermont in 1964 for the summer, and permanently settled there in 1968. Jim Rader, a friend from my student days at the University of Chicago, whose acquaintance I renewed in

Vermont, mentioned to me that the Liberty Union Party was
holding a meeting at Goddard College in Plainfield. I'd heard of
the Liberty Union, a small peace-oriented third party which had
run candidates in Vermont's previous election. Jim's information
rattled around in my brain for a few days, and I ended up going to
the Plainfield meeting.

Why did I go? I really don't know. I had been active in radical
politics at the University of Chicago, where I was involved in the
civil rights and peace movements, and had worked very briefly for a
labor union. I grew up in a lower-middle-class home in Brooklyn,
New York—and knew what it was like to be in a family where lack
of money was a constant source of tension and unhappiness.

My father worked hard as a paint salesman—day after day,
year after year. There was always enough money to put food on
the table and to buy a few extras, but never enough to fulfill my
mother's dream of moving out of our three-and-a-half-room
apartment and into a home of our own. Almost every major
household purchase—a bed, a couch, drapes—would be accompanied by a fight between my parents over whether or not we
could afford it. On one occasion I made the mistake of buying the
groceries that my mother wanted at a small, local store rather
than at the supermarket where the prices were lower. I received,
to say the least, a rather emotional lecture about wise shopping
and not wasting money.

I was a good athlete, and there was always enough money for
a baseball glove, sneakers, track shoes, and a football helmet—
but usually not quite of the quality that some of the other kids
had. While I had my share of hand-me-downs, there was enough
money for decent clothes, but only after an enormous amount of
shopping around to get the "best buy." At a very young age I
learned that lack of money and economic insecurity can play a
pivotal role in determining how one lives life. That's a lesson I've
never forgotten.

When I was graduating James Madison High School in
Brooklyn, New York, I applied for admission into college. My

father had his doubts. He had dropped out of high school in
Poland and come to this country as a young man, worked hard all
of his life and, with vivid memories of the Depression, wondered
whether a solid job after high school wasn't a safer route than
spending four more years as a student. My mother, who had
graduated high school in the Bronx, disagreed and thought it
important that I go to college.

My parents always voted Democratic, as did virtually every
other family in our Jewish neighborhood, but they were basically
nonpolitical. My family went to only one political meeting that I
can recall, when Adlai Stevenson spoke at my elementary school,
P.S. 197, during one of his presidential campaigns. It was my
brother Larry who introduced me to political ideas. He became
chairman of the Young Democrats at Brooklyn College and, fulfilling his sibling duties, dragged me to some of his meetings.
More importantly, he was a voracious reader and brought all
kinds of books and newspapers into the house, which he discussed with me.

I spent one year at Brooklyn College and four years at the
University of Chicago, from which I graduated with a BA in 1964.
I got through college with student loans and grants and through
part-time work. I was not a good student. I took some time off
from my studies when a dean suggested that, perhaps, I should
"evaluate" my commitment to higher education. The truth is,
though, that I learned a lot more from my out-of-class activities
than I did through my formal studies. At the university I became
a member of the Congress on Racial Equality (CORE), the
Student Peace Union (SPU), and the Young People's Socialist
League (YPSL). I participated in civil rights activities related to
ending segregation in Chicago's school system and in housing,
and I marched against the proliferation of nuclear weapons. I also
worked, very briefly, for a trade union, the United Packinghouse
Workers. At the end of my junior year I worked in a mental hospital in California as part of a project for the American Friends
Service Committee.

While coursework didn't interest me all that much, I read everything I could get my hands on—except what I was required to read for class. The University of Chicago has one of the great libraries in America, and I spent a lot of time burrowed deep in the "stacks"—the basement area where most of the books were stored. I read mostly about American and European history, philosophy, socialism, and psychology. Among many other writers, I read Jefferson, Lincoln, Fromm, Dewey, Debs, Marx, Engels, Lenin, Trotsky, Freud, and Reich. I also discovered the periodicals room.

In any case, there I was on a beautiful fall day in 1971 in a room full of strangers at a meeting of a group called the Liberty Union.

When I arrived, I soon discovered that the purpose of this meeting was to nominate candidates for the U.S. Senate and the U.S. House of Representatives. Vermont's senior senator, Winston Prouty, had died on September 10, 1971, and the state's lone congressman, Robert Stafford, had decided to give up his House seat to run for the open Senate post in a special election to be held in January. That left two positions vacant, with no incumbents contesting either race.

The small Liberty Union Party was not exactly overflowing with individuals who were interested in running for the two seats. So, full of enthusiasm for what I believed was right and just, I raised my hand and offered my views on education, the economy, and the war in Vietnam. An hour later, I had won the nomination as the Liberty Union candidate for the open Senate seat. Talk about grassroots democracy! That meeting also allowed me to meet two lifelong progressives who have remained close friends ever since, Dick and Betty Clark of Chittenden.

When I say "won" I am being overly generous to myself. I was chosen as the candidate unanimously because there was no competition. By day's end, I had embarked on the first political campaign of my life. Together with Doris Lake, who was selected as the candidate for the House, I was to present Vermont voters with a political perspective from outside of the two-party system.

At the beginning of the campaign I participated in my first ever radio broadcast—a talk show in Burlington. And what a show it was. I was so nervous that my knees shook, literally bouncing uncontrollably against the table. The sound engineer frantically waved his arms at me through the glass partition between the studio and the control room. The sound of the shaking table was being picked up by the microphone. A strange thumping noise traversed the airwaves as the Liberty Union candidate for the U.S. Senate began his political career. And the few calls that came in expressed no doubt that this career was to be short-lived. "Who *is* this guy?" one of the listeners asked.

Despite such inauspicious beginnings, I enjoyed the experience of running for office very much. What excited me most was the opportunity to express to the people of Vermont views which many of them had not heard before. Although Vermont is a very small rural state, it has dozens of radio stations, eleven daily newspapers, and over thirty weekly newspapers. As it turned out, much of the local media was delighted to report the strange opinions of the Liberty Union's candidate. Again and again during that summer and fall I stressed my opposition to the war in Vietnam, and articulated my belief in economic democracy and social justice.

My political opponents in Vermont often accuse me of being boring, of hammering away at the same themes. They're probably right. It has never made sense to me, then or now, that a tiny clique of people should have incredible wealth and power while most people have none. Justice is not a complicated concept, nor a "new" idea. Tragically, most politicians do not talk about the most serious issues facing our country, or the real causes of our problems. So I do. Over and over again. This drives the media and my opponents a bit crazy, but most Vermonters seem to appreciate that I address the issues most relevant to their lives. And should we ever achieve economic and social justice in this country, I promise that I'll write some new speeches.

Just prior to the 1970 election, the Banking Committee of the U.S. House of Representatives published a report documenting the degree to which large banks in America controlled many major corporations, exerting enormous economic influence over our society. (Little would I, or anyone else in Vermont, have believed then that twenty years later I would be a member of that committee.) I lugged that report all over the state, quoting from it extensively.

I used the publication to talk about the phenomenon of "interlocking directorates," showing how a handful of very powerful people were making decisions affecting one major sector of the economy after another. I contrasted the reality of corporate domination with the lives of ordinary working people—laborers, farmers, shop owners—who had little or no say over what happened to them on the job.

Time after time, I pointed out that such disparity in the distribution of wealth and decision-making power was not just unfair economically, but that without economic democracy it was impossible to achieve genuine political democracy. The message could be reduced to a simple formula: wealth = power, lack of money = subservience. How could we change that? How could we create a truly democratic society?

For me, one of the highlights of that campaign was the public debates which I had with Republican congressman Robert Stafford and the Democratic candidate, state representative Randy Major. More often than not, the audience was sympathetic to the views I expressed—especially the call for economic justice. Although I was the candidate of a minor party, people were listening to what I had to say and they often supported my position.

The lesson I learned from those debates and the audience response—a lesson that remains with me today—is that the ideas I was espousing were not "far out" or "fringe." Frankly, they were "mainstream." They were concepts that a majority of people would support, if they had an opportunity to hear them. In short, social justice was neither "radical" nor "un-American."

But another political fact became clear to me during this first campaign: the perpetual bane of American third parties. "I fully agree with what you're saying, Bernie," someone in the audience would invariably tell me after a debate. "But I don't want to waste my vote on a third-party candidate." How many times over the years have I heard that view?

That first campaign also provided a good introduction to the role of the media in politics. It was an unforgettable experience. The Democratic candidate, state representative Randy Major, was not widely known and was considered a long shot in our (then) very Republican Vermont. So Major devised a plan to attract media attention by "skiing around the state to meet the voters." It was a brilliant publicity gimmick, and it worked wonderfully. Throughout the campaign, people were talking about the skiing lawmaker.

In fact, far more press attention was paid to the condition of Major's ailing feet than the "issues" facing Vermont and the nation. Here I was, giving long-winded statements to a bored media about the major problems facing humanity, and the TV cameras were literally focused on Randy's blisters. It was "new," fast-breaking news. Would he be able to continue his ski effort the next day? Tune in and find out. In any case, neither my "in-depth analyses" nor Randy's skiing made much of a difference to the election outcome. In January 1972, Bob Stafford won the special election by thirty-one percentage points. Spending less than one thousand dollars, I came in a very distant third, with only 2 percent of the vote.

But if the truth be told, I was proud of the campaign that I had run. The low vote I got did not depress me. I understood that making political change was a long process, and that we had achieved an important kind of success. The Liberty Union, with a few campaign workers and limited financial resources, had exposed tens of thousands of people to new perspectives. Some Vermonters were seeing politics beyond the prism of the two-party system.

Six months later, in the general election of 1972, I ran for governor of Vermont. During that campaign I naturally concentrated on the state and local issues that a governor deals with. The interest in my campaign increased but my percentage of the vote declined. This time, I ended up with only one percent. Now that's quite an experience—getting one percent of the vote. However, the issues that I and other Liberty Union candidates raised during that campaign helped play an important part in the election results and eventually resulted in changes in public policy.

Thomas Salmon, a Democrat, upset the Republican candidate, Fred Hackett, and was elected as only the second Democratic governor in the state's history. During the campaign, Salmon very shrewdly and effectively picked up on two issues that the Liberty Union was fighting for: property tax reform and dental care for low-income children. Under the Salmon administration, a popular property tax rebate program was established, as well as a "tooth fairy" program which went a long way toward improving dental care for kids. Despite our paltry one percent, the Liberty Union made an impact on major legislation.

1972 was the year Richard Nixon won a landslide victory over George McGovern. During that campaign, the Liberty Union threw its support behind the presidential candidate of the People's Party, Dr. Benjamin Spock, the world-famous pediatrician. A delightful man, Spock campaigned in Vermont on several occasions. Because he was one of the "major" candidates for president, Spock was provided with Secret Service protection and was guarded in exactly the same way as Nixon and McGovern. Some twenty-five agents watched over him, in shifts, twenty-four hours a day.

As the Liberty Union candidate for governor, and the head of our ticket, I was given the responsibility of meeting Spock at the airport when he came to Vermont. I was broke at the time, and needed to borrow a few bucks to put gas into my old VW bug just to get there. At the airport, after convincing the Secret Service that I really was a candidate for governor, I was able to welcome Spock to Vermont.

Later in the afternoon, Spock, I, and other Liberty Union candidates walked down Church Street, Burlington's main thoroughfare, and campaigned under the very watchful eyes of the Secret Service. I remember the incongruity of it all. Here I was, without a dime in my pocket, about to get one percent of the vote, being protected by a dozen well-armed agents of the federal government.

During that trip, Spock and I spoke at Johnson State College. In the midst of his speech, which was very well attended, a student ran into the auditorium and screamed out, "Is there a doctor in the house? There's been a car accident." Some drunken students had driven their car off the side of the road, and it overturned. Can you imagine their surprise when they found Dr. Spock and the U.S. Secret Service tending to their needs? Probably sobered them right up.

I ran for the U.S. Senate again in 1974. That election, in which I was vying for the seat left open when the venerable George Aiken retired, was a very close, hard-fought contest. While most of the state focused on the major party candidates—Patrick Leahy, a Democratic state's attorney from Chittenden County, and Richard Mallary, the incumbent Republican member of the House—I doubled my highest previous vote total, now reaching 4 percent. Leahy pulled off a major upset in that election and became the first Democrat ever elected to the U.S. Senate from Vermont.

1974 was a very exciting year for the Liberty Union, and the high point of its existence. Michael Parenti, who had been dismissed from his teaching post at the University of Vermont because of his antiwar activities, ran an excellent campaign for the U.S. House and received 7 percent of the vote against Republican Jim Jeffords (who won) and a Democrat—an extraordinary showing for a third-party candidate. Michael, who remains a good friend, eventually left the state and has since become an outstanding progressive writer.

The Liberty Union also put up strong candidates that year for governor, lieutenant governor, and for a number of seats in the state legislature—and many of them did well. Martha Abbott, our candidate for governor, and Art DeLoy, our candidate for lieutenant governor, each received about 5 percent of the vote. Nancy Kaufman, a young attorney who was the Liberty Union candidate for attorney general, received over 6 percent. (Twenty years later, Martha Abbott was elected to the Burlington City Council as a Progressive, where she continues to play a leadership role in the progressive movement.)

In 1976, as the now "perennial candidate" of the Liberty Union, I ran for governor again, this time against Republican Richard Snelling and Democrat Stella Hackel. With a solid performance in a prime-time television debate and greatly increased name recognition, I ended up with 6 percent of the vote. An increase to be sure, and an all-time high for me, but a long way from victory.

After that campaign I decided to leave the Liberty Union Party. It was a painful decision. I was proud of what a small number of people could accomplish in terms of running good campaigns, fighting utility rate increases, and supporting striking workers. We had done extremely well with limited resources, had brought a number of serious issues before the public which otherwise would not have been aired, and we affected public policy. With almost no money, our candidates received as much as 8 percent of the vote in three-party statewide elections. Further, since many of our candidates were women, we played a role in breaking down sexism in statewide politics. We also provided excellent political opportunities for working people and low-income citizens. One of our candidates for lieutenant governor, Art DeLoy, was the leader of one of Vermont's largest unions—the first time in memory that an active trade unionist had run for office.

But as is often the case for small third parties, we were not attracting new members, new energy, or new leadership. Virtually all party responsibilities continued to rest with a handful of dedicated activists—including me. Enough was enough. My political career was over. With politics behind me, I set out to make a living and began building, reasonably successfully, a small business in educational filmstrips. I wrote, produced, and sold filmstrips on New England history for elementary schools and high schools. It was a lot of fun. In the process, I improved my writing skills and learned something about photography, marketing, and door-to-door salesmanship. I also met a lot of fine educators around Vermont.

In 1979, after discovering that the vast majority of college students I spoke to had never heard of Eugene Victor Debs, I produced a thirty-minute video on his life and ideas. Debs was the founder of the American Socialist Party and six-time candidate for president. During his lifetime, Debs had a profound impact on American politics and the lives of American workers. Many of his ideas about trade unionism laid the foundation for the growth of the CIO in the 1930s and '40s. The Debs video was sold and rented to colleges throughout the country, and we also managed to get it on public television in Vermont. Folkways Records also produced the soundtrack of the video as a record.

Debs died in 1926, but his vision and the example of his life still resonate today. Unfortunately, his ideas remain sufficiently dangerous for them not to be widely taught in schools or discussed in the mass media. He fought to achieve a truly democratic society in which working people, not big money, would control the economic and political life of the nation. He founded the American Railway Union and led a bitter strike against some of the most powerful forces in the country. He believed in international worker solidarity and spent years in jail for his opposition to World War I. In 1920, while in jail for opposing that war, he ran for president—receiving close to one million votes. Eugene Victor Debs remains a hero of mine. A plaque commemorating him hangs on the wall in my Washington office.

Although I now had a business career, in an important sense my political work had not ceased. I was educating people, not from a podium or in a radio interview, but by resurrecting the heroes of our nation's political past. The Debs video was a success, and I was now beginning to think about a video series on other

American radicals—Mother Jones, Emma Goldman, Paul Robeson, and other extraordinary Americans who most young people have never heard of. For better or worse, my media production career came to end in 1980.

☞

B ut forward now to 1996, when aspects of the campaign are worrying me deeply, and getting me depressed. Too many questions are unanswered, and there are too many loose ends.

How do we relate to Vermont Democrats? In Congress, I chair the fifty-two-member House Progressive Caucus which has fifty-one Democrats and me, people with whom I have an excellent relationship. But things are different in Vermont where, among others, Governor Howard Dean is a moderate-to-conservative Democrat.

How do we relate to President Clinton, who is rapidly moving to the right? Should we establish links with his Vermont campaign? How should I respond to the Ralph Nader presidential campaign? Nader is a personal friend and an exemplary progressive, and his supporters have asked me to endorse his candidacy.

What should the progressive movement in Vermont do for this campaign? In addition to my own race for reelection, should we put up a full slate of candidates for office? Should we at least run a candidate for governor?

In Burlington, Progressives have won seven out of the last eight mayoral elections. I was mayor from 1981 to 1989; Peter Clavelle from 1989 to 1993. After losing to a Republican in '93, Clavelle was reelected in 1995. That same year, Progressives also took control of the City Council. But how do we strengthen the progressive movement throughout the state, beyond Burlington? We have had minimal electoral success in legislative races. Over the last six years, two or three Progressives have held seats in the legislature. Terry Bouricious, who served on the Burlington City Council for ten years and has worked with me over the last twenty, was elected in 1990, '92, and '94. Dean Corren was elected in '92 and '94, and Tom Smith, also a former Burlington city councilor, was elected in '90 and '92. But although we have strong pockets of support in communities around the state, never has a Progressive or Independent from outside Burlington captured a legislative post.

These are a few of the questions that I and other progressives are wrestling with as we begin organizing in earnest for the campaign.

In terms of who to support for president, the choice is really not difficult. I am certainly not a big fan of Bill Clinton's politics. As a strong advocate of a single-payer health care system, I opposed his convoluted health care reform package. I have helped lead the opposition to his trade policies, which represent the interests of corporate America and which are virtually indistinguishable from the views of George Bush and Newt Gingrich. I opposed his bloated military budget, the welfare reform bill that he signed, and the so-called Defense of Marriage Act, which he supported. He has been weak on campaign finance reform and has caved in far too often on the environment. Bill Clinton is a moderate Democrat. I'm a democratic socialist.

Yet, without enthusiasm, I've decided to support Bill Clinton for president. Perhaps "support" is too strong a word. I'm planning no press conferences to push his candidacy, and will do no campaigning for him. I *will* vote for him, and make that public.

Why? I think that many people do not perceive how truly dangerous the political situation in this country is today. If Bob Dole were to be elected president and Gingrich and the Republicans were to maintain control of Congress, we would see a legislative agenda unlike any in the modern history of this country. There would be an unparalleled war against working people and the poor, and political decisions would be made that could very well be irreversible.

Medicare and Medicaid would certainly be destroyed, and tens of millions more Americans would lose their health insurance. Steps would be taken to privatize Social Security, and the very existence of public education in America would be threatened. Serious efforts would be made to pass a constitutional amendment to ban abortion, affirmative action would be wiped out, and gay bashing would intensify. A flat tax would be passed, resulting in a massive shift in income from the working class to the rich, and all of our major environmental legislation would be eviscerated.

The Motor Voter bill would be repealed, and legislation making it *harder* for people to vote would be passed. Union-busting legislation would become law, the minimum wage would be abolished, and child labor would increase. Adults and kids in America would be competing for $3.00-an-hour jobs.

You think I'm kidding. You think I'm exaggerating. Well, I'm not. I work in Congress. I *listen* to these guys every day. They are very serious people. And the folks behind them, the Christian Coalition, the NRA, the Heritage Foundation, and others, are even crazier than they are. My old friend Dick Armey is not some wacko member of Congress laughed at by his colleagues. He is the Majority Leader of the U.S. House of Representatives. Check out his views. No. I do not want Bob Dole to be president. I'm voting for Bill Clinton.

Do I have confidence that Clinton will stand up for the working people of this country—for children, for the elderly, for the folks who are hurting? No, I do not. But a Clinton victory could give us some time to build a movement, to develop a political infrastructure to protect what needs protecting, and to change the direction of the country.

This is more than utopian fantasy. First of all, there are some promising developments in organized labor. Several months ago the Progressive Caucus met with John Sweeney, the new president of the AFL-CIO, who told us that there will be a greater AFL-CIO commitment to union organizing, and more energy and resources spent in the political process. This has been long needed and is a very welcome development.

The great political crisis in American society is the quiescence of working people. If 5 percent of unionized workers became politically active, we could radically transform economic and social policy in this country. Today, most low-income workers do not vote, and many have very little understanding of the relationship of politics to their lives. The average American worker has come to accept that he or she has no power on the job. The company is moving the plant to Mexico. How can I stop it? The CEO earns 173 times more than the average worker. Who am I to contest management prerogatives? Corporations are asking for a give-back in health care, despite record profits. What authority do I have to challenge big capital? In our "democracy," the vast majority of working people feel helpless—*are* helpless given the current political structure—to protect their economic interests or chart their future.

If you have no influence over your own working conditions, what kind of power can you have over the economics and politics of the entire country? Why bother to vote? Why bother to pay attention to politics? And millions don't. In Vermont and throughout the country, the rich ante up $500 or $5,000 at a fundraising event to support the candidate who will represent their interests. Meanwhile, the majority of the poor and working people don't even vote. No wonder the rich get richer and everyone else gets poorer. Are we really living in a democracy?

Certainly, some of the more powerful unions, with entrenched bureaucracies and leaders disinclined to rock the boat, have contributed to this malaise. For many years, the AFL-CIO, under Lane Kirkland, was extremely conservative and inactive. A few years ago I was asked by some union leaders to speak with Kirkland at a dinner during the AFL-CIO convention in Florida. My mission was to radicalize him. I tried. I didn't succeed. "Lane, what about a national AFL-CIO cable TV station which could educate working people about what's going on in our society and give them information they never get on commercial TV?" I asked. "Can't be done," he replied. "What about more organizing efforts? What about more political activity?" Not much of a response. Kirkland impressed me as an intelligent and thoughtful man with no energy or interest in making change. He was totally resigned to the status quo.

During the spring, 300 Vermont workers came out to hear Rich Trumka, former president of the United Mine Workers and new secretary-treasurer of the AFL-CIO. He gave a rousing speech which was very well received. The new president of the Vermont AFL-CIO, Ron Pickering of the Paperworkers, is doing an excellent job in reactivating the union movement in Vermont. One of the main goals of the "Sanders for Congress" campaign is to involve more and more working people in the political process. I look forward to working with Ron as the campaign progresses. We're going to receive substantial financial help from the unions, but we want rank and file grassroots support as well.

In June, there was a founding convention in Cleveland of the Labor Party, an organization which, at its inception, was supported by labor bodies representing over a million American workers. These union workers see no fundamental difference between the Democratic and Republican parties—and are starting a new party. It was an important political event, yet it received virtually no media coverage. Not one word in the *New York Times*, the *Washington Post*, or the *Wall Street Journal*. Hey! Only representatives of a million workers coming together to form a new political party. And now for another story about our favorite billionaire, Ross Perot, and *his* third party.

The Labor Party convention grew out of several years of organizing by people from the Oil, Chemical and Atomic Workers, the United Electrical Workers, and other progressive unions. These union activists have long understood that negotiating a good contract for their workers is only part of their job, and that working people will continue to get the short end of the stick unless we have a government that represents *their* interests. The slogan of the Labor Party is, "The bosses have two parties. We need one of our own." Hard to argue with that.

oliticians often claim that they are running for office because "the people urged me to do it." This is rarely true. But in late 1980, it was true for me. Well, not exactly "the people." It was my good friend Richard Sugarman.

Richard, talk show aficionado, baseball statistician, brilliant philosopher, and professor of religion at the University of Vermont, suggested that I run for mayor of Burlington against the five-term incumbent Democrat, Gordon Paquette. In Richard, you could not have found a more unlikely political adviser. As a Hasidic Jew, professor, and writer, he is deeply involved in the interpretation of sacred texts; as a philosopher, he is immersed in the abstract thought of Plato, Nietzsche, Sartre, and Levinas. But he also has a very pragmatic side. Richard is one of the sharpest political observers I have ever known.

His idea, however, seemed more than a little farfetched. "Richard, why should I run for office when I'm happily retired from politics? How could I possibly win against an entrenched political machine? And what the hell would I do if, by some miracle, I actually won?" Those were only a few of my questions as he dragged me into the Burlington city clerk's office in late fall 1980.

With the help of an employee in the office, Richard and I discovered the musty binder which contained the official Burlington election results from way back when. We went through and analyzed the 1976 gubernatorial election results. Patiently, he showed me a ward-by-ward breakdown of the election results, indicating how city residents had voted. Richard had a point to make: even though I received only 6 percent of the vote statewide, in Burlington I carried 12 percent, and in the two working-class wards of the city, over 16 percent.

On the basis of this showing, Richard reasoned that if all of our energy were concentrated on my hometown, we might win the upcoming mayoral election. For days and nights, friends and I argued about the wisdom of running and, if I did run, what kind of strategy made sense. Finally, convinced that for the first time I might have a real chance not only to educate the public but actually win an election, I decided to run as an Independent. I collected signatures on nominating petitions, submitted them to the city clerk, and the campaign was on its way.

And what a campaign it was! Talk about coalitions. By the time Election Day rolled around, we had brought together leaders of the low-income community, college professors, the Burlington Patrolmen's Association, environmentalists, and conservative homeowners worried about rising property taxes.

This was not to be an "educational" campaign. The goal of this contest was to win. For this reason, the campaign was issue-oriented, focused on the most serious problems facing Vermont's largest city, problems ignored by city government. While I often placed these issues within the context of what was going on nationally, and made it clear that a fundamental change of priorities was needed at the national level, virtually all of my energy was spent addressing the concerns that faced the people of Burlington. I was running for mayor, not U.S. senator. The people of the city wanted to know how I would improve the quality of life at the local level if I became mayor. Those were the issues I addressed.

Our electoral strategy was straightforward, aimed at creating a broad-based, grassroots constituency. Starting with the low-income and working-class wards, I knocked on as many doors as possible. As I walked through the neighborhoods, I told people that I would do my best to represent those in the city who had long been locked out of City Hall. I listened to their concerns and supported their grievances. For instance, public housing tenants told me how unhappy they were with the ineffective leadership of the Burlington Housing Authority. They had almost no voice in decision making, maintenance was poor, and there were virtually no recreational activities for their children. In Lakeside, a working-class neighborhood in the south end, I walked a picket line with residents who had, for years, been asking the administration to repair an underpass which, in rainy weather, became impassable and left the entire neighborhood dangerously isolated from the rest of the city.

As I sat in kitchens and talked on front stoops in low-income neighborhoods, I heard the bitterness in their voices. They were well aware of the inequitable provision of municipal services. They knew that street and sidewalk paving, police protection, park maintenance, and snow clearing were less available to them than to upper-income neighborhoods. So I made alliances with neighborhood organizations in the low-income and working-class areas who believed, rightly, that their communities were not getting a fair shake from city government.

I tried to speak for those who had never had a voice in City Hall. Landlords in Burlington had all the power in tenant/landlord relations, so I pledged to the city's tenants that, for the first time, they would have a strong ally in the mayor's office. I championed the rights of tenants and came out in support of their fight for rent control legislation.

One of my most widely noticed positions was strong opposition to a huge increase in the property tax proposed by Mayor Paquette. He calculated that with only token resistance (mine), he could slip the tax hike by without suffering any negative political effects. I kept stressing my opposition not only to this particular tax increase but also to the very concept of the property tax. Property taxes are highly regressive and hurt, in particular, low- and moderate-income citizens, especially senior citizens. During the campaign, I proposed that Burlington break its dependence on the property tax and develop a fair and progressive tax system to fund municipal services and local education. Day after day, door after door, I was pleasantly surprised by the kind of support I encountered. Either people were not being honest with me or we were going to do a lot better than the pundits expected. It turned out that Burlingtonians *were* honest.

Our campaign had a great deal of energy, but little sophistication. My campaign manager, Linda Niedweskie, an aspiring nutritionist who had recently graduated from college, had never before been involved in politics. Linda provided us with a strong sense of organization and kept everyone focused. Two low-income advocates, Dick Sartelle and John Bartlett, did a great job, and a number of former Liberty Union members, including John Franco and Terry Bouricious, also played active roles. David Clavelle, who had worked for a while for Senator Leahy, taught us how to make voter ID telephone calls. What a remarkable idea! Using the telephone for a campaign. None of us had thought of that. Together with a lot of volunteers who were energized by the remote but real possibility that we could win and develop a radically new politics for the city, we worked to canvass every home and apartment in Burlington.

The campaign itself functioned as a crash course in Burlington's problems and politics. In truth, I knew very little about Burlington city government. I had attended two Board of Aldermen meetings in my life—and had fallen asleep at one of them. They were boring. When the campaign began, I hadn't a clue where Ward 1 was, or the political difference between Wards 4 and 2. Not only did I have to become familiar with city problems and solutions, I had to learn to place those issues in a relevant context and devise viable solutions. In some ways, running for statewide office was easier than running for mayor because I was more familiar with the terrain of national and statewide politics.

Even though my campaign was geared toward lower- and middle-class people, a number of Burlington's upper-income citizens voted for me. One reason for this was that I attacked a plan to build high-rise condominiums on the city's waterfront. Burlington is a beautiful city, located on the eastern shore of Lake Champlain, with stunning vistas of the lake and New York's Adirondack mountains. A real estate developer had proposed building luxury high-rise condominiums along the choicest sections of the waterfront. When I vigorously opposed that project, many citizens concerned about the environment and preserving the natural beauty of the city decided that my candidacy was worth serious consideration. By the end of the campaign a local artist, Frank Hewitt, had designed an effective poster which boldly proclaimed, "Burlington is not for sale."

I spoke out against the planned expansion of the local hospital, primarily because it would burden the community with increased health care costs. But I also knew from going door to door that neighborhood residents were angry that the unnecessarily large expansion would replace a popular sledding hill with a large decked parking lot. So I stood up for local families who wanted children and past custom to count for more than cars and cement.

Again and again, in varying ways, our campaign reminded the people of Burlington that the incumbent mayor and his local Democratic machine were in cahoots with the downtown business community and irresponsible "pro-growth" forces, and out of touch with the concerns of the average citizen. My basic campaign message was that if I were elected mayor, I would open City Hall to *all* the people. I would run the city by responding to the best interests of working people, low-income people, and the middle class—the very folks who had largely been frozen out of the decision-making process.

But as it turned out, of all the issues I raised, the one that gave the greatest impetus to my candidacy was my support for municipal workers who were frustrated that the incumbent mayor and treasurer had refused, year after year, to negotiate in good faith with their unions.

The problem with a third-party or independent candidacy, as I had learned back in my Liberty Union days, was that although people will often agree with the candidate's position, they are skeptical of his or her "electability." So it was of major importance that, shortly before the election, the Burlington Patrolmen's Association endorsed my bid for mayor. They did so because I promised to listen to the concerns of cops on the beat and open serious labor negotiations with their union. In supporting my candidacy the police union and its leader, Joe Crepeau, showed enormous courage. If I lost (which most people expected) they would be even deeper in the city doghouse with the incumbent mayor.

Needless to say, their endorsement became a monumental

campaign event and a major news story: a leftist populist, a former opponent of the war in Vietnam, had gained the support of
the blue-collar forces of law and order! The coalition we had
brought together—low-income people, hard-pressed working-
class homeowners, environmentalists, renters, trade unionists,
college students, professors, and now the police—reinforced each
other in the belief that together we could win the election.

I cannot emphasize enough how important it was that we

developed a "coalition politics." The way to rekindle hope in America, we learned in our small New England city, is to bring people together. After all, most people share things in common with their neighbors. They work hard to make a living, they are concerned about their children, they want to drink clean water and to feel safe in their homes. Reminding ordinary people that government can and should work for them, speak with their voice, is the great strength of coalition politics, and the hope, I believe, for America's future.

Being a congressman is tougher than you think. And it's even tougher than that when you're a serious legislator, trying to accomplish things in Washington while, at the same time, you're running for reelection in a difficult campaign. And it's even tougher than *that* when you're an Independent, taking on half the world in D.C. and the other half of the world back home. (Then again, some of my friends say I have a tendency to exaggerate.)

I come home to Vermont every weekend. That's where I live. I'm always surprised when people assume that I live in Washington. No way. I *work* in Washington. I *live* in Vermont. During the six years that I've been in Congress, I've spent two weekends in D.C. I come home to Vermont for several reasons. That's where my family and friends are. Vermont is where I want to spend my time. I couldn't be a good congressman if I weren't in constant touch with my friends, neighbors, and constituents. It's not just the many town meetings and conferences I hold or the schools and meetings that I attend. It's the walk downtown. It's the ride in the country. It's getting a sense of the weather. It's seeing the local papers rather than reading faxes. It's watching the local TV. It's getting a *feeling* of what's going on, and what people are thinking about.

I know members, especially some who have been in Congress

for a while, who believe that they *live* in D.C. They go back to
their districts now and then. But their hearts are in Washington.
That's dangerous. When that happens you run the very real
danger of forgetting where you come from, and what you're
supposed to be doing.

There are great differences between being a mayor and a congressman. A mayor is a big fish in a little pond. A congressman is
one body out of 535 (not to mention the president). But the main
difference to me is physical proximity. When you're a mayor,
you're *always* home and on the job. In fact, the problem is you can't
get away for a minute. The phone rings at your house at 4 a.m.
because the snow plows have blocked somebody's driveway and
she can't get to work. A neighbor collars you in the produce section of the grocery store to report his annoyance with a zoning
ordinance. You're running around the city checking out the condition of the streets when it snows. You're talking to kids at the Teen
Center. It's very different from being in Congress. In Congress, you
may be working on a multibillion dollar issue which affects millions of people, but nobody back home knows what you're doing.
And you don't even know what the weather is like.

In the middle of a campaign it seems that everything comes to
the fore. All your neuroses, all your fears, all your weaknesses.
You're *on* all the time, and you're often tired, stressed out, prone to
make mistakes. And a mistake in a campaign can be very costly.
And I am tired. The past two years have been very tough. It's one
thing to criticize intellectually the policies of Gingrich and the
right wing. It's another thing to be locked in the day-to-day struggle, to be in a committee meeting or on the floor of the House, and
to see and feel the ugliness and irrationality of much of what goes
on. It is depressing and debilitating. But now I'm beginning a campaign. It's time to go forward.

I remember when I began my reelection effort for mayor in
1983. I was absorbed in city issues and neglected the upcoming
campaign. The first debate was held one afternoon in a radio
station. I stayed too late at City Hall and came flying into the

station just in time. I was unprepared for the event and did poorly. Getting beaten in that debate immediately jolted me into the real world of politics, and into understanding the significant difference between being an officeholder and a candidate. It was a lasting discovery. No matter how hard I work, no matter what I accomplish, somebody else will always want my job. That's democracy. Okay. Time to figure out how I get reelected. Don't worry about the last two years. Don't worry about being tired. Start moving forward in this campaign. Focus. Focus. Focus.

Phil Fiermonte, a former AFT union organizer and the head of my congressional outreach effort, keeps reminding me that we should begin to organize the campaign. "It's getting a little late, Bernie," he says. "We need money. We need a staff. Gotta get moving. It's going to take some time to get a good campaign manager." "Hey, Phil. You want to be campaign manager?" "No. Definitely not. I don't like campaigns. I'll help out, but I want to stay in the congressional office."

But deep down Phil knows that he is a doomed man. He will have to jump-start the campaign, work eighty hours a week, and deal with terrible pressure. I know all of the progressives in Vermont and Phil, by far, has the best organizational capabilities and temperament for the job. Further, he knows me well and tolerates my many foibles.

We briefly consider the possibility of hiring out of state, but dismiss the idea. You just can't put an ad in the *New York Times* saying "Wanted. Campaign manager for the only Independent in Congress. Knowledge of democratic socialism and independent politics required. Familiarity with Vermont and rural life a must. Eighty hours a week. Terrific responsibility. Low pay." Frankly, there aren't too many folks around who would respond to that ad. I'll stick with the Vermonter.

Phil, Jane, myself, and a few close friends discuss some of the immediate challenges. As we talk, I compile a list of the major concerns we face in the campaign. It looks like this:

MONEY

STAFF

STYLE

GUNS

MEDIA

MY HEALTH

OUR "MESSAGE"

To many people this list might seem like a strange hodge-podge. Political issues, fundraising, media strategy, and my personal concerns logically should be in separate categories. But when you sit down to a political meal, you don't find meat on one platter and vegetables and potatoes in separate bowls. A campaign is like a stew. Everything is in one pot. All the issues are mixed up together.

MONEY

When Sweetser announced her candidacy in November, she refused to discuss campaign spending limits, which meant that her wealthy friends were going to supply her with a bundle. Last campaign, we raised over $700,000. This time we'll need more, probably $900,000, which is a lot considering that my campaigns are financed primarily from small individual contributions. We also receive PAC money from labor unions, senior citizen organizations, environmental, women's, and children's groups, but the bulk of our funds come from ordinary people with limited resources. Since we have been criticized in the past for raising too much money out of state (even though we always have many more Vermont individual contributors than any other candidate), we are determined to raise substantially more in Vermont. Our supporters don't have a lot of money and we can't hold $500-a-plate fundraisers. But we can do much better than in the past.

STAFF

Finding people skilled in the intricacies of campaign work is more difficult than it sounds. Most people do not sit at home for a year and a half, waiting to work on a campaign. Sometimes you luck out and get experienced, mature people inbetween jobs. Sometimes you don't. One of the problems with our last campaign was that our staff was young and inexperienced and they didn't get along terribly well. They were all terrific and hard-working people but there were clashes of personality. In fact, as I later learned, chairs occasionally went flying across the room. This time we wanted to hire a more mature and compatible staff.

STYLE

I had not run a good campaign in 1994, and when I assessed its weaknesses I had to acknowledge that it was me, not the staff, that was the major problem. My style of campaigning had been too passive. I had been reluctant to respond quickly and vigorously when I was attacked. My attitude was: "The people aren't going to believe this nonsense. They know what I stand for. I don't have to respond to every stupid criticism." Wrong. This time we would respond immediately and forcefully. Further, we would not allow ourselves to be on the defensive. My opponent had served four years in the state senate, and had a record. We would let Vermonters know about it.

GUNS

During the 1994 campaign the National Rifle Association (NRA) had played a very forceful role against me. They distributed widely a "Bye, Bye, Bernie" bumper sticker, held press conferences and public meetings, placed radio ads, made phone calls—and it was effective. There is no question that we lost many working-class men in that election because we handled the gun issue badly.

Vermont is a rural state in which tens of thousands of people enjoy hunting and own guns. During hunting season thousands of kids go out with their fathers and mothers to hunt and enjoy the outdoors. Vermont is an "outdoor" state—and hunting is a key part of that way of life. I am pro-gun, and pro-hunting. But I don't believe that hunters need assault weapons and AK-47s to kill deer. I voted for the ban on assault weapons, which brought the wrath of the NRA down on me.

For this campaign, we devise a three-pronged strategy on the gun issue. First, according to a number of polls, the vast majority of Vermonters (and Americans) *support* the ban on assault weapons. Susan Sweeter's position—the straight NRA line, which is opposition to all gun control—is way out of touch with what Vermonters believe. We are going to make that clear. Second, we will bring into the campaign a number of hunters who support my position on the ban on assault weapons. Third, we will ask friends who *disagree* with the ban to publicly support my candidacy by stating that guns are only one issue among many. As one NRA friend told me, "You can't buy an AK-47 without a job. Let's get our priorities straight."

MEDIA

For most of my political life I've had a problem with WCAX-TV, the largest television station in the state. Pure and simple, it's a Republican station. The owner of WCAX is a wealthy, conservative Republican and major contributor to the state party. Unsurprisingly, the news division often reflects his views. The station is not a right-wing wacko operation; many of its political stories are fair and accurate, and it has a number of good reporters. But overall, and in a consistent way, there is a very clear Republican bias to its reporting, which usually becomes more conspicuous as election time draws near. And I'm not the only target. Other progressives, liberal Democrats, Senator Leahy—all have been skewered by WCAX at one time or another. Positive stories are ignored, negative stories are played up. There is no easy way of dealing with this. It's hard to win a fight against someone behind a TV camera. We need to keep thinking about it.

HEALTH

In modern politics, the personal becomes the political whether we like it or not. And I am facing personal difficulties which could have troublesome implications for the upcoming campaign. Ever since the end of the last campaign, my voice has been hoarse, sometimes almost inaudible. Once, on the floor of the House, I could barely complete a speech. I must drink water constantly while I'm talking, and I can't speak publicly without a microphone. More and more my voice seems unnatural and strained. Personally, it is getting to be a real drag, and I think it is hurting me politically.

Doctors have diagnosed the problem as a nodule on my vocal cords, and recommend surgery. I have never had a serious medical problem in my life. I haven't spent a night in the hospital since I was born. I don't want a doctor scraping away at my vocal cords and making me sound like Donald Duck.

I'm trying for a "natural cure." I drink all kinds of weird teas. I've taken homeopathic remedies. I'm supporting the cough drop industry. I'm trying to change my way of speaking. It's all very interesting, but none of it is working.

I don't want to do it, but if my voice doesn't get better soon, I'm going to have the surgery. I can't go through the campaign like this. A reporter recently asked me, "Do you have throat cancer?" Every time I'm on the radio someone asks me about my voice. If people think that I am in poor health, I'm not going to win this election.

MESSAGE

It may seem surprising, but of all the challenges ahead the decision of what my overall campaign message will be is the easiest to address. For two years I've been listening to the garbage of Gingrich and his right-wing friends. And for two years I've been fighting them. This campaign is going to be about the Gingrich agenda.

If elected, Ms. Sweetser will vote for Gingrich as Speaker of the House. If Vermonters want massive cuts in Medicare,

Medicaid, education, veterans' programs, and environmental protection, together with huge tax breaks for the rich, Ms. Sweetser is going to be elected the next representative from Vermont. Frankly, I don't think that's going to happen.

Nonetheless, I know that Sweetser will be a very tough opponent. She is bright, articulate, attractive, and very popular. Further, she has an unusual history indicating a great deal of courage and strength. Kevin J. Kelley described Sweetser in a November article in the *Vermont Times*, a weekly newspaper.

> Susan Sweetser brings several assets to her race against Congressman Bernie Sanders. Foremost among them is her standing as one of the most popular young politicians in Vermont. After only a single term in the legislature, the 36-year-old Republican finished first in 1994 in the crowded and highly competitive field of candidates vying for state senate seats from Chittenden County. Sweetser is a rising star likely to shine brightly for many years in state—and possibly national—politics.

> Sweetser is still associated in the public mind mainly with her courageous decision in 1989 to reveal that she had been raped nine years earlier. In acknowledging that she had been sexually assaulted, Sweetser defied the social taboo that requires women to remain silent and not to challenge the unwarranted sense of shame felt by many rape victims.

> Having helped initiate a candid discussion on a sensitive subject, Sweetser went on to campaign tirelessly on behalf of "victims' rights." She founded Survivors of Crime, Inc., a group that advocates tougher penalties and preventive measures in regard to crimes of violence. Sweetser's effectiveness in this area also results from what Elizabeth Ready, a state senate colleague, describes as her "spunky spirit." Sweetser exemplifies the sort of determined, do-it-yourself approach to life sure to appeal to many Vermonters.

Yes, this is going to be a tough election. The early polls show that. On February 28, a *Rutland Herald* poll has me ahead by 47 percent to 32 percent. Maybe that sounds good, but it's not. I am much better known than Sweetser, and early polls almost always give an advantage to the incumbent. In fact, as the *Rutland Herald* points out, a poll which they did in late June 1994 had me almost thirty points ahead of my opponent that year, John Carroll, and I won by only three points. Sweetser is starting her campaign much earlier than Carroll did, and already has better name recognition than he did. *Roll Call*, a Washington political newspaper which analyzes congressional races, calls the race a "toss up." I can't disagree with that assessment.

☞

Election Day, or Town Meeting Day as we call it in Vermont, was March 3, 1981. I got up at five o'clock in the morning, ready to go. As I drove down North Avenue I saw telephone poles plastered with red-and-white "Sanders for Mayor" posters. Campaign volunteers, mostly from the low-income housing projects, had been up early, and the signs served notice that our election-day effort was proceeding as planned. Their presence seemed a good omen: we were everywhere, we were ready for the final day.

As I continued the drive from my apartment to the north end of the city, I noticed a young nurse, dressed for work later that morning in her white uniform, holding up a "Sanders for Mayor" sign at a major intersection. I had not expected to see her out there, shivering in the early morning cold, symbolic of the energy and commitment that had propelled our campaign. Another good omen.

Still, I was far from confident that the day would be ours. There was a chance that we would surprise everyone and walk away with the election. A nice comeuppance for the newspaper columnist who the day before had predicted that I would lose by twenty points. Still, as had always been the case for me in the past, I could get obliterated. Conventional wisdom was with the newspaper columnist: despite the surprising endorsement of the Patrolmen's Association, despite the wide support we seemed to be drawing throughout the city, Bernie Sanders and the progressive effort could still get hammered.

What no one anticipated, but what in fact happened, was a nailbiter.

The day was a blur. I made appearances at each of the six ward polling places. I kept checking with Linda Niedweskie at campaign central to see how things were going and what the voter turnout was like. The good news for us was that voting was heavier than usual, 25 percent higher than in previous mayoral elections. Supporters wished me well. Campaign workers ferried elderly and low-income voters to the polls in the car pools we had organized.

The polls closed at seven. In each ward the votes were tallied by ward officials, most observed by members of our independent coalition. As my friend Richard had predicted months before as we pored over those musty polling books in City Hall, I did extremely well in the working-class districts. In fact, we carried Wards 2 and 3—traditionally Democratic and working class—by almost two to one over Paquette.

As the vote totals rolled in, it appeared that the election would be very close. Our strong performance in the low-income and working-class wards was being offset by a less than inspiring performance in the more affluent wards. Apparently, speaking forthrightly about the needs of working people made wealthy folks nervous. With all of the machine ballots counted, and with the absentee ballots tallied everywhere but in Ward 3, we were ahead, though not by much. Only the paper absentee ballots in that one Democratically controlled ward remained to be counted. We waited anxiously.

What seemed like an interminable amount of time passed, and still there was no word from Ward 3. Finally, surrounded by lawyers and supporters, I marched into the ward polling place to see what was going on. A few minutes later, a group of ward functionaries came out from behind a closed door, where they had been counting the ballots. Even though I had won the ward by two to one on the voting machines, it seems I had lost the absentee ballot count by the same amount.

Yet, to my surprise, to Mayor Paquette's shock, to the business community's alarm, and to the deep interest of Vermonters throughout the state, when the absentee votes were tallied in with the rest, I found myself elected mayor of Burlington—by a mere fourteen votes. For once, the old saying was really true: every vote had counted. So stunning was the upset that nine years later the state's largest newspaper would still be referring to it as "the story of the decade."

But the evening did not end with our victory and my live appearance on late-night news, ferried to the state's largest television station by a reporter with a siren on the roof of his car. With such a close election there would be a recount, and City Hall had possession of all the ballots. After a great deal of legal mumbo jumbo among my lawyer friends, meeting in the midst of total chaos in somebody's office, it was decided that we should try to get the ballots out of City Hall.

So, in the middle of the night—at three o'clock in the morning to be precise—a lawyer and I traveled down a dirt road and woke up a judge to request that the election ballots be impounded. The judge granted our request. The next morning the ballots were moved to the state courthouse.

One month later, I was sworn in as mayor of Vermont's largest city, the only mayor in the entire country elected in opposition to the two major political parties. I would be reelected three times, and then move on to the U.S. House of Representatives, the first Independent in the Congress in four decades. But that March night in 1981 was the event which made possible all that came after.

We were a coalition of ordinary people, none of whom had any real access to power in the conventional scheme of things, but we had contested an important election—and we had won. If an independent progressive movement could win in America's most rural state—and until recently, one of America's most Republican—then it might be possible for progressives to do likewise anywhere in the nation.

Socialism in One City

"They're playing you for a fool and they've already taken away your right to representation in Congress. Who are 'they'? The leftists, extreme liberals and radicals all over the country. From Berkeley, California to New York's Greenwich Village, thousands of these people, that's right, thousands of them, have been contributing to and working hard for the election of Bernard Sanders to Congress."

This, from a fundraising letter widely distributed throughout Vermont, is the gist of Sweetser's campaign strategy: a slightly retooled version of '50s-style redbaiting. The people of Vermont have been duped. Bernie Sanders does not represent their interests. He owes his allegiance to left-wing "outsiders" who control him through their purse strings.

Every campaign has an official beginning. Mine was May 27, 1996, the day I made the formal announcement of my candidacy. The first of five such announcements scheduled for each region of Vermont took place in Burlington, my hometown and the state's largest city. Symbolically, we held the event in the Community Boathouse on the waterfront, one of the major accomplishments of my time as mayor. We organized the announcement as we had two years ago. The campaign staff—Tom Smith, John Gallagher, and Brendan Smith—brought together leading representatives of our various constituencies, the backbone of our support. Each of them spoke for a few moments about issues of importance to them and reasons why they wanted me reelected. Tom Smith, a former Progressive in the state legislature, emceed the event. We had a very good crowd, over 150 people at noon. It was a beautiful Vermont spring day.

Ron Pickering, the head of the Vermont AFL-CIO, was there, representing 20,000 union workers and retirees. So were Representative Bobby Starr, the chairman of the House Agriculture Committee and a leading voice for family farmers in the state legislature, and Sally Conrad, a former state senator and one of the strongest advocates for women and the poor. Stan LaFlamme, a disabled Vietnam veteran who was a member of my Veterans Council, delivered a very poignant speech. Ned Farquar of the Sierra Club spoke for the environmental community, Mira Fakiranada for the low-income community, and Alice Cook Bassett for senior citizens. We heard from Will Rapp, the owner of Gardener's Supply and a successful and environmentally conscious small businessman. Liz Ready, a progressive Democrat in the state senate, recalled her encounters with Susan Sweetser. And Peter Clavelle, who was director of economic development in my administration and was now in his third term as the Progressive mayor of Burlington, talked about my mayoral record.

These folks, many of them personal friends, represented the progressive coalition that we had worked hard over many years to bring together: workers, family farmers, women's advocates, low-income people, veterans, senior citizens, environmentalists, and small businesspeople. Together, they stood for the vast majority of the people in Vermont. Together, we would win this election.

I wrote my announcement speech the night before. As usual, when I was speaking my voice was hoarse and strained, and I had to stop a couple of times to down some water. In the speech, I tried to frame the central issues of the campaign. This is how it began:

Six years ago, I asked the people of Vermont to do something that had never been done before in the history of our state, and had not been done for forty years in the United States of America. And that is to send an Independent to Congress—someone not affiliated with the Republican Party or with the Democratic Party.

When I first ran for Congress, I asked the people of Vermont to send me to Washington so that I could fight for those people who can't afford to attend $500-a-person fundraisers like the one my opponent recently held; and who can't afford to have well-paid lobbyists in Washington protecting their interests. That's the promise that I made, and that's the promise that I've kept.

I asked the people of Vermont to send me to Congress so that I could stand up to a Republican president when he was wrong, and a Democratic president when he was wrong; to stand up to a Democratically controlled Congress when they were wrong and a Republican controlled Congress when they were wrong. And that's what I've done.

Mostly, I asked the people of Vermont to send me to Congress so that I could fight for justice—a concept we don't hear too much about anymore. To fight for justice for working families and the middle class—80 percent of whom, since 1973, have experienced a decline in their standard of living or, at best, economic stagnation—while at the same time the people on the top have never had it so good.

During the 1980s, the top one percent of wealth holders in this country enjoyed two-thirds of all increases in financial wealth. The bottom 80 percent ended up with less real financial wealth in 1989 than in 1983—and that trend continues. Today, tragically, the United States has the most unfair distribution of wealth and income in the entire industrialized world.

Justice. An economy in which all people do well, not just the very rich. And that's what I've been fighting for.

I then described some of what I had seen in Vermont as I traveled around the state during the two preceding years.

I talked about the meeting I had with a woman in Danville, who told me that both she and her husband were working sixty hours a week in order to save money to send their daughters, excellent high school students, to college. But despite their backbreaking efforts, they didn't know if they would succeed—given the high cost of college and the enormous debt they would have to sustain.

I talked about the young farmer I had met in Troy. She and her husband go out milking at 5 a.m., seven days a week. But despite their hard work and their love of the land, they didn't know if they would be able to stay on the farm because of the collapse of milk prices.

I talked about the senior citizens I met throughout the state who, despite Medicare, were unable to afford their prescription drugs. And how some of them were forced to choose between adequately heating their homes in the winter, or buying the food they needed.

And I talked about the young workers who had no health insurance and dead-end jobs.

My point was that while the economy might have been working well for the people on top, it was leaving many, many people far behind.

Next came my legislative achievements. For years my opponents had been telling Vermonters that as an Independent I couldn't pass major bills or amendments. It was important to set the record straight. In fact, I had an impressive legislative record.

I had helped lead the effort to raise the minimum wage and to pass the Northeast Dairy Compact, legislation of great importance to Vermont farmers. It was my amendment that passed the House and told the president that he couldn't put $50 billion at risk bailing out the Mexican economy on behalf of Wall Street investment banks. Another amendment of mine stopped an outrageous example of corporate welfare—a $31 million Pentagon bonus for the board of directors and CEO of Lockheed-Martin for merging their companies and laying off 17,000 workers. In Vermont it gets cold in the winter, very cold, so my office led the effort in the House to stop Gingrich's attempt to eliminate the fuel assistance program, LIHEAP, restoring almost full funding for it, as well as seeing through a major amendment for affordable housing. Further, I passed legislation which prevented insurance companies from discriminating against battered women, and an amendment which said that an HMO or insurance company could not force a woman and her newborn baby out of the hospital before they were ready to go. And there were other successful amendments and bills which I had authored. The important point was to show Vermonters that an Independent could pass legislation relevant to our state and to the nation.

But then came, perhaps, the most important point that I wanted to make. I continued:

> What this election is about is whether Newt Gingrich, Dick Armey, and the Republican Party are going to have another two years to push through the most reactionary, extremist agenda in the modern history of America—or whether we stop them cold right now and tell them that greed and bigotry and scapegoating are not what America is all about.
>
> What this election is about is whether Gingrich and Armey and the Republican Party are going to be successful in slashing Medicare, Medicaid, education, environmental protection, veterans' programs, nutrition, affordable housing, and a dozen other programs impacting tens of millions of Americans—while at the same time they give huge tax breaks to the rich and large corporations, and build B-2 bombers and Star Wars gadgets that the Pentagon doesn't want.

Finally, I concluded by emphasizing what is too frequently ignored in politics: that despite all of the problems and pettiness that take place every day in the political world, it is imperative for progressives to maintain a vision—a vision that has been carried forth generation after generation after generation—a vision that cries out for social justice and the attainment of the true potential that this country can become.

I ended my remarks by stating:

> It is vitally important to the future of this country and our state that we defeat the Republican agenda, and that we prevent the Republicans from recapturing the Congress and taking the White House. That is enormously important. But it is even more important that we as progressives and as Vermonters hold on to that special vision that has propelled us forward for so many years.
>
> A vision which says that in this richest of all nations all of our people, and not just the wealthy, should enjoy the fruits of their labor with decent jobs and benefits that allow them to live in dignity. That we cannot continue to have the highest rate of childhood poverty in the world, while the number of millionaires and billionaires continues to increase. A vision which says that every man, woman, and child in this country is entitled to health care as a right of citizenship, and that the United States must join the rest of the industrialized world by enacting a national health care system, a single-payer health care system. A vision which says that lifelong quality education is the essence of what being alive is about, and that all of our citizens, no matter what their incomes, should be able to receive a higher education.
>
> A vision which says that we respect the struggles that women have been waging for so many years, and that the very personal decision of abortion must be decided by the woman herself—and not Newt Gingrich or the United States government. A vision which says that we judge people not by their color, their gender, their sexual orientation, their nation of birth—but by the quality of their character, and that we will never accept sexism, racism, or homophobia.
>
> A vision which says that there is no conflict between respect for the environment and job growth, and that, in

fact, our economy improves when we stop environmental degradation. A vision which says that a society is ultimately judged by how we treat the weakest and most vulnerable among us—the children, the elderly, the sick, the disabled. And that we do not cut back on programs which help the weak and the powerless, in order to give tax breaks to the rich and the powerful.

The announcement event in Burlington was a terrific success. It was great to see so many of my old friends again, people who had been part of our efforts in Burlington when I was mayor, people who had worked with me for years. I was honored and humbled to be part of a coalition of such good, decent, and down-to-earth people. It was a completely different world from the backbiting of Washington. I was very proud to be a Vermonter.

But the warm feelings lasted only until the evening news was broadcast. We were then reminded very pointedly that in politics there's reality, and there's perception of reality as portrayed on television. The official campaign had just begun, and voters were forming their first impressions. And what they saw on TV was very different from what had actually taken place.

My Republican opponent, Susan Sweetser, held a press conference immediately after my announcement. Her attack on me for attacking her (which I didn't—I never even mentioned her) dominated the news. She was particularly successful at turning our announcement to her advantage on the largest television station in the state, WCAX-TV, which gave as much time to Sweetser's response as to my speech. In the midst of their coverage, they felt it necessary to report, incorrectly, that I had spent almost $200,000 more than my Republican opponent in the *last* election—they simply "forgot" to mention the independent expenditures made on his behalf by the Republican Party, including money paid to WCAX.

Stuart "Red" Martin, the conservative Republican who owns WCAX, had already contributed $2,000, the maximum amount allowed by law, to the Sweetser campaign. Recently Peter Freyne, a columnist on the Vermont weekly newspaper *Seven Days*, quoted

Martin as saying that he wanted "to chip in as much as I can ... I feel I'm doing a public service if we remove Bernie Sanders." From the beginning, we had worried about how WCAX would cover this campaign. Now we knew. We were off to a very bad start.

In effect, my opening announcement on TV became a pro-Sweetser promotion. The strategy of her campaign handlers is the essence of modern TV-oriented campaigning: when your opponent makes a speech, respond very quickly so that the television report focuses more on the response than on the original statement. In general, sound-bite television likes the idea of "conflict" more than the simple reporting of information. This works especially well when a TV station is sympathetic to a particular point of view.

Increasingly, both with regard to the campaign and my congressional duties, I worry about the role of television "news" in the life of our country—regardless of the political orientation of the station. The simple fact of the matter is that no one, not Bill Clinton, not Bob Dole, not Bernie Sanders, can deal with complex issues in a seven-second sound bite. The rapid pace of TV "action news" makes it virtually impossible for there to be serious reflection on important issues. Further, there is little sense of proportion in the coverage given to issues. TV news wants *new* developments, and smart press secretaries cater to this craving by concocting gimmicks and photo ops—anything to get their bosses on the tube.

Meanwhile, the deepest and most profound issues facing the country rarely get discussed because they don't fit the format. Several years ago, I attended a meeting with the head of a network news division. He described the extraordinary commitment of labor and money to coverage of an airplane crash—routine procedure for a disaster story. Someone asked him about his network's reporting of the savings and loan scandal (a real disaster). His reply: "We didn't do much. It wasn't good television. Too boring."

Every night, television news offers colorful, fast-paced, and exciting coverage—but of what? Ultimately, Americans who depend on TV for information learn very little about how and why things really happen in their country. Good entertainment? Yes. Knowledge for a democracy? No.

There is no question that Sweetser's people will be doing a lot of instant response "spin." Pretty sophisticated stuff for a small state like Vermont. Much better than I've done in past campaigns. I didn't even know until later that her campaign manager was at my announcement with a tape recorder. It is now clear what their strategy will be. Every time I speak they will be there, almost literally "in my face." On the other hand, whether that sort of attack strategy will succeed in Vermont remains to be seen. Vermont is not California or New York. I'm not so sure that Vermonters will enjoy the spectacle of an in-your-face style of campaign.

While my opening announcement was poorly covered by television, the newspaper coverage was excellent. The three major print media, the *Burlington Free Press,* the Vermont Press Bureau (representing the second and third largest papers in the state, the *Rutland Herald* and the *Times-Argus*), and the Associated Press (which covers for all the papers), described the event accurately on their front pages and provided ample coverage of my remarks. In print, Sweetser's statement that "Bernie Sanders represents the tired failed ideology of left-wing extremism," didn't play as well as it did for the television cameras, especially given that I was surrounded by representatives of the vast majority of the people of Vermont. Her attack on my support for the needs of working people and the middle class sounded as if she were unaware that a majority of Vermonters are not as supportive of Gingrich as she is.

I wish I could say that I was enthused once the campaign had begun officially. After all, it was great to see so many old friends show up, people who have been with me through so many struggles. But even that had its down side. It reminded me that a major challenge of this campaign is not only to get people involved, but to get them involved in a meaningful way. In the 1994 campaign, we recruited very few new campaign workers. No one wants to sit around an office waiting for orders from on high. How do we develop a structure that attracts volunteers and gives them significant work to do? How do we develop a sense of excitement? That's tough. But we must do better than in 1994.

It's also tough being an incumbent. Yes, I know. You're not feeling sorry for me. Incumbents, you say, have all kinds of advantages. You're right. We have staff, access to information, an ability to make news and play the "Rose Garden strategy" by simply doing our jobs. That's true. But there are also serious disadvantages.

One of the very real problems I have in this campaign, one I felt severely two years ago, is that I have to spend much of my time in Washington while my opponent has seven days a week in the state of Vermont. She's on local radio shows. She's constantly talking to groups. She's getting interviewed by reporters in small towns. Meanwhile, I'm stuck in Washington, dealing with congressional business (my job, after all) which isn't likely to be reported in the local news, or facing tough votes which will offend one or another constituency.

But I'm not the only member of Congress having to worry about the incumbency predicament. Gingrich's freshman class of "revolutionaries" want to go home too. They're in trouble, and they want to campaign in their districts. The good news, therefore, is that we may get out of the Capitol earlier this year than last election.

The recount was completed two weeks after the election. My lead dropped from fourteen to ten votes. But still, I am elected mayor of Burlington, the only candidate in America to buck the two-party system, the only socialist mayor in the country.

I was inaugurated in April 1981, before a huge crowd at City Hall. I was pleased with the speech I delivered, tying local issues to the broader national and international context. For the first time in anyone's memory, local radio carried a mayor's speech

live. Later, a reporter asked me for a copy of the speech, and I handed her my pages of scribbled notes on a yellow legal pad. That's too bad. I wish I had that speech today.

Hysteria reigned. The establishment was in total shock. The director of the hospital later wrote that when he heard the news on the radio, he nearly drove his car off the bridge he was riding over. The local bankers, who had scheduled a meeting for the day after the election, tried to figure out how they would communicate with the new mayor. Did anyone know this guy? I got a call from the Democratic lieutenant governor. "Don't do anything rash," she said.

I became a celebrity, of sorts. The local media was ecstatic: this election was the biggest Vermont political story in years. And it went beyond Vermont. The *New York Times*, the *Boston Globe*, and many other national papers featured stories on the "socialist mayor." Phil Donahue invited me to be on his show for a full hour. I declined, choosing not to be the spokesperson for the American socialist movement. I did accept NBC's offer to fly Jane and me to Chicago for a ten-minute Donahue interview on the "Today Show." And there was Canadian television, and the BBC. Somebody told me that I was even broadcast on Chinese radio.

Garry Trudeau of Doonesbury fame came to Burlington and we had breakfast together. This was just after the Socialist Party and François Mitterand had taken power in France. Not long after a Doonesbury cartoon appeared that read, "As goes Burlington, so goes France." And then there were T-shirts, with several variations on "The People's Republic of Burlington." All and all, it was a very heady experience for a guy whose last bid for public office garnered only 6 percent of the vote.

An immediate crisis involved purchasing clothes suitable for a mayor. At the time, I didn't own a suit, just one or two corduroy sports jackets and a few ties. While it wasn't my intention to become the best-dressed mayor in America, or even to wear a tie all that often, I thought a little sprucing up wouldn't hurt. Overnight, my wardrobe doubled.

More importantly, I had to put together an administration. Under Burlington's charter, the mayor has the right to appoint a city attorney, clerk, treasurer, constable, and a number of other positions. I needed to find competent, experienced people who shared my political views. And beyond this more immediate concern was the monumental task of transforming city government.

How would we implement our campaign promises? How would we democratize Burlington politics and open up city government to all the people? How could we break our dependency on the regressive property tax? How could we protect the environment and stop unnecessary road construction? How would we address the needs of low-income and working-class neighborhoods? How would we bring women into a city government that had been dominated by an old boys' network? What could we do for the kids and teenagers of the city, and for the seniors? How could we treat city employees fairly, not only through decent wages and working conditions, but by involving them more in the decision making of their departments? How would we make Burlington a city in which all people have access to the arts, not just those with money? Above all, how could we accomplish all of this with only two supporters on a thirteen-member City Council, and virtually no support on the various commissions that directed most of Burlington's departments?

My "shadow cabinet" and I organized a series of task forces to begin addressing these questions. Essentially, we opened the doors of City Hall and invited all interested people to come in and suggest the best ways forward. We were delighted by the response. Hundreds of people from all walks of life attended a wide variety of meetings. Many of them had great ideas.

Out of these task forces came a number of Mayor's Councils: on youth, the arts, women, senior citizens, health care, and tax reform, among other issues. Over the years, and after great political struggle, some of these councils were incorporated into the structure of city government. In the early days of my administration, however, they served almost as a parallel government.

Those early days at City Hall were exhilarating, but very tense. To be more accurate, there was a civil war taking place in Burlington city government. Conservative Democrats had controlled Burlington city government for decades and, with their Republican allies, they were surely not going to give up their power without a fight. The Board of Aldermen (as it was then called) consisted of eight Democrats, three Republicans, and two supporters of mine—Terry Bouricious and Sadie White.

At twenty-seven, Terry became the first Citizen Party candidate in America elected to public office. I had known Terry since his student days at Middlebury College, where he participated in the Liberty Union and helped in my 1976 gubernatorial race. While Terry ran his aldermanic campaign more or less independently of my mayoral race, he was a strong socialist and a natural ally, and he is a leader of the Vermont progressive movement to this day. After five terms on the Board of Aldermen, Terry was elected to the state legislature, where he is now serving his fourth term.

Sadie White, at seventy-nine, also defeated the Democratic machine to become an alderwoman. But her story is quite different from Terry's. For many years Sadie had been a Democratic state representative in the legislature. Her independence and willingness to stand up for her working-class constituents earned her the enmity of the machine, and they dumped her. Sadie had the last laugh, however. She came back with a vengeance, winning election to the Board as an Independent. Despite enormous pressure to return to the Democratic Party fold, she has remained an unwavering ally and good friend, during her stint on the Board and to this day.

At my first official meeting as mayor, the Board of Aldermen fired my secretary, the only person I had been able to hire. They claimed I hadn't hired her in the proper way. (They allowed me to rehire her soon after.) Two months later, on the day that the mayor formally announces his choices for administration posts, the Board rejected all of my appointees. The situation was absurd: I was expected to run city government with the administration of the guy I had just defeated in a bitter election, and a group of people who vigorously opposed my political goals. We were outflanked by the opposition on every major decision. The votes were always the same: eleven to two, the eight Democrats and three Republicans on one side, Terry and Sadie on the other.

The Democrats' strategy was not too complicated: they would tie my hands, make it impossible for me to accomplish anything, then win back the mayor's office by claiming that I had been ineffective.

And what was our strategy? First, we were going to do everything that a mayor could possibly do without the support of the City Council. Second, we were going to expose the local Democrats and Republicans for what they were—obstructionists and political hacks who had very few positive ideas. Third, and most important, we were going to build a third party in the city to defeat them in the next election.

During this first term, I discovered that the city was wasting substantial sums of money on its insurance policies. Local companies, year after year, were getting the city's business at substantially higher than market rates. I instituted a radical socialist concept, "competitive" bidding, which saved the city tens of thousands of dollars. We were showing that to be "radical" did not mean that we wasted taxpayer dollars. Quite the contrary. For those of us committed to the idea that government should play an important role in the life of our community, it was absolutely necessary to show that we could run a tightfisted, cost-effective administration. There is no excuse for wasting taxpayer money.

We also started a successful Little League program in the city's poorest neighborhood, and began what was to become a citywide tree-planting program that transformed block after block in Burlington. We began a very popular summer concert series which drew thousands of people to a beautiful waterfront park, where they listened to great music and watched the sun set over

Lake Champlain. We did all this and more by scratching together a few bucks here and a few bucks there.

As the year progressed, it became clear that the only way we could carry out effective policy for the city was by electing a majority of Progressives to the Board of Aldermen—which meant the creation of a new political entity. In the beginning we called it the Independent Coalition. Later, it was renamed the Progressive Coalition. The Coalition existed only in Burlington. While not a political party under state law (because it is not a statewide organization), it operates in Burlington as if it were exactly that.

In the winter of 1981–82, we recruited aldermanic candidates from each of the city's wards for the election in March. Rik Musty, a psychology professor at the University of Vermont, was our candidate in Ward 1; Zoe Breiner, a young worker at IBM, in Ward 2; Gary DeCarolis, a mental health worker for the state, in Ward 3; Jane Watson, an attorney, in Ward 4; Joan Beauchemin, a long-time community activist, in Ward 5; and Huck Gutman, co-author of this book and UVM professor of English, in Ward 6.

It gets very cold in Vermont in the winter, with lots of snow and ice. Frankly, it's not always fun knocking on doors when the weather is below zero. But that's what we did. Without exception, all of our candidates mounted vigorous campaigns, knocking on almost every door in their wards. I went out with our candidates as often as possible. We were motivated, to say the least. The themes of the campaign were crystal clear. First, our candidates ran on a progressive platform. Second, they were taking on Democrats and Republicans who were preventing the mayor from doing his job.

Voter turnout for the aldermanic elections hit an all-time high, and on election night, March 2, 1982, we had one wild cele-bration. Ward 1—victory. Ward 2—victory. Ward 3—victory. Ward 4—defeat. Ward 5—a runoff election between the Progressive and the Democrat as neither candidate received 40 percent of the vote. The Republican was defeated. Ward 6—a runoff between the Progressive and the Republican. The Democrat was defeated.

If my mayoral victory one year before had been regarded by some as a fluke, there could be no mistaking what was happening now. A political revolution had occurred in Burlington. The people had spoken, loudly and clearly. With a very high voter turnout, the citizens of Burlington informed the Democrats and Republicans that they wanted change—*real* change. Progressives were on the move.

As expected, the Democrats and Republicans combined their efforts for the runoff elections in Wards 5 and 6. The Republicans supported the Democrat in Ward 5, and the Democrats backed the Republican in Ward 6. Although our candidates ran very hard, both Joan and Huck lost.

Consequently, we did not capture a majority of the thirteen-member Board. (And we never did in my eight years as mayor.) But with the votes of Rik, Zoe, and Gary added to Sadie's and Terry's, we now at least had veto power. We could block any Democratic-Republican initiative. They had no other choice but to work with us. There was a new balance of power, and we could go forward.

My life as mayor was immediately made easier when the Board of Aldermen, suddenly seeing the light of day, decided to accept my appointments to various city positions. After a year as mayor, I finally had an administration. No longer would the mayor's advisers have to meet around my kitchen table to write the budget as volunteers. Now we could actually work at City Hall, and they would get paid for their work.

I was able to bring in a topnotch financial analyst, Jonathan Leopold, as treasurer. Jonathan revamped the city's entire financial operation, saving Burlington substantial sums of money. Barr Swennerfelt as assistant treasurer, Peter Clavelle as personnel director, Jim Dunn as assistant city attorney, Jim Rader as city clerk, David Clavelle as constable, and Steve Goodkind as city engineer rounded out my early appointments.

The Sanders administration and the Progressive Coalition were aggressive on all fronts. We were a very activist city government. The property tax, the major source of funding for education and municipal services in Vermont, is regressive because it is not based on ability to pay. Many senior citizens and working people were (and are) paying far more in property taxes than they can afford on their limited incomes. For seven straight years I did not raise the general property tax for homeowners in Burlington. At the same time, I fought hard for more progressive forms of taxation.

While I had strong backing from city residents in this fight, I did not have the support of the state legislature. In Vermont, municipalities must get approval for charter revisions from the state legislature. Time and again the legislature refused to approve the progressive charter changes that the people of Burlington had voted for—sometimes overwhelmingly. It was very disheartening, and one of the reasons I ran for governor in 1986. But more on that later.

Nonetheless, we did become the first municipality in Vermont to develop alternatives to the property tax. After a major struggle against many of the restaurant owners, we implemented a one percent room-and-meal tax. We also passed a classification system of taxation which raised to 120 percent the tax rate on commercial and industrial property. After a court battle, the utilities were forced to pay for the damage done when they tore up our streets for utility work. Following a heated battle with a cable TV company, and an effort on our part to create a municipally owned system, we managed to get substantial revenue from them and reduced rates for seniors.

The large tax-exempt institutions in the city, the University of Vermont and the Medical Center Hospital, successfully resisted most changes to the status quo. However, we did substantially increase payments from them for police and fire service. As a result of opposition from the governor and legislature, we were unable to generate the revenue we wanted from the municipally owned airport in South Burlington. But by taking over the administration of the large parking lot there, and deploying our own police officers for security, we did improve our cash flow.

Needless to say, our administration and movement were about more than progressive tax policy and efficient government. We were also about involving people in the process, about community, empowerment, fun, and excitement. For instance, the Mayor's Council on Women, which soon became the Burlington Women's Council, brought together women's organizations representing diverse professions and political orientations, from radical gay feminists to conservative businesswomen. Initiatives by the Women's Council included legislation, far ahead of its time, on domestic violence and specialized training for the police department, a study of "comparable worth" which resulted in a financial upgrading for many female municipal employees, and funding for a very successful program which trained low-income women in male-dominated, nontraditional types of employment, such as the building trades.

Jane O'Meara Driscoll, who later became my wife, headed up our Youth Office—first on a volunteer basis, later on the payroll. Jane launched a very successful municipally funded child care center, as well as a Teen Center. Everyone yells at teenagers and tells them to stay out of trouble and not do drugs. We offered them a social space, and opportunities for music and dance. Jane developed an afterschool program for younger kids, a youth newspaper, a theater program, a youth employment program, a summer garden project, and a public access TV show. She also implemented Operation Snow Shovel, a wonderful service program through which young people cleared snow for the elderly and disabled.

We started a number of cultural activities which took art into the streets. A jazz festival—with free concerts and music on our buses. A blues festival. A reggae festival. A country music festival. A chew-chew festival. Free summer concerts in the park. A First Night event on December 31, attended by thousands of people. Almost all of these events continue to this day.

One of my favorite evenings was a poetry reading in which Allen Ginsberg joined Burlington school children to read their poems in Burlington City Hall. Noam Chomsky, perhaps the best known radical author in America, spoke to a full house in City Hall. Studs Terkel visited us during a Workers' Rights celebration. Abbie Hoffman, Dave Dellinger, and I spoke on a panel in what turned out to be a very amusing evening. Ella Fitzgerald showcased a jazz festival. Burlington was becoming one of the most exciting and culturally alive small cities in the country.

These brief descriptions of the councils' work imply that implementation of their programs was a breeze. But the creation of the councils was a major political struggle, complete with blood, sweat, and tears. Almost every funding request was accompanied by vituperative and vicious debate. Everything was partisan. Nothing came easy.

I remember a letter to the editor written by an older man which said: "I don't know anything about this socialism, but Sanders is doing a good job repaving the streets." My administration never lost sight of the fact that, while broadening the scope of city government and developing new policy were important and satisfying, we could never forget about taking care of the basics. And in this area, we out-Republicaned the Republicans.

We expanded and improved the Police Department, and began the process of paying our officers a living wage. Ironically, one of my major allies in improving the Police Department was Tony Pomerleau, the chairman of the Police Commission and one of the wealthiest people in the state. (It was Tony's disastrous high-rise condominium waterfront development project that I had campaigned against in 1981.) Tony became such a good ally on police matters that he lost the support of the Democrats and Republicans and had to be reappointed with Progressive votes.

We upgraded the very expensive and life-saving trucks and apparatus used by the Fire Department. We merged the Street and Water Departments, and created a much more efficient Public Works Department, with new and more capable leadership. We developed and implemented a major street repaving program. We purchased an entirely new fleet of snow removal vehicles, and developed a new and more effective snow removal plan. And we brought in competent managers to run the city departments.

We instituted the largest and most costly environmental improvement program in the state's history: a $52 million city-state-federal project to rebuild our sewer system, upgrade our wastewater plants, and stop the pollution of Lake Champlain. We shut down the environmentally unsound landfill, and killed a proposed trash-burning plan which would have been both an environmental and fiscal catastrophe.

We initiated an extensive waterfront beautification plan. The previous mayor had supported a disastrous high-rise condominium project for the downtown waterfront. After an enormous amount of public discussion and fierce debate, we ended up with a very successful people-oriented waterfront of public parks, a nine-mile bike path, and a community boathouse. Today, cyclists can travel from one end of Burlington to the other. Swimming is free of charge at any one of four public parks. We've got some nice athletic facilities as well.

We also developed some very innovative concepts in affordable housing. Against opposition from a segment of the local real estate industry, we became the first city in America to fund community land-trust housing. Through the Burlington Community Land Trust, working-class people were able to purchase their own homes at a lower cost than offered on the commercial market. The housing remains affordable in perpetuity because the owners must agree not to resell the property at market rates, accepting only a reasonable and limited return on their investment.

Working with a tenant organization and nonprofit housing groups, we prevented the largest subsidized housing development in the state, Northgate, from being converted into expensive condominiums. With a federal grant secured by Senator Leahy, and other sources of funding, we managed to convert that develop-

ment into a cooperatively owned housing project—and saved 336
units for people with modest incomes. Through a variety of
mechanisms, we were also able to build a number of units of
affordable housing.

We also improved life for low-income people in Burlington's
public housing. Every year I was able to appoint one new member
to the Burlington Housing Authority. At the end of three years we
finally had a majority, at which point we brought in an outstanding new director, Mike McNamara, who made major improve-
ments in city-run low-income and senior citizen housing.

While we were able to pass the most sweeping tenants' rights
legislation in the state, we were not successful in our major pro-
tenant initiative, rent control. In 1982, the landlord organization
defeated us decisively in a citywide vote on that issue. They raised a
substantial sum of money, hired a consultant, and outpoliticked us.

In 1983, working with a citizen's committee led by local businessman Tom Racine, we managed to bring minor league baseball to Burlington. After interminable discussions with the owner
of an AA Eastern League franchise and the Cincinnati Reds,
minor league baseball returned to Burlington after a hiatus of
thirty years. We worked out a deal with the University of
Vermont to use their field, and the Vermont Reds became a huge
success. In their first year, they drew over 120,000 fans. The team
won three straight Eastern League championships and, amazingly, were one of the great minor league teams of their time. At
least a half dozen players on the Vermont Reds became major lea-
guers, including such stars as Kal Daniels, Paul O'Neill, Chris
Sabo, Jeff Montgomery, and Jeff Treadway.

I happen to think that Burlington is one of the most beautiful
cities in America. But the truth is that a number of cities have
nice waterfronts, good streets, honest police departments, and
even minor league baseball. But how many cities of 40,000 have a
foreign policy? Well, we did.

As you may recall, I was not the only elected official in
America during the 1980s. There was that other fellow, Ronald

Reagan. Many Burlingtonians, including myself, supported the
Sandinista government in Nicaragua. President Reagan did not.
We disagreed with him. We expressed our displeasure.

Somewhere in the Reagan archives, or wherever these things
are kept, is a letter from the mayor of Burlington on this subject.
There are also official proclamations from the Burlington Board
of Aldermen, made after long and emotional public hearings.
"Stop the war against the people of Nicaragua! Use our tax dollars
to feed the hungry and house the homeless. Stop killing the innocent people of Nicaragua."

This was an issue that many of us in the progressive movement felt very strongly about. Not only was the war against
Nicaragua illegal and immoral, it was an outrageous waste of taxpayer money. As a mayor, I wanted more federal funds for affordable housing and economic development. I did not want to see
taxpayer dollars going to the CIA for an appalling war. While
most of the Democrats and Republicans on the Board of
Aldermen disagreed, to us this was very much a municipal issue.

In 1985, I was invited by the Nicaraguan government to visit
Managua for the seventh anniversary of the Sandinista
Revolution. I was—believe it or not—the highest ranking
American official present. The competition wasn't too keen. I
think the only other elected American official was a school board
member from Berkeley, California.

The trip to Nicaragua was a profoundly emotional experience. Along with other "foreign dignitaries," I was introduced
to a crowd of hundreds of thousands who gathered for the
anniversary celebration. I will never forget that in the front row
of the huge crowd were dozens and dozens of amputees in
wheelchairs—young soldiers, many of them in their teens, who
had lost their legs in a war foisted on them and financed by the
U.S. government.

During the trip I had an opportunity to meet with Daniel
Ortega, the president of Nicaragua, as well as other government
officials. I also met with some of the opposition, including Jaime

Chamorro, the editor of the opposition newspaper, *La Prensa*. Father Miguel D'Escoto was then the Nicaraguan foreign minister. I met him in a small church in Managua where he was lying in bed, fasting in protest against U.S. support for the contras.

This trip took on special significance because I was accompanied by a reporter from our local newspaper, the *Burlington Free Press*, the largest paper in the state. The reporter, Don Melvin, covered the City Hall beat. He found out that I was going to Nicaragua and somehow managed to convince his editors that if his job was following the mayor, then that meant following him to Nicaragua. Don filed a story each night from Nicaragua which made the front pages of the paper. Our relationship remained entirely professional, and I had no clue as to what he was writing until I returned home. As it happened, he did an excellent job of describing what he saw, and his articles succeeded in countering a lot of the lies and distortions about Nicaragua trotted out by the corporate media.

One of the most moving experiences of the trip occurred on our very first day there. Shortly after we arrived in Managua, we boarded a small plane and flew to the town of Puerto Cabezas, on the Atlantic coastline. Before I left Burlington, the city had agreed to develop a sister-city program with Puerto Cabezas. I went there to meet with local officials and work out the details. News had just reached the town, which had a heavy Miskito Indian population, that some people who had returned to their home on the Rio Coco had been killed, and their bodies were being transported back to Puerto Cabezas.

Eighteen hours earlier, Don and I had been breakfasting together in Burlington. And now, on that same unbelievably long day, somewhere in an Indian village on the Atlantic coast of Nicaragua, we listened to the wailing of family members who received their dead relatives back into the village. It was an unforgettable experience.

The sister-city program with Puerto Cabezas was very popular and continues to this day. Out of that program came many trips back and forth of Vermonters and Nicaraguans, and the development of many friendships. The people of Burlington provided a significant amount of material help in terms of medical supplies, school equipment, and other desperately needed goods. In return, we had the opportunity to learn about a courageous people and a very different culture.

On May 28, 1988, Jane and I were married. The marriage ceremony was held—where else?—in North Beach, a public park on Burlington's waterfront. A lot of people attended.

On the next day we began a quiet, romantic honeymoon. We went to Yaroslavl, in the Soviet Union, along with ten other Burlingtonians, to finalize our sister-city relationship with that city. Trust me. It was a very strange honeymoon.

Like the Puerto Cabezas project, the sister-city program with Yaroslavl has been very successful. Each has different constituencies of support. Puerto Cabezas mostly attracted the energy of left-wing activists who were initially involved because of their support for the

Sandinista Revolution and opposition to U.S. intervention in Central America. The Yaroslavl project received more broad-based backing, including from a number of business people in the city.

In 1987, the Leningrad Youth Choir gave a magnificent concert at Memorial Auditorium, our largest facility. The audience was especially moved when the young people from Leningrad performed alongside high school students from throughout Vermont. We also played host to a number of Soviet students who visited Burlington High School as part of an exchange program.

Jane and I visited Cuba in 1989. I had hoped to meet with Castro, but that didn't work out. But I did meet with the mayor of Havana and other officials.

Burlington had a foreign policy because, as progressives, we understood that we all live in one world. We understood that just as actions taken outside of our city affected us, we could have an impact on national and international developments. If children in Nicaragua were suffering because of U.S. policy, it was our responsibility to try to change that policy. If children in the United States were going hungry because the federal government was spending more than was necessary on the military, we also had a responsibility to work on changing that.

As the mayor of Burlington, and someone committed to grassroots democracy, I saw no magic line separating local, state, national, and international issues. How could federal cuts in education not be a local issue? They affect our public schools. How could environmental degradation not be a local issue? It affects the water we drink and our health. How could issues of war and peace not be a local issue? It is local youngsters who fight and die in wars. Ultimately, if we're going to revitalize democracy in this country, local government will have to assume a much stronger and more expansive role.

I think back on my eight years as mayor of Burlington with enormous satisfaction. We had shown that good people could come together, take on very powerful special interests, and successfully fight for social change. We had shown that if you open the doors to City Hall and are prepared to fight for the interests of ordinary people, they will come in and join the struggle.

But let me be very clear: a major factor in our success was that we worked *extremely* hard. We had to in order to survive. Year after year. Yes, the movement was filled with bright people who had loads of creative ideas. Yes, we ran attractive and articulate candidates, and enlisted people who became excellent administrators. But unless you are ready to hit the streets, knock on doors, and communicate with your constituents, you're not going to be successful.

We did not accomplish all that we set out to do, and we made our share of mistakes. But no one, not even our worst enemies, could accuse us of being armchair radicals. We outworked our opponents in every campaign. Remember that in Burlington, elections are held every year when half the Board comes up. That's a lot of work.

In 1983, the *Burlington Free Press*, the city's daily newspaper and voice of the business community, urged the Democratic and Republican parties to join forces around one candidate in order to defeat my reelection bid. Gee. Here I was, year after year, telling people that there wasn't a helluva big difference between the two major parties, and the *Burlington Free Press* agreed with me.

But the two parties did not combine in 1983. Instead, they ran separate candidates. Judy Stephany, a leader in the Vermont House of Representatives, ran as the Democratic candidate; Jim Gilson, the chairman of the school board, was the Republican candidate. The election night results were Sanders 52 percent, Stephany 31 percent, and Gilson 17 percent. The Progressives were also successful in reelecting two members to the Board of Aldermen.

In 1979, before the progressive movement was active in Burlington, 7,000 people had voted in the mayoral election. In 1981, when I was first elected, participation went up to 9,300—a 30 percent increase. In 1983, when I was reelected, 13,320 people voted, almost twice as many as in 1979. The citizens of Burlington had seen a local government working for their interests, and they came out in large numbers to support it. In the low-income and working-class wards, I won close to 70 percent of the vote in a three-way race, and our aldermanic candidates won landslide victories.

Interestingly, as Burlingtonians paid more and more attention to local elections in March, they also voted in far larger numbers in the national elections in November. In 1984, 18,129 Burlingtonians voted in the presidential elections, a 23 percent higher turnout than in 1980. In the national election, the city voted strongly Democratic.

In 1985, I ran for a third term against the former lieutenant governor of Vermont, Democrat Brian Burns. The Republican candidate was Diane Gallagher, a member of the City Council. In that election, I received 55 percent of the vote, Burns 31 percent, and Gallagher 12 percent.

When I announced for reelection for a fourth term in 1987, I stated that, if I won, this would be my last two years. In that election, somewhat belatedly, the Democrats and Republicans finally heeded the advice that the *Burlington Free Press* had given them in 1983. They rallied around one candidate, Paul Lafayette, who was a Democrat on the City Council. Needless to say, taking on the combined parties wasn't easy, and Paul ran a smart campaign. When he was nominated by the Democrats in a contested caucus, close to a thousand people, a huge turnout, attended the meeting. After six years out of the mayor's office, the Democrats were very anxious to regain City Hall. We were very happy, therefore, when we defeated Lafayette, 54 to 46 percent.

Despite a poll showing me with a very high favorability rating and no serious opposition, I left office in April 1989. Eight years was enough. At the end of the month I attended my last Board of Aldermen meeting as mayor of Burlington. I was very happy that this meeting ended on a better note than my first. The Democrats, Republicans, and Progressives presented me with a beautiful newspaper collage, highlighting some of the outstanding events of my tenure.

I was also delighted that my replacement as mayor would be Peter Clavelle, a Progressive. Peter had served in my administration for a number of years, most recently as the director of economic development, where he did an outstanding job. Peter became mayor by defeating a candidate supported by both the Democrats and Republicans. I was leaving the city in good hands.

This whole campaign fundraising situation stinks to high heaven. In the past, I have fought hard for campaign finance reform which limits the amount of money that can be spent in an election and which emphasizes public funding of elections and small individual contributions. Ordinary Americans should have a chance to win elections, not just the rich or representatives thereof. If reelected, I will accelerate my efforts in this area.

Ironically, Susan Sweetser is attacking me on the issue of fundraising. She criticizes the fact that I do not list every contribution under $200. (Federal Election Commission law mandates only that contributors of $200 or more be itemized.) And in press conferences and press releases, she points out that I receive much of my support from out of state. Hence the strategy of tying me to a national cabal of left-wing extremists.

For years, Vermont Republicans have been furious that I have been able to raise money and run strong campaigns. They understand, as I do, that a winning campaign is well nigh impossible without adequate financial resources. In 1988, it is likely that if I had been able to spend as much as my Republican opponent, Peter Smith, I would have won. In 1990, while we were outspent again by Smith, we raised enough money to mount a forceful campaign—and win. I was not outspent in 1992 or '94.

As the only Independent in Congress, I face unique fundraising handicaps which my campaign works very hard to overcome. Unlike Democrats and Republicans, I do not receive any funds from a political party. I do not benefit from the coordinated campaigns that Democrats and Republicans utilize. My campaign does not get support from a party organization which provides staff, polling, literature, offices, mailings, voter checklists, and other services. Further, as a Progressive, I have adamantly refused financial support from Big Money interests. Throughout my political career, I have never accepted one penny from a corporate PAC. (Of the Banking Committee's fifty-two members, only two, including myself, receive no PAC funds from interests associated with the corporate financial community.)

Most importantly, the vast majority of my contributors do not have a lot of money and are unable to give large amounts. In campaign after campaign, I receive *more* individual contributions from Vermont than my opponents, but *fewer* total dollars. Our average campaign contribution is less than $35. My Republican opponent will always have a much higher average contribution. Sweetser, for instance, is collecting many $1,000 checks from some of the richest people in the state, not to mention the $30,000 she raised at the $500-a-plate function attended by Dick Armey.

So, how have we raised money in the past, and what are we doing this campaign? Simple. We play to our strengths. While our average campaign contribution is small, we receive an enormous number of contributions from middle-class and working people, in Vermont and throughout the country. This campaign we hope to receive some 20,000 individual contributions, an incredible number. As the only Independent in Congress, and as a progressive, working people from every state have contributed to my campaigns. If the Republicans think I'm embarrassed by this, they can think again. I'm proud to have the support.

Raising money from so many people takes an enormous amount of work and record keeping. We have to record every contribution that comes in and make certain that our bank deposits are correct. We also have to fill out the FEC reports several times during the campaign—and make sure that they are right. Tineke and Jerome Russell and Sara Burchard have volunteered for this massive undertaking for the last two campaigns. They have done an extraordinary job.

It is unlikely that we will ever be able to raise as much money in Vermont as a strong Republican like Sweetser. The arithmetic is simple. If 400 wealthy individuals made an average contribution of $500, Sweetser would raise $200,000 in Vermont. That is much more than we have ever raised, or are ever likely to raise. You just can't accumulate that kind of money when your average contribution is less than $35, and when you get thousands of contributions from people who are doing the best they can by sending a check for $10 or $20. I would need close to 6,000 contributions averaging $35 to match her $200,000, not to mention the greatly increased costs and the labor associated with actually raising that much money from so many people.

While I will not accept PAC money from corporate America, I gladly accept PAC contributions from organizations fighting to improve life for ordinary people. Over the years, my campaigns have received strong financial support from PACs associated with organized labor, the environment, women, senior citizens, human rights, and the needs of children. That is continuing in this campaign.

The general ignorance surrounding the issue of campaign financing is frustrating. My opponents call me a "hypocrite" for accepting PAC money. How can I accept PAC money, they say, and then claim that I am fighting against "special interests"? Isn't a PAC, by definition, a "special interest"? Aren't all PAC contributions the same? Does it make any difference who the PAC represents?

Such questions, which are repeated ad nauseam in the media, reflect a lack of understanding of the role of money in politics. So, let me be very clear about this. I do *not* believe that working people are a special interest. I do *not* believe that hungry kids are a special interest. I do *not* believe that fighting for the right of women to control their own bodies is a special interest. I do *not* believe that protecting the environment is a special interest.

Believe me. The problem with Washington, and politics in the United States, is *not* that ordinary people have too much power and influence. It's not that too much attention is being paid to low-income children. It's not that the needs of the rich and large corporations are ignored.

The problem, for those who have just crawled out from under a rock, is that groups representing the wealthiest people in this country are able to decisively influence the legislative process so that public policy reflects the interests of the privileged few and not the needs of the general population. And if you don't understand this simple fact, you haven't a clue as to what politics in America is all about.

In this campaign, my opponent has been promised $153,000 from the Republican national party, which will come directly from some of the richest people in America. She has already received, and will undoubtedly continue to get, heavy contributions from some of the largest corporations in America and from groups which represent multi-billion dollar corporate interests. She is obtaining significant support from some of the wealthiest people in Vermont. She indicated at the very beginning of the campaign that she did not want a limit on the amount that could be spent.

Bottom line. If people, including the media, do not understand the difference between one candidate who receives the bulk of his support from organizations and individuals who represent working people and the middle class, and another candidate who receives the bulk of her support from the wealthy and large corporations, than they do not know much about what goes on in Congress. I am going to do my best to prevent the wealthy and corporate interests from buying this election.

The Long March Forward

In 1986, I ran for governor as an Independent. I was still in my third term as mayor of Burlington. I ran because the state legislature continually denied Burlington and other communities the democratic right to reform their regressive property tax system. We voted for change but, despite all the lip service to "local control," the legislature and the governor refused to allow us to change our city charter and implement progressive legislation. They simply nullified what we were attempting to do. In Burlington, we were showing that grassroots democracy could work. In the state capital, they were thwarting our efforts and trying to destroy our momentum.

I also ran for governor because I feared that the "Burlington Revolution" would suffocate if we didn't expand beyond one city. People all over the state believed in progressive politics and wanted to be involved in electoral activity. We needed new energy. We also needed to make a political connection between the rural and urban areas of the state.

Madeleine Kunin, the former Democratic lieutenant governor, had been elected the first woman governor of Vermont in 1984, and was running for reelection in 1986. Peter Smith, the lieutenant governor, was the Republican candidate. Kunin was a liberal, strong on women's issues and the environment. We had very serious disagreements, however, not only on the issue of "local control" and the need for Vermont to break its dependence on the property tax, but on health care, child care, utility rates, the needs of the poor, and involving working people in the political process. In any case, I mounted a campaign to become the first Independent governor in Vermont's history. The campaign was a near disaster, and came very close to ending my political career.

The major tactical error that we made was transferring our campaign office from Burlington to Montpelier, where we had a strong but inexperienced base of support. I wanted to physically separate my work as mayor from that of the campaign office, and allow a new group of progressive activists to play leading roles. I also wanted Vermonters to feel that this was a statewide effort, not something emanating from the Burlington progressive community.

It just didn't turn out the way it was supposed to. Our central Vermont activists were smart, hard working, and dedicated, but they lacked the day-to-day experience of running a campaign. Further, and even more importantly, the race against Kunin was very difficult. Liberals were angry that I was running against a female Democrat, as were some environmentalists.

Midway through the campaign, as we were running out of money and going nowhere in the polls, my campaign manager resigned. There was a growing feeling from supporters, and the media, that I should and would drop out of the race. This was the lowest point in my political career. What to do?

I did not quit the race. After a lot of soul-searching and planning, what was left of the campaign limped back to Burlington and regrouped. The campaign was now back in the hands of people who had been with me through the mayoral elections.

Jane and I flew to California, where I gave speeches in Los Angeles and San Francisco. Through the efforts of such progressives as Sherri and Leo Frumkin and Peter Camejo, we were able to raise $6,000. Not a great deal of money, but it all helped. Our fundraising in Vermont also began to pick up.

Some of the people who worked with me at City Hall decided to use their free time to help out. Forty hours at City Hall, forty hours on the campaign. A long week. Jane, city treasurer Jonathan Leopold, Sue Trainer, and a few others jumped head first into the campaign. They were joined by Jeff Weaver, a young man from St. Albans, Vermont, who had been expelled from Boston University for protesting racial discrimination. Jeff would work with me for much of the next eight years.

Slowly the campaign rejuvenated. There were a number of debates, some on television, and I did well. We held lively rallies. Despite the fact that the polls put me far behind and that conventional wisdom suggests that a third-party candidate will fade under such circumstances, we kept gaining momentum right up to Election Day.

Kunin received 48 percent of the vote, Smith 37 percent. I ended up with 14.5 percent. We had lost badly but, if the truth be known, we felt pretty good. We raised the right issues, won the support of many working-class people from all over the state, and had come back from near political death. It could have been a lot worse.

In 1988, Senator Robert Stafford retired after sixteen years, and Republican Congressman Jim Jeffords ran for the vacant post. Vermont's sole seat in the U.S. House was open, and I decided to run for it. Peter Smith, who finished second in the governor's race against Kunin in 1986, was the Republican candidate, and Paul Poirier was running for the Democrats after winning a tough, three-way primary.

In many ways that congressional campaign was the turning point for me in statewide politics. I began the race as the "spoiler." (Oh, how I love that word, with all its implications about the sacrosanct nature of the two-party system.) Would I take enough votes away from the Democrat to elect the Republican? But a funny thing happened on the way to Election Day. I wasn't the spoiler, after all. The Democrat was.

Looking back, the 1988 campaign was actually a lot of fun. Smith was a moderate Republican who had received positive recognition for helping to start the Vermont community college system. Poirier was the majority leader in the Vermont House, a moderate-to-liberal Democrat. Paul was a former teacher and was widely considered a decent, down-to-earth guy. And then there was me.

Vermont is a small state, and Smith, Poirier, and I knew each other pretty well. In fact, we liked each other. That campaign was what Vermont politics should be about. The three of us had strong differences of opinion, but we ran civil, issue-oriented campaigns. The debates were respectful and there was no negative advertising, no desire to "destroy" the other person. Boy, does that seem like a long time ago.

That fall, Harry Reasoner and the crew of "60 Minutes" came to Vermont to film me and the campaign. They had heard that an Independent, and a democratic socialist, had a chance to win a congressional race. It was a good story for them. While they were there, I held a press conference about agricultural issues on a farm in central Vermont. The Associated Press, the most important print media organization in the state, did not show up— which was getting to be a habit with them.

When you're a politician dealing with the media, life is difficult. If you're getting screwed by the media, you don't have much recourse. Who can you complain to? They own the camera. They print the news. What are you going to do about it?

Finally, for the one and only time in my life, I did have a recourse. I had "60 Minutes" following me around. I could expose the AP to the world. A politician's dream come true.

"Come on guys," I told my staff. "We're going to visit the AP and talk about fair news coverage." Ten minutes later I was walking up the stairs of the AP office in Montpelier, the camera and microphone of "60 Minutes" right behind me. This time *I* was asking the questions. "Okay, how come you never cover my press conferences? You have time for the Republicans. You have time for the Democrats. Why not an Independent?" The AP had heard it all before. Except this time the cameras of "60 Minutes" were rolling, and AP was on the defensive. It was delicious.

I had a lot of fun that afternoon. Of course, I paid for it later. You never beat the media. After I was elected in 1990, the AP chief went to Washington to do a long series on whether or not I was an effective congressman. Guess what he concluded?

But that's all over now. It's water over the dam. It's hardly worth remembering. The AP and I are friends now, and we have a truly professional relationship. Right? Right? Hello. Hello.

While I was heavily outspent by Smith, our campaign did a good job of raising money. Unfortunately, we ran out of funds one week before Election Day and were going to have to take our TV ads off the air. Jane and I discussed the matter, went to the bank, took out all the money we had—$10,000—and gave it to the TV stations.

On the evening before the election I bumped into Smith as we were campaigning in Montpelier, our state capital. We embraced and congratulated each other on a good campaign. Election night was an emotional roller coaster. The returns first came in from Burlington and surrounding towns, where I usually do well. We were ahead by ten points. Then, as the night wore on, our lead dropped to five points. Then we were in a dead heat. Finally, three points behind. And that's where we stayed, hour after hour. Three points. At one o'clock in the morning, I called Smith and conceded. We were very disappointed, but we had run an excellent campaign. The final results: Smith 41 percent, Sanders 38 percent, Poirier 19 percent. I would never again be called a spoiler.

Needless to say, "60 Minutes" did not run the profile on Bernie Sanders. This is America. Winner take all. Who wants a story about a guy who *almost* became a congressman?

Aside from my own campaign, 1988 was an interesting political year for me because I became a Democrat—for all of one night. This was the year that Jesse Jackson waged an exciting and strategically important battle for the Democratic nomination for president. Within the progressive movement in Vermont, there were differing opinions as to what our role should be in Jackson's efforts. While almost everyone was impressed by his campaign, some progressives thought that we should not get involved because Jackson was running within the Democratic Party. On the other hand, strong Vermont progressives like Ellen David Friedman, Liz Blum, Chris Wood, and others had formed a Vermont chapter of the Rainbow Coalition, which was working hard and effectively for Jackson. After a good deal of debate, the Burlington Progressive Coalition decided to endorse Jackson.

The Rainbow Coalition garnered significant support for Jackson statewide. In central Vermont, they mobilized a huge crowd for his appearance in Montpelier. Burlington and Chittenden County progressives also worked hard, and I campaigned with Jackson when he visited Burlington. On the evening of the nonbinding Vermont Democratic Party caucus, which was held in towns throughout the state, I participated in a formal Democratic Party function for the first and last time in my life. (In Vermont the primary process was then absolutely open. Anyone could identify with any party.) Along with many other progressives, I attended the Democratic Caucus in Burlington.

As mayor of the city, I gave the nominating speech for Jackson. Governor Madeleine Kunin, who also lived in Burlington, gave the nominating speech for Dukakis. Given that progressives had replaced Democrats as the governing party in Burlington, not everyone there greeted my presence with enthusiasm. In fact, a number of old-line Dems staged a silent protest by standing up and turning around as I delivered my speech. And when I returned to my seat, a woman in the audience slapped me across the face. It was an exciting evening. By the way, Jackson won the Burlington caucus overwhelmingly. He also carried the state.

By the spring of 1989, my term as mayor of Burlington was over. I was unemployed and began looking for a job. Unlike some former elected officials, I was not flooded with invitations to prestigious institutions. Actually, I didn't get *any* job offers. My particular skills, it seems, were not too marketable. Panicking a bit, I sent off letters to every college in the country. I was interested in both speaking engagements and a teaching job. I also had illusions about writing a syndicated column.

In the fall of 1989, I taught at the Institute for Policy Studies at Harvard University's Kennedy School of Government. They offer a sensible program which brings real-life politicians (not infrequently folks who have lost their last election) to the campus to give students a sense of real-life politics. I taught a course on third-party politics which was well attended. Jane took some courses at the Kennedy School and two of our children, Carina and David, attended the local public schools. I went to more football games that fall than I had in twenty years, and became addicted to the cinnamon raisin buns at Au Bon Pain at Harvard Square. I know that conservatives worry a great deal about Harvard. They see it as a bastion of progressive thought, the brain trust for the revolution. Trust me. They can stop worrying. Harvard has many wonderful attributes, but the revolution will not start at Harvard University.

In the spring I went to Hamilton College in Clinton, New York. Dennis Gilbert, a professor of sociology there, arranged for me to teach in his department for a semester. I taught one course on politics and another on urban issues. Dennis has since become a very good friend, and remains a part of our political family. I also taught a course for adults at a satellite location through the State University of New York in Binghamton.

In May 1990, I had to make a decision about my future. I had three options. The first was to do what almost any sane human being would choose—drop out of politics. I had served eight of the last twenty years as mayor. I had run in ten elections with my name on the ballot, and I had played an active role in another five or six. I could give the people of Vermont, myself, and my family a break—and return to producing radical educational media, which I had enjoyed so much in the years before I became mayor. The idea of making videos, records, and tapes was attractive.

I loved the work, and could probably bring in a decent income. I could also teach, lecture, and write—and spend time with my wife and four kids. All in all, this was a very appealing option.

My second option was to run for governor. In 1990, Governor Kunin decided not to seek a fourth term. Former governor Richard Snelling became the leading candidate and a number of Democrats were considering a run. Within the progressive movement, there was a lot of interest in having me run for governor. The truth is there was (and is) a lot more interest in what happens at the state level than in that faraway place called Washington, D.C. A "Sanders for Governor" campaign would create a great deal of excitement, bring together the various elements of the progressive coalition, sharply raise political consciousness in the state, and might very well result in victory in a three-way race. It was an option that I, and other progressives, gave serious consideration.

The negatives of a run for governor were that it would be, in Yogi Berra's words, déjà vu all over again. If the Establishment had gone berserk when I was mayor, what would they do if I were governor and the stakes were much higher? We would most certainly face enormous political and economic opposition, and some of us wondered whether we had the statewide political infrastructure and strength to sustain ourselves against such an onslaught.

If I won we could expect that the Democrats and Republicans who controlled the legislature would vigorously oppose the progressive initiatives I brought forward. Would I be able to win more than a few votes on our key pieces of legislation?

There would also be enormous opposition from the big money interests. If we demanded that the wealthy and large Vermont corporations pay their fair share of taxes, would some of them leave the state and throw Vermont workers out on the streets? As we fought for a statewide health insurance program for all Vermonters, would the insurance companies and health care establishment sabotage our efforts and cut back on medical services? Would Wall Street lower Vermont's bond ratings and plunge us into a financial crisis? Would we be able to get our point of view out through the conservative media organs? Most importantly, did we have a strong enough political organization to keep our supporters mobilized and fighting? Could we hang in for the long haul, or would they blow us away after two years?

There was also a practical consideration: it was unlikely that I would carry 50 percent of the vote in a three-way race. The Vermont Constitution mandates that if no candidate wins 50 percent, the legislature elects the governor. While there would be a tremendous uproar if the legislature failed to seat the candidate with the most votes, it was a distinct possibility. Many Republicans and Democrats in the legislature would *never* cast a vote for Bernie Sanders.

My third and final option was to run for Congress against Peter Smith, again. While it is very tough to knock off an incumbent, I had lost the last race by only three-and-a-half points. Given the fact that the Democrat in 1988 had come in a distant third, it was unlikely that a strong Democrat would enter the race. It was probable, therefore, that I could get the lion's share of the 19 percent that Poirier had received. Further, the developing savings and loan fiasco—which in the end cost taxpayers hundreds of billions of dollars—had revealed the degree to which both parties in Congress worked to represent the interests of wealthy special interests, and exemplified what I had been talking about for years.

Should I run for governor? Should I run for Congress? After a great deal of discussion with progressives all over the state, and amid enormous media speculation, I decided to make another run against Smith.

If the congressional campaign of 1988 had been friendly, positive, and issue-oriented, the election of 1990 was the very opposite. It was one of the most bitter campaigns in Vermont history. It was not fun.

But there were a number of key elements in my favor. First, Smith had voted for the 1990 budget reconciliation bill, which proposed major cuts in Medicare. He had to make a tough choice, and he made the wrong one. I strongly opposed that legislation, and the bill was unpopular in Vermont. Senior citizens in Vermont were strongly Republican or Democrat, and not necessarily comfortable with a progressive Independent. After Smith's vote, however, I began to win more support among seniors.

Second, the 1990 congressional session went on and on and on. Smith was trapped in Washington for much of the campaign. Unlike in 1988, when I had the responsibility of being both a mayor and a candidate, I could campaign full-time in Vermont. I didn't have to spend half my time running a city. That was a clear advantage which allowed me to get around the state and meet voters.

Third, the National Rifle Association turned against Smith. In 1988, the NRA had supported both Smith and Poirier, and had opposed me. During that campaign, I was very clear that while I opposed the Brady bill because I felt that a handgun waiting period could be dealt with at the state level, I supported a ban on certain types of assault weapons, which was clearly a national issue. Both Smith and Poirier adopted the anti–gun control position of the NRA.

A few months after taking office, Smith suddenly announced that he would now vote *for* the ban on assault weapons. The NRA and other elements in Vermont's sportsmen community were furious at his about-face. They felt betrayed and worked hard to defeat him. While the NRA has never endorsed me or given me a nickel, their efforts against Smith in 1988 clearly helped my candidacy. (I should add here that in 1992, '94, and '96, the NRA strongly opposed me.)

Fourth, as I expected, no strong Democrat entered the race. Dolores Sandoval, a professor at the University of Vermont, ran a weak campaign with little party support.

Fifth, many Republicans thought Smith had been rude and disloyal to President Bush, who flew into Vermont to stump for him. At a big Republican fundraiser in Burlington, with the president at his side, Smith announced that he disagreed with Bush and supported increased taxes on the rich. Since everyone in Vermont knew that this had been my position from day one, many Republicans felt that Smith was being opportunistic, and should not have embarrassed the first sitting president to visit Vermont in many years. Republican support for Smith turned tepid.

Last, the political climate in Vermont and America was changing. The excesses of the 1980s were becoming more and more apparent, and it wasn't just the S&L scandal. The rich were getting richer, the middle class was shrinking, the new jobs being created were low-wage jobs, and the people of Vermont were increasingly dissatisfied with status-quo politics. The idea of going outside of the two-party system became more and more appealing. In this context, an Independent candidate began to look attractive.

Throughout the campaign, polls indicated that the race was close, with Smith slightly ahead. After Smith voted for the budget bill and the cuts in Medicare, however, the momentum shifted to us. Several weeks before the election, we were up by four to six points. Smith then panicked and made the biggest mistake of his campaign: he listened to his Washington consultants and produced the most negative television ads that anyone in Vermont had ever seen. One of the ads, taking a statement of mine out of context, described me as becoming "nauseous" upon hearing John F. Kennedy's inaugural speech. Another redbaited me by putting me on a split screen with Fidel Castro.

A week before the election, Dennis Gilbert, who was rapidly becoming a very adept pollster, put together a quick tracking poll. Not being "sophisticated" and having the poll done by big time operators in Washington, we were able to tabulate the polling information immediately. In fact, Dennis and I counted some of the results in my car after picking up the raw data from one of our volunteer phone banks. The poll confirmed what we had been feeling out on the streets: Smith's ads were backfiring, and we were winning big. The people of Vermont did not like ugly, negative advertising.

Our momentum was palpable. Everywhere I went there was tremendous support. As I walked down streets, people honked their horns and shouted from their cars, "Give 'em hell, Bernie," "Shake 'em up." Hester McKinney, our office manager, was fielding calls of support from all over the state. Our campaign slogan was, "Making History in Vermont." That's what we were about to do—and everyone knew it.

Election night was euphoric. As television stations reported victories for us in town after town, what stuck in my mind was how two years before we had been ahead early in the evening, but had ultimately lost. The last thing in the world I wanted was to show up at the celebration, presume victory, and then lose. So my family and I, along with some close friends, waited out the long night at home.

But 1990 was not 1988. Our support was amazingly strong all over the state, and we carried thirteen of Vermont's fourteen counties. The final results were Sanders 56 percent, Smith 40 percent, and Sandoval 3 percent. When we finally headed off to the celebration, well over a thousand people had already filled the basement of Memorial Auditorium. There was pandemonium. I could barely fight my way to the podium.

It is hard to describe my feelings at that moment. We had come such a long way, against such incredible odds. So many wonderful people, from one end of the state to the other, had come together to make this victory possible. Twenty years before, I had run for statewide office and had received 2 percent of the vote. As I climbed onto the platform for my victory statement, I was now the congressman-elect from the state of Vermont, the first Independent elected to Congress in forty years. It was almost incomprehensible.

All of us were exhausted, but the adrenalin of victory kept us afloat for many days. There were people all over the state to visit and thank, and a million phone calls to make. There were radio, TV, and newspaper interviews to do all across the country. I was a true novelty: the only Independent in Congress *and* a socialist.

Whatever "socialist" might mean to the media, it was sure new
and different. Media heaven. Among other shows, I appeared on
"Nightline" with Ted Koppel. Paul Wellstone, who had just been
elected to the Senate, and Gary Franks, the first black Republican
in Congress, were also on that night. I did the show from the ABC
affiliate in Burlington, and it was the first time that I had to
answer questions while staring into a blank camera. It was a dis-
concerting experience. A short time later I appeared on Larry
King's radio program. King and I reminisced about Brooklyn,
where we had
both grown up.
    A new mem-
ber of Congress,
whether a socialist
Independent or a
right-wing
Republican, must
deal immediately
with housekeep-
ing chores. I
headed for
Washington and
jumped in. First, I

had to familiarize myself with a congressman's annual budget,
about $877,000, and the legal guidelines for allocating funds to
staff, mailings, general office expenses, etc. Along with other new
members, I had to select an office in one of the House office buildings—Rayburn, Cannon, or Longworth—by drawing a number
out of a box. I ended up with an office in Cannon, on the fifth
floor. Coincidentally, this same office was used a few decades
before by an aggressive young congressman from California,
Richard Nixon. Now where did he hide those tape recorders?
    Bells sound in the office buildings fifteen minutes before a
vote, and it's down the elevator, through the halls, and across the
street to the Capitol. On a vote-heavy day, you can spend an hour

on trips to the Capitol and back. It's one way to stay in shape. The best offices (in the Rayburn building) are closest to the Capitol. Needless to say, new members don't get them.

The next order of business was organizing district congressional offices, along with assembling a competent staff, installing telephones, figuring out which outrageously expensive computer system worked best for my needs, and requisitioning furniture from the General Administrative Services. (We inherited some of Peter Smith's old desks.) Burlington is the largest city in Vermont, and that's where I decided to open the main district office. However, during the campaign I had promised the people of Bennington, who are in the southern tip of the state and often feel slighted by Vermont government, that if I were elected I would also establish an office there. That we did.

Unless you're a total nut who wants to make some kind of weird political statement by sleeping in your office (as some freshmen Republicans did in 1995), you need to find a place to live. Jane and I wanted to live on Capitol Hill, and be able to walk to work. We found an apartment about five blocks from the office that turned out to be too big and expensive. We later took an efficiency one block from the office.

Now that I was a congressman, I had to establish goals for the next two years and decide what I could realistically accomplish. An important component of this agenda-setting was selecting the appropriate committees to serve on. This involved an enormous amount of political maneuvering.

Dealing with all of these matters at the same time must be difficult for any congressman. But they are even tougher without a party apparatus behind you and when you're the lone representative from your state. (Vermont, Alaska, Delaware, Montana, North Dakota, South Dakota, and Wyoming are the seven states with a single representative in Congress.) Patrick Leahy, Vermont's senior senator, kindly offered me the use of his offices during the transition period, and I began tackling what needed to be done.

Jane, who became an unpaid "special assistant," and Jeff Weaver took turns covering the orientation for Chiefs of Staff, sifted through hundreds of resumés, and interviewed potential staff members. A young man named George Stephanopolous, who at that time was an aide to Dick Gephardt, proved very helpful in showing us the ropes in Congress. He later went on to become George Stephanopolous.

To head the D.C. office, I brought in Doug Boucher, a former college instructor and environmental writer, who was extremely knowledgeable on foreign policy issues and Latin America. Ruthan Wirman, a veteran on Capitol Hill, came aboard as our office manager, and John Franco and Jeff Weaver took on the legislative work. A remarkable young woman named Katie Clarke was assigned phone duty, and within a few years became our legislative director. Carolyn Kazdin, who had worked on several of Jesse Jackson's campaigns, focused on economic issues and our relationship to organized labor.

For the Vermont staff, I hired Anthony Pollina, the founder and director of Rural Vermont, as district director. Saving the dwindling number of family-owned dairy farms in Vermont was a priority, and Anthony is one of the most knowledgeable people around on agricultural issues. He also has a great deal of expertise on environmental matters. Rachael Levin, who had helped manage the campaign, came on board as our office manager. (Rachael's mother Ruth had been a member of the Liberty Union twenty years before, and I remembered Rachael as a baby.) Jim Schumacher, who had been active in Burlington city government for many years and served very effectively as our field director during the campaign, became our outreach director. Liz Gibbs West took over scheduling and general office management.

In Vermont, we put together a strong office which placed a great deal of emphasis on constituent services. Whatever else I and my staff would accomplish, I wanted the senior citizens, veterans, and working people of Vermont to know that if they were having trouble getting what they were entitled to from the fed-

eral government, our office would be there for them. While constituent service is not a very sexy issue, it's something that my
office has always taken very seriously, and every year we respond
to the concerns of thousands of constituents. Lisa Barrett, who
had been a poverty lawyer for many years, did a great job in organizing that office. In recent years, David Weinstein has done an
outstanding job.

Initially, I decided to break with congressional precedent and
not hire a press secretary. Why should I pay someone to talk to
reporters for me? It was a waste of taxpayer money and an ego
trip. I would do it myself. Was I wrong! Six months later, I hired
Debbie Bookchin, who had written for the *Rutland Herald*. Tina
Wisell, who had done radio work in northern Vermont, eventually replaced Debbie and has been with me for several years.

In December, Jane and I borrowed some money from a friend
(we were flat broke) and went to Mexico for a week. Away from
the political turmoil, I was able to think about what my office
would focus on, and how we could be most effective.

A delightful surprise of my first few weeks in Washington was
the wonderful "Welcome to D.C." party put on by the progressive
community there. With Jesse Jackson and Ralph Nader as the
main speakers, some 500 people crowded into the Eastern Market.
Clearly, for many of those people, I was more than the congressman from Vermont. All over the country there was a growing dis-
satisfaction with politics-as-usual and the two-party system, and
the turnout reflected that.

Until recently, the House leadership sponsored a bipartisan
orientation for incoming freshmen, usually held at Harvard. The
purpose of this was to provide new members with boilerplate
information on the workings of Congress as well as expert opinion from leading thinkers on the economy, social issues, and foreign policy. While there is a time and place to hear opposing
points of view, this was not one of them. I personally was
offended to hear from some of the leading scholars in the Reagan
administration. I had not come to Congress to hear about the

virtues of supply-side economics. Other new members, with different political perspectives, had similar objections. Ironically enough, it was Newt Gingrich who called a halt to the bipartisan orientations in 1994. He was quite right.

The orientation did, however, give me a first taste of my new status as a member of Congress. It was a bit heady, to say the least, to fly from Andrews Air Force Base via military transport into Boston, have my bags delivered by the military, and then ride to the hotel in a bus escorted by local police cars with lights flashing.

Although I didn't get much out of the lectures except for a few arguments, I did have the opportunity to establish friendships with members of my class, the 102nd Congress, including Neil Abercrombie (Hawaii), Maxine Waters (California), Pete Peterson (Florida), Jim Backus (Florida), Bill Jefferson (Louisiana), Rosa Delauro (Connecticut), Chet Edwards (Texas), Jim Moran (Virginia), Bud Cramer (Alabama), Tim Roemer (Indiana), Eleanor Holmes Norton (D.C.), Collin Peterson (Minnesota), and John Cox (Illinois). While most of my congressional friendships, then and now, are based on shared political views, I have grown to like a number of members with whom I have very little in common politically.

As part of orientation, the new members were invited to the White House for a social occasion to meet with President and Mrs. Bush and Vice President and Mrs. Quayle. Both the president and his wife were gracious and friendly to Jane and me, and seemed quite familiar with my victory. Jane had a long chat with Mrs. Bush, who said something to the effect that "Oh, your husband defeated that man who was so rude to the president." Go figure. On the other hand, Dan and Marilyn Quayle were decidedly unfriendly. Also, in case you're interested, the food was terrific.

My primary concern during the orientation period was how I would be treated with regard to committee assignments and seniority. I was the first Independent in forty years. What would they do with me? Committee assignments are sorted out by the parties, and

I was affiliated with neither of them. Would I get on *any* committee? In Congress, the longer you serve the higher up you move in the committee structure. Would I move up if I were reelected or would I always be at the bottom of the pecking order—the last to speak, never gaining a chairmanship or ranking position?

During the campaign, I had publicly stated that I would seek entry into the Democratic Caucus, while remaining an Independent. I had spoken to some of the caucus leaders, and they were not unsympathetic to such an approach. Unfortunately, not all Democrats were in agreement. Charlie Stenholm of Texas, a leader of the conservative Blue Dog Democrats, led the opposition. He was of the opinion that having a socialist in the caucus would not sit well with folks back home.

Stenholm distributed a document containing some of my less than flattering observations on the Democratic Party. Frankly, I was surprised by the quality of his research (my introduction to Lexis/Nexis)—the quotes were accurate. Over the years I had been extremely critical of the Democratic Party and its tepidness about fighting for the working families of this country. While party liberals were willing to support my entry into the caucus, the conservatives dug in their heels. At this point I worked out a compromise with Speaker Tom Foley and Majority Leader Dick Gephardt which remains in effect today: I would not become a member of the Democratic Caucus, but in terms of committee assignments and seniority, I would be treated as if I were a Democrat, as the last-ranking member of my class.

Freshmen members are entitled to pick one "major" and one "minor" committee. I selected Banking and Community Development (very major) and Government Operations. I made those choices because both committees were chaired by progressive Democrats, and more importantly, because their jurisdictions dovetailed with my interests. The S&L fiasco had figured largely in my campaign speeches: it was my opinion that working people should not have to pick up the tab for the bailout, and that legislation should be passed to protect them. As a former mayor, I was also interested in creating affordable housing, maintaining community development programs, and developing other progressive initiatives for cities and towns. All of this fell within the domain of the Banking Committee, which was chaired by Henry Gonzalez, one of the strongest progressives in Congress.

The Government Operations Committee has oversight responsibility for all departments and agencies of the federal government. This committee can determine whether and why a department or agency is not adequately performing its mandate. It has wide investigative capabilities. Government Operations was then chaired by John Conyers of Michigan, with whom I had shared podiums as mayor of Burlington. I respected John, a longtime progressive, and looked forward to working with him.

Most Americans don't know the seating arrangements for members of Congress. I didn't before I arrived. In the Senate, each member has his or her own desk, and the Republicans and Democrats are on different sides of the room. I assumed the House was organized in the same way, and wondered whether a new section would have to be created for me. But House members are not assigned permanent seats; we sit wherever we want. The Democrats usually face the Speaker's chair on the left side, while the Republicans take the right. I sometimes hang out with the Illinois crowd on the Democratic side.

The Democrats and Republicans each have a "cloakroom," located just off the floor. I use the Democratic room. It's a place where you can make a phone call, grab a sandwich, watch TV, or sack out on the couch if it's 2 a.m., you need a nap, and you don't want to make the trek back to your office.

Posted on the walls of the Capitol and House office buildings are directories listing the rooms and phone numbers of members of Congress. Question: How do you tell a Democrat from a Republican from an Independent? Answer: The Democrats are in roman type, the Republicans are in italic, and there I am, all by myself, in SMALL CAPS. My election also created problems for C-Span. They had to add a new line to their congressional record graphics. Now, when C-Span records House votes, there is a line for Democrats, a line for Republicans, and a line for the Independent. Back home everyone says, "Bernie, we always know how *you* vote." Lucky me.

We Win Some Victories

On August 2, 1996, the House finally gets a chance to vote on raising the minimum wage, and the measure passes overwhelmingly.

After months and months of dealing with destructive and reactionary legislation—slashes in Medicare, Medicaid, and education; the evisceration of important enviromental legislation; limiting a woman's choice regarding abortion; and punishing children—the U.S. House of Representatives finally passed something to *improve* the lives of tens of millions of Americans who are in desperate need of help.

I have worked to raise the minimum wage from almost my first day in Congress. In 1993, I introduced a bill which would have immediately raised the minimum wage to $5.50 an hour and indexed it to inflation. The only other person in the House to introduce similar legislation at the time was Marty Sabo of Minnesota.

It's easy to forget what real life is about when you make $133,000 a year as a congressman. It's easy to forget what low-income workers feel when you're one of the twenty-nine millionaires in the Senate. It's easy to forget that most people don't drop $50 on lunch when you hang out at the country club with people whose income makes *you* look like a minimum wage worker.

But there are 12 million American workers earning less than $5.15 an hour, or $10,712 a year. And no, these are not all middle-class teenagers earning a little mad money. Three-quarters of them are adults, mostly women, trying to keep themselves and their families alive. These are people who take on two and three jobs, because forty-hour-a-week jobs are hard to come by, who have to walk to work or wait long periods for a bus because they can't scrape together enough money to buy a car, who sleep in emergency shelters or in campgrounds because they can't pay the rent.

The national minimum wage today, in terms of purchasing power, is 26 percent less than it was twenty years ago. If the minimum wage had kept pace with inflation from 1968, it would be $6.45 today. The increase passed by Congress—$4.70 on July 1, 1996, and then to $5.15 on July 1, 1997—is totally inadequate but it *is* at least a step forward. Further, millions of workers making slightly more than the minimum wage—$5.00 to $6.00 an hour—will also get a bump upward.

Since the 1930s, when minimum wage legislation was first enacted, much of the business community and their representatives in Congress have fiercely opposed raising the minimum wage. Executives make millions of dollars a year in income, and yet they oppose a $2,000 a year increase for a fellow American making $8,840. They send forth their lobbyists to do battle—from the U.S. Chamber of Commerce, from the National Federation of Independent Businesses, from the National Association of Manufacturers. Pathetic.

The way the debate on the House floor shaped up was nothing new. Same old lies. Same old bullshit. Same old empty sound-and-fury. Suddenly Dick Armey, Newt Gingrich, and others who had received millions in contributions from corporate America and the rich were deeply concerned about the well-being of low-income workers. Raising the minimum wage, they declaimed with melodramatic handwringing, would *hurt* the poor, not help them. So deeply pained were they by the plight of low-income workers, they could barely hold back the tears. The right-wing think tanks, which are funded by corporate America, had come to the same conclusion, based on "scientifically" assembled empirical data: raising the minimum wage would result in job loss. Companies would not be hiring young workers.

After these same congressmen had just passed legislation to throw millions of poor people off welfare, to make major cuts in food stamps, to slash affordable housing, forgive me for thinking that their sudden display of concern for low-income workers seemed a bit insincere. The theatrics bordered on the comic. Armey vowed to fight an increase in the minimum wage "with every fiber of his being." And he did. The Republican leadership stalled a vote for as long as possible. John Boehner, chairman of the House Republican Conference, threatened to kill himself if a minimum wage increase was passed. He didn't. Where is Republican honor when you really need it?

But there was a new, even more insidious, element in this year's debate. In 1989, President George Bush signed a minimum wage increase which had the support of most Republicans, including Newt Gingrich. It was a reasonably bipartisan effort. It is an indication of how fast and far Congress has veered to the right that in the early phase of the 1996 debate virtually no Republicans would back a minimum wage increase. Even more incredible, there were now a significant number of Republicans who wanted to *abolish* the concept of the minimum wage altogether, and grant American workers the "freedom" to work for $3.00 an hour. What had once been the dream of the lunatic fringe had now moved into the mainstream of the Republican Party.

The law of the jungle, the survival of the fittest. Employers want to pay workers bottom dollar, and workers are too desperate to refuse. Voilà. The "magic of the marketplace" at work, brought to us by people who make $133,000 a year. How very civilized.

Millions of Americans are now working for starvation wages. To add insult to injury, these low-wage jobs cost *taxpayers* huge amounts of money in corporate welfare. When fast-food chains, grocery stores, and service industry employers pay $4.50 or $5.00

an hour, their employees often need additional support in order to eat, pay the rent, and take care of their kids. These are the workers who receive Medicaid, food stamps, subsidized housing, and other resources through government programs.

In 1993, when I introduced my minimum wage legislation, I was only able to secure fifty cosponsors, almost all progressive Democrats. No Republicans signed on. President Clinton was also opposed, as I discovered at a meeting with him in the Oval Office. Clinton confers regularly with the congressional leadership of the Democratic and Republican parties. In a phone conversation, I suggested it might be appropriate for him to meet with the leadership of the "Independent Caucus" as well. He was kind enough to schedule me for a fifteen-minute session. I stayed for half an hour.

Our discussion centered on three issues. First, I tried to win his support for raising the minimum wage. He said that he was not unsympathetic to the idea, but that it couldn't be done while his health care proposal was being debated. Second, I commiserated with him about the savage attacks he had been receiving from the media. He and Mrs. Clinton were being ripped apart by Rush Limbaugh and other right wingers every day of the week. I asked him to think about the very serious problem of corporate control of the media and what, if anything, could be done about it. Lastly, I asked for his support of the Northeast Dairy Compact, which would greatly assist Vermont's dairy farmers. Vermont farmers are going out of business in large numbers because they receive a very low price for their milk. The Compact, which is supported by all six New England states, would allow the Northeast region to set a fair price for the milk their farmers produce. Clinton understood the concept and indicated that he was not unsympathetic.

Despite the importance of the issue and the desperate straits of a core constituency of the electorate, there was practically no discussion in 1993 by the Democratic Party about raising the minimum wage. Now, in 1996, with a presidential election coming up, and tired of being on the defensive over the Republican agenda, the Democrats finally recognized it as a good political issue: polls showed that over 80 percent of the people were sympathetic to raising the minimum wage. The Democrats correctly perceived that making a pitch for low-wage workers would boost their campaign against Gingrich and Bob Dole, and their woeful record on the needs of working people.

To give the Democrats due credit, once they decided to push the issue, they did a very effective job. House Majority Leader Dick Gephardt organized an impressive press conference at which low-wage workers had an opportunity to air their views. It was unusual and refreshing for workers to have a platform on Capitol Hill. Ted Kennedy, Paul Wellstone, and a few other senators spoke, as well as a number of us from the House.

From then on, the Democratic leaders placed the issue at the forefront of their agenda. They had members raise the issue during the "one minutes" at the beginning of the day, and worked hard and creatively to get the legislation attached to various other bills that the Republican leadership was bringing up. For once, they were focused and determined to press a piece of legislation to its conclusion.

In one of the few instances since Gingrich ascended to the Speaker's chair, the Republicans couldn't hold their members in line. Faced with the unpleasant task of explaining to low- and moderate-income workers in their districts why they were not willing to support a long overdue increase in the minimum wage, six northern Republicans broke away from Gingrich and backed the legislation. Soon after, another fourteen Republicans were prepared to bolt, with more waiting in the wings. Finally, a majority of the House supported raising the minimum wage— and Gingrich and Armey, kicking and screaming, were forced to call a vote.

The debate itself was quite extraordinary. In effect, Republicans argued that miserable wages are good for America because they keep the country competitive. For workers, of course, this "competition" means a race to the bottom:

responding to wages paid in China, sometimes as low as twenty cents an hour.

But the major battle on the floor involved the Goodling amendment, designed to exempt businesses with $500,000 or less in profits from paying the minimum wage. By itself, this amendment would have taken away minimum wage protection from new applicants for some 10.5 million jobs. More importantly, it would have paved the way for the eventual elimination of the minimum wage concept altogether. The proposal to remove minimum wage requirements for small businesses was defeated on a close vote of 229 to 196. One hundred and eighty-nine Republicans voted for it.

During the debate, the only valid point that the Republicans made was to ask why the Democrats, if they were so concerned about low-wage workers, had not passed a minimum wage increase two years earlier when they had the majority in the House and Senate? I agreed, and got some time from Scott McInnis, a Republican from Colorado, to express my views.

While Republicans were incorrect in claiming that a small increase in the minimum wage would lead to job loss, their argument hid a more important issue. The major crisis of the current period is not unemployment, but the rapid decline in working-class wages. While unemployment remains too high—and it is far higher than "official" statistics indicate—the more serious problem is that real wages for American workers have declined by 16 percent over the last twenty years. In 1973, the average American worker was earning $445 a week. Twenty years later, that worker was making $373 a week in real dollars.

The situation is even more acute for low-wage workers and workers who lack a college degree. Real wages for male high school graduates in entry-level jobs plummeted a full 30 percent in the past fifteen years, while wages have fallen 18 percent for young women. During the 1980s, about three-quarters of the new jobs created in America were poverty-level jobs, many temporary and part-time.

"Welfare reform" has deepened the crisis. What happens to wages when millions of the working poor lose their safety net and are forced to compete with other low-wage workers? What happens to public employees and their wage scale when they are replaced by former welfare recipients forced into workfare programs?

The minimum wage bill passed by a vote of 354 to 72. Interestingly, 160 Republicans ended up voting for the bill, when just a few months before none of them had supported it. Many people might find this conversion puzzling. In fact, it is the predictable result of an important political dynamic.

The forces of reaction work most effectively behind closed doors, hidden from public scrutiny. When debate on an issue is pushed into the open, in this case, onto the floor of the House, when the close link between special interests, the wealthy, and their "representatives" in Congress is threatened with exposure, the opposition will often surrender rather than resist.

Force a vote, so that the public can see the position of their representatives, and often the common good will prevail. This is what happened, to my great surprise, with an amendment I introduced in September 1995, seeking to eliminate outrageous corporate bonuses at Lockheed-Martin.

One of Burlington's largest employers was Martin Marietta. When that defense contractor merged with Lockheed to form Lockheed-Martin, I was more than usually attuned to the implication of that deal—the downsizing of 17,000 American workers. For making the "tough decision" to fire all those workers, the executives of the newly merged company decided to pay themselves $91 million in executive bonuses. Ninety-one million dollars as a reward for obliterating 17,000 jobs.

Some of the major recipients of that bonus were the CEO of the company, Norm Augustine ($8.2 million); former Tennessee governor and presidential aspirant Lamar Alexander ($236,000); former secretary of defense Mel Laird ($1.6 million); and retired general and former member of the Joint Chiefs of Staff John Vessey ($372,000).

Now, a $91 million bonus for executives who were laying off 17,000 workers is obscene enough. Even worse, Bill Goold, my legislative director, discovered that fully one-third of that money, $31 million, was to come from the Pentagon as "restructuring costs." As soon as I learned about this outrageous federal give-away, I drafted an amendment to prevent the Pentagon from paying the bonus. Imagine: workers thrown out of their jobs paying taxes so that the bastards who fired them could stuff their pockets. Bill termed the legislation the "payoffs for layoffs" amendment.

When I brought that amendment to the floor, I thought I'd have a very hard fight on my hands. But to my surprise, John Murtha, the ranking Democrat on the Defense Appropriations Committee and consequently the person responsible for Democratic strategy on the bill, said they were going to support it. He discussed the amendment with Bill Young, the Republican chairman of Military Appropriations, who signed on without hesitation. The amendment passed by voice vote.

Here was a controversial piece of legislation—challenging corporate America, and in particular the right of the wealthy to pay themselves handsomely for eliminating the jobs of working people—which was being endorsed by both parties. The truth is, nobody wanted to defend, either on the floor of the House or especially to constituents, the government's use of taxpayer money to pay bonuses to executives (already making millions) who had just laid off thousands of American workers.

In politics, if you are not continually learning, you lose ground fast. I learned something from that success, both about the political process and about the rivers of "corporate welfare" that pour out of the Pentagon. Those lessons, along with some excellent work on the part of my staff, later enabled us to pull off another truly significant coup.

We learned, after much probing, that the Pentagon bonuses to Lockheed-Martin executives were merely the tip of the iceberg in terms of corporate welfare for the defense industry. Clinton's secretary of defense, William Perry, had instituted a new policy under which the Pentagon provides "restructuring costs" to companies that undergo a merger. Through this policy, the federal government offers corporations huge sums of money to encourage mergers in the defense industry. Corporate "efficiency" is the ostensible goal; there is no concern with the mergers' inevitable result, the laying off of many thousands of American workers.

Further, there is absolutely no evidence that fewer companies and diminished competition within the defense industry will save taxpayers one nickel. Lockheed-Martin already controls a dangerous 32 percent of defense business. Increased concentration by large companies will not lower our taxes, nor enable the Pentagon to purchase products for lower prices.

In any case, this is a perverse sort of government involvement in the economy. I subscribe to the concept of industrial policy, where the government plays a role in *creating*, with the private sector, decent-paying jobs. I do not believe that the government should offer incentives to lay off tens of thousands of workers.

In studying this issue, we learned that Lockheed-Martin alone had close to a billion dollars of "restructuring costs" in the pipeline. Another company had already received $200 million, and there were thirty-two other corporations in the process of applying for money to subsidize "restructuring." Needless to say, despite the huge amount of money involved, this was an issue that had not received much attention, either by Congress or the media.

We managed to create a very interesting left-right alliance on the issue. New Jersey representative Chris Smith is a conservative Republican with whom I had been only slightly acquainted. He is best known as one of the foremost opponents of abortion rights in Congress. But Lockheed-Martin closed down a plant in his district, a plant which had employed 3,000 workers. Smith believed that the shutdown was encouraged by the Pentagon's financial assistance. After I introduced an amendment to end the incentive program, Smith supported it. That made it the Sanders-Smith amendment. Then a moderate Democrat, David Minge from

Minnesota, a progressive, Peter DeFazio from Oregon, and others, signed on as original cosponsors. The amendment would come before the House with truly broad-based support.

Again, both John Murtha, ranking Democrat on the Defense Subcommittee of the Appropriations Committee, and the Republican leadership accepted the amendment without a fuss. Nobody wanted to oppose such a sensible amendment—not on the floor, in any case—especially with tripartisan support. Nobody wanted to have to explain how using taxpayer dollars to lay off workers would benefit America.

The only controversy regarding the amendment was what it would be called. Would it be the Sanders-Smith amendment, or the Smith-Sanders amendment? Smith's version was similar to mine, but mine was stronger. But Smith is a Republican in a Republican-controlled House. We agreed that my version would be adopted, but it would be called the Smith-Sanders amendment. The legislation attracted significant attention. A substantial article in the *Los Angeles Times* called it a "major defeat" for the defense industry. Of course, getting it through the House was only the first step. It had to survive conference committee and pass the Senate. The next day, to my delight, my office received four calls from senators requesting information on the amendment: Barbara Boxer, John McCain, Chuck Grassley, and Tom Harkin. Two Republicans and two Democrats—a good sign.

By developing that amendment, I touched on a major issue which had been well hidden, and which had apparently never before been discussed on the floor of the House. To my mind, I was doing what, as an Independent, I had been elected to do. I have come to understand that one of the most important roles I can play in Congress is to raise issues which, for a variety of reasons, other people choose not to deal with. Just shifting the framework of debate can have enormous consequences.

Frankly, the big money interests do not intimidate me—not the medical-industrial complex, not the military-industrial complex, not Wall Street or the American Bankers Association.

Exposing the outrageous practice by which the Defense
Department subsidized corporate mergers and the laying off of
tens of thousands of workers is precisely what I was elected to do.

Still, when the total Defense Authorization bill came to the
floor, I ended up voting against it, even though it included the
Smith-Sanders amendment. Sometimes it's difficult to explain
this sort of action to people who do not follow Congress. Simply
put, I try to make each and every bill better by drafting and, hope-
fully, passing good amendments. When the final bill comes up, I
weigh the good elements against the bad and, sometimes, even if
I've
improved it
with amend-
ments, I still
end up vot-
ing against it.
In this
instance, the
bill con-
tained far
too much
money for
the military—$10 billion more than the president had wanted,
and he wanted too much.

Sanders heats up defense-bonus criticism

Lockheed Martin payment at issue

By Patrick Sloyan
Newsday

WASHINGTON — The leader of a congressional effort to block a Clinton administration payment of $31 million in executive bonuses for Lockheed Martin Corp. has asked the Pentagon for key documents that would justify the windfall for the nation's largest defense contractor.

Rep. Bernie Sanders, I-Vt., asked the Defense Department's inspector general to provide Congress with executive agreements between the company and the Pentagon that permit use of taxpayer money to help finance $92 million in payments the executives gave themselves for completing the merger of Lockheed Corp. and Martin Marietta Corp.

Burlington is the headquarters of Lockheed Martin Armament Systems, a unit of Lockheed Martin that produces Gatling guns and ammunition loading systems. The plant, which employs about 725 people, also is developing a light armored vehicle and a rotary engine for unmanned planes.

Sanders' request reflects growing suspicion in Congress and among some Pentagon auditors that the $31 million payment might violate defense regulations, which specifically prohibit reimbursing costs associated with a change in management. Earlier this month the House approved Sanders' amendment to stop the Pentagon payment. But the provision was unlikely to survive a House-Senate conference on the defense appropriations bill, according to congressional sources.

"Since one-third of the payments are to be provided from public funds, the executive agreements are public documents," Sanders wrote Inspector General Eleanor Hill. Hill's deputy, Derek Vander Schaaf, is monitoring a Pentagon audit of the bonus package scheduled to be finished Saturday. Vander Schaaf declined comment.

Major stockholders objected to the $92 million bonus package that primarily went to Martin-Marietta chief Norman Augustine and 439 executives.

But the one-time, lump-sum payment was the result of an anti-takeover provision adopted by Martin-Marietta after an abortive hostile acquisition attempt in 1982 by Bendix Corp.

However, Pentagon regulations governing defense contracts forbid using public funds to cover such payments.

In addition, Pentagon veterans said the $31 million payment violates important defense contracting precedents. "We do pay bonuses, but only as an incentive for meeting production goals or other achievements that save taxpayer money," said an Air Force official.

Defense Secretary William Perry has defended the Pentagon's share of the bonus package, arguing it was money that would have been paid to Martin Marietta even if a merger had not occurred. Perry has favored mergers as a means of reducing defense spending by cutting overhead costs.

☞

Susan Sweetser's new Federal Election Commission report has
just been made public. Lockheed-Martin has contributed $10,000
to her campaign, the maximum allowed by law. What a shock.

So much to do. So little time to do it in. On Friday, after the
week's battles in Congress, I fly from Washington to Hartford,
Connecticut, where Phil Fiermonte picks me up and we drive to
Brattleboro, in southern Vermont, for the second of my campaign
announcements. This one is much like the Burlington event, but

features speakers from Windham County. All the seats are filled in the Town Hall by a crowd of about sixty or seventy people. A good sign. Also, the media coverage is good.

The highlight of the Brattleboro event is an electrifying speech delivered by a young high school student, Acacia Fanto. I am so engrossed by what she says that I don't mind being upstaged.

I first met this young woman when she came to the Vermont youth conference sponsored by my office last year. The conference brought together students from ten different high schools to give talks on issues they felt Congress should be addressing. The presentations, which in a number of cases required substantial research by the students, were excellent. The idea for the student hearing came from Tim Kipp, a personal friend who teaches social studies at Brattleboro Union High School. Acacia was his student, and her message is simple but profound: in order to preserve democracy, it is imperative that young people be actively involved in the political process. Without them, democracy will not survive. Her short speech is cogent and deeply touching.

Traveling through Vermont, I try to schedule opportunities to speak in the schools whenever I can. Over the past five years, I have spoken in almost every high school in the state as well as many elementary schools. It's important that young people get a chance to talk to their congressman, to express their concerns and opinions. Many of these students have very little understanding of the relationship of politics and government to their lives. Teachers tell me that it is surprising how many kids become more interested in the political process after meeting their congressman face to face.

Peter Shumlin, the Democratic minority leader in the state senate, endorses my candidacy at the Brattleboro meeting. Peter has not been publicly supportive in the past, but feels it is important to play a role in defeating the Gingrich agenda. After spending the night with Tim Kipp and his wife Kathy Keller at my longtime home away from home in Brattleboro, Phil and I drive to Bennington on Saturday morning for another opening announcement. Bennington and Brattleboro, the two major towns in southern Vermont, are only forty miles apart over the Hogback mountains but they are as different as night and day. Brattleboro is the most countercultural town in the state, while Bennington is solidly working class.

The turnout at the meeting in Bennington is respectable, especially considering it is the kind of beautiful spring day when Vermonters hate to be inside. After a long Vermont winter, indoor meetings on a beautiful spring day are not usually a big draw. A highlight of the announcement is the talk by Mark Santelli, the former president of the UAW local at the Johnson Controls battery plant in Bennington.

On a Sunday in August 1993, I had marched with the UAW at the Battle of Bennington parade. The next day, workers learned that Johnson Controls was closing their plant, and 269 decent-paying union jobs would be lost when production was shifted to Mexico. Mark's valiant effort to keep the plant in Vermont had failed. My office was helpful in getting the laid-off workers some additional benefits under the NAFTA legislation. Mark is not only a respected union leader, he is also active in the hunting community and, like me, does not believe hunters need AK-47s to kill a deer. His support is much appreciated.

Next stop, Rutland. A political campaign is always full of surprises. This time it is a veteran, Jeffrey Hatch, who gives a terrific speech. As it happens, I had never met him before. He is very articulate and direct. "I'm a Republican, I'm a veteran, and I'm supporting Bernie Sanders because he's been good on veterans' issues." In Rutland, the speeches are wonderful, but the turnout poor.

Now it's on to St. Johnsbury, the third and last stop of the day. St. Johnsbury is the "capital" of the Northeast Kingdom, the most rural, the most rugged, the poorest, and in some ways the most beautiful part of Vermont. Our activist support in the Northeast Kingdom is almost all working class: low-income advocates, family farmers, veterans. Two couples, Bob and Kay Perkins and Marvin Minkler and Mary Strole, organized the event. A number

of seniors attend, but the crowd is small. One of my favorite people in the state, Jenny Nelson, a farmer from Ryegate, gives a terrific speech. Jenny and her husband Bill own a beautiful farm
which has been in the Nelson family for generations. Like many
other Vermont farmers, they work incredibly long hours and are
fighting hard to hold onto their land. Jenny, who is one of the
leaders of Rural Vermont, a progressive family farm organization,
talks about how we have worked together over the years on a
number of projects to save family farms.

Phil and I rack up 500 miles on the odometer that weekend.
Every mile is worth it. The campaign kickoffs in Brattleboro,
Bennington, Rutland, and St. Johnsbury bring our supporters
together and receive generally good news coverage. But they are
also important because they remind me on a deep, emotional
level why I am a congressman, and how fortunate I am to have
such great people behind me. Having all those people supporting
our effort is a source of great pride. It sustains me when I go back
to the inside-the-beltway mentality of Washington.

☞❚

Along with 434 others, on January 3, 1991, I was sworn in as a
member of the United States Congress. On that day, as is custom-
ary, new members hosted receptions in their offices for friends
and family who came by to wish them luck. We held a reception
in our office, too. Unfortunately, I was unable to attend. I was at
meetings trying to prevent a war.

On August 2, 1990, Saddam Hussein, a former ally who was
well supplied with American equipment, invaded Kuwait. On
August 9, U.S. troops sent by President Bush began arriving in
Saudi Arabia to prevent further Iraqi aggression. Now, in early
January, Bush was seeking congressional authority for an all-out
war with Iraq. I was opposed to giving him that authority.

From the very beginning of the Persian Gulf crisis, I was of the
belief that the United States could push Saddam Hussein out of

Kuwait without having to resort to war. Diplomacy, economic
boycott, isolation, financial leverage: we had many means for
reversing the invasion. I was not only opposed to the war because
of the potential destruction and loss of life, but also because I
believe it *is* possible for the major countries of this planet, and a
virtually united world community, to resolve crises without car-
nage. If this matter could not be solved without massive bombing
and killing thousands of people, then what crisis could ever be
solved peacefully?

Further, I was angry that the Iraqi situation was deflecting
attention from the serious domestic crises that we faced, problems that I was anxious to tackle. (Some would argue that deflecting attention away from domestic injustice is one of the major
functions of war.) Twenty percent of our children live in poverty,
millions of Americans lack decent housing, workers' standard of
living is in free-fall, and we need a major overhaul of our health
care system to ensure affordable medical care for everyone. And
now we were going to spend months engaged in a war with a two-
bit tyrant.

In those early days of the 102nd Congress, several members,
among them Ron Dellums and Tom Foglietta, organized an antiwar caucus in the House. What should our overall strategy be in
trying to prevent the war? What alternatives were available to get
Saddam Hussein out of Kuwait without bloodshed? How could we
affect public opinion? How could we win more votes in Congress
for our position? These were some of the questions we wrestled
with at meeting after meeting in the first days of the new Congress.

In Vermont, I spoke at a large antiwar demonstration at the
state capital. About 1,500 people attended. In Washington, I was
appearing in the national media as a critic of the drift toward war.

In early January, I attended a meeting in which Speaker Foley
and the Democratic leadership—Gephardt, Bonior, and others—talked about the upcoming vote. At that time the
Democrats had a strong majority in the House and Senate.
Simply stated, if the Democratic leadership wanted to block the

war, they had the votes to do it. My friend Tom Andrews, a fellow antiwar freshman from Maine, asked a straightforward question: Would the leadership impose party discipline on this vote, and refuse to give Bush the authority to declare war? Foley looked straight at Tom and told him that there would be no party discipline. While he, and every other member of the leadership, was going to vote against giving the president the authority to send our troops into battle, he was not going to demand that all Democrats support that position.

At that moment, I knew the war was inevitable. Ostensibly, the Democrats controlled the House. Yet, on the most important issue facing the country, the Republicans were going to win. It was clear that there would be enough Democrats joining the Republicans to give Bush the necessary votes.

On January 15, just before the war broke out, I spoke on the floor of the House: "Mr. Speaker, let me begin my saying that I think we all agree in this body, and throughout this country, and throughout virtually the entire world, that Saddam Hussein is an evil person, and what he has done in Kuwait is illegal, immoral, and brutal. It seems to me, however, that the challenge of our time is not simply to begin a war which will result in the deaths of tens of thousands of people, young Americans, innocent women and children in Iraq, but the real challenge of our time is to see how we can stop aggression, how we can stop evil in a new way, in a nonviolent way.

"If ever there has been a time in the history of the world when the entire world is united against one small country, this is that time. It seems to me a terrible failing, and very ominous for the future, if we cannot resolve this crisis, if we cannot defeat Saddam Hussein in a nonviolent way. If we are not successful now, then I think all that this world has to look forward to in the future for our children, is war, and more war, and more war."

My speech, and many other fine speeches, had little impact. Bush had the votes. On January 17, 1991, American planes attacked Iraq with a massive show of force.

On January 18, 1991, I once again spoke on the House floor: "Mr. Speaker, a few months ago the entire world rejoiced that the Cold War had finally ended, and that the hundreds of billions of dollars being spent on bombs and tanks and missiles could finally be used to improve human life, not to destroy human life.

"Mr. Speaker, a major war in the Persian Gulf, costing us thousands of lives and tens of billions of dollars, could well be a disaster for the people of our country—especially the working people, the poor people, the elderly, and the children. I predict that this Congress will soon be asked for more money for guided missiles, but there will be no money available to house the homeless. I predict that this Congress will soon be asked for more money for tanks, but there will be no money or effort available to develop a national health care system, guaranteeing health care for all of our people—as virtually all of the industrialized world has.

"I predict that this Congress will soon be asked for more money for bombs, but there will be no money available to reindustrialize our nation so that our working people can have decent-paying jobs. There will be no money available for education and for our children—25 percent of whom live in poverty. There will be no money available for the environment, or to help the family farmer—many of whom are being forced off the land today in my state of Vermont and throughout this country.

"Mr. Speaker, I predict that in order to pay for this war, there will be more cutbacks in Medicare for the elderly, and even an effort to cut back on Social Security payments."

For me personally, this was a very depressing period. I am not a pacifist. I believe that there are times when war is legitimate, when the alternative is existence under a horrendous status quo. I think those instances, however, are much rarer than most government leaders admit.

It would seem that after thousands of years in which one group or country has resolved its problems by killing the people of another group or country, the human race should be ready to learn something about resolving differences nonviolently. I had been a vocal opponent of the Vietnam War, an opponent of the war against the people of Nicaragua, an opponent of the U.S. invasions of Grenada and Panama. Now, as a U.S. congressman, I had voted against the Persian Gulf War.

As the bombs began falling and American troops entered combat, I learned a very painful lesson about congressional politics.

A resolution was brought before the House on January 18—a Republican-drafted document endorsed by the Democratic leadership. The resolution urged congressional support for our troops in combat and simultaneously commended "the efforts and leadership of the President." An amendment on March 5 praised the president for "his decisive leadership, unerring judgment, and sound decisions with respect to the crisis in the Persian Gulf." I was incredulous. Unerring judgment? Not only did this phrase sound like some Stalinist propaganda of the 1930s, it directly contradicted what 183 members had said through their votes against the war less than two months earlier.

It was one thing, now that the war had begun and American troops were fighting for their lives, to express support for them. I was ready and willing to do that. But it seemed to me that it was a very different thing to declare that President Bush had been right all along regarding the situation in the Persian Gulf, and that war had been the only solution. After all, almost half of Congress had opposed the president's militarism. Sending in the troops and bombers changed the situation for soldiers, but it did not nullify our basic argument that peaceful solutions are preferable to military ones. We had not been wrong, but that is exactly what the resolution asked us to say.

In the face of a growing and massive media campaign to justify and celebrate the war, it was hard to vote no this second time. A week earlier, 183 members had voted to support a continuation of economic sanctions, and against a war. Now, as I looked up at the vote tally board, *everyone* was voting yes. I remember putting my card into the machine—we vote on the floor by using a card with a magnetic strip to activate a voting machine, and then pressing either the yes or no button—and thinking to myself, "This is going to be a short congressional career." I pressed the no button. Only five other members did the same. The vote was 399 to 6.

That vote would haunt me. In every election since, political opponents charge, "In the middle of a war, Bernie Sanders did not vote to support the troops." It's a lie and a distortion of reality, but it works well in a thirty-second radio ad.

I had been in Congress for less than a month, and already I was feeling awfully lonely. But how I was feeling personally or politically was a lot less important than what was happening in the country.

And what was happening was frightening. A more or less totalitarian system was kicking into effect. Even a longtime critic of the media like myself was stunned by the servility of the media, by how quickly they fell into line behind the militaristic impera-tives of the president and Pentagon. Their obedience paid off. When I returned to Vermont, there was a yellow ribbon on what seemed like every house and tree. The media had succeeded in creating a national war mood.

Television gave virtually no coverage to people who opposed the war. Reporting was tightly controlled and totally one-sided. A study done several years later found that prowar National Football League players got more air time to discuss their views on the Persian Gulf War than the whole antiwar movement put together. During the early days of the war, Jesse Jackson led a large march on Washington, and it received almost no coverage. Simply stated, there was massive censorship of dissent, criticism, debate.

Clearly, the government had learned a lesson from the Vietnam War. This time, the media would not play a role in pro-viding information to support any sort of antiwar sentiment. No Americans would be televised coming home in body bags. No photos of American atrocities would reach the evening news. No critics would be heard above the din of the president's pumped-up war rhetoric.

And it was not just the national television. It was the radio, the newspapers, the magazines. I tried to get news in Washington from the supposedly liberal National Public Radio network, but they were as bad as everyone else. In fact, there was no pretense at objectivity. The government *announced* that it was censoring the news. Instead of contesting this flagrant violation of the public's right to be informed, the media submitted to the blackout and lapped up the government's doctored reports. Before Congress had voted to give the president authority to send troops into combat, polls showed the country was pretty evenly divided on the wisdom of U.S. involvement. Three weeks into the war (and a massive media campaign), the overwhelming majority of Americans supported it.

One of the very few newspapers courageous enough to oppose the war was located in my own state. Stephen Faye, the editor of the *Brattleboro Reformer*, withstood criticism from some of his advertisers, and wrote forceful editorials against the war week after week. Tragically, in those emotional days, there were very few journalists with that sort of courage.

Six years after the war, I wonder how many Americans have seen even one story about the enormous loss of life suffered by the women and children of Iraq. An estimated 200,000 noncombatants died in that war, killed by our "smart bombs." This figure does not include the terrible loss of life incurred after the war as a result of hunger, contaminated water, lack of health care, and the destruction of the Iraqi infrastructure. Though brief, the war caused enormous slaughter and suffering for the ordinary people of Iraq. No, our "smart bombs" did not avoid "collateral damage." No, it was not just Iraqi soldiers who died.

The president and the Pentagon claimed the war was a success: we achieved our objectives with very little loss of American life. What they did not tell us was that some 70,000 American soldiers returned with a variety of ailments commonly referred to as Persian Gulf syndrome. In fact, ever since the war, the Pentagon has lied and attempted to conceal almost all information about the devastating effects of the war on American soldiers. It took five years for the military to even acknowledge that American troops had been exposed to chemical warfare agents when they blew up an Iraqi munitions depot in the town of Khamiseyah. Even today, it is difficult for those of us in Congress who are demanding adequate treatment and compensation for these hidden casualties of the war to get the truth from the Pentagon.

And let me be very clear. Given their enormous success in selling the Persian Gulf debacle, there is no reason to expect that the government and the media will behave any differently when the next war comes. If they could win massive public support for defending "freedom" in Kuwait, they can use the same techniques to build support for *any* war. After all, Kuwait was, and is, a country controlled by billionaire emirs. Kuwait is not so free that it allows women to vote, or even to drive automobiles. It is not so free that the Christian and Jewish soldiers we sent to defend Kuwait were allowed to celebrate Christmas or Hanukkah when they were there.

Hard as it was to be in Washington in those days, it was even harder to be in Vermont. I recall, with deep hurt, seeing off a unit of the Vermont National Guard as they departed for the Gulf. I was booed by a few people there, one of the few times in my political career that had ever happened to me. War is a very strange phenomenon. I do not claim to understand its psychological effects. Here I had done my best to prevent young Vermonters and other Americans from getting killed, and I was being booed for my efforts. One day I was at the airport waiting for a flight to Washington, and a woman said to me, "My son is over there. I'm appalled that you're not supporting him." That wasn't true, but nothing I said would convince her otherwise.

On a more optimistic note, a poll came out during that period which found my "favorability" ratings reasonably high. Apparently, a number of Vermonters respected my standing up for what I believed, even if they disagreed with my position on the war.

Those early days in Congress were very tough. I even managed to make a fool of myself at a nationally televised Washington event. To this day, whenever the subject of that night comes up, my wife, who saw it on TV in Vermont, involuntarily winces and shakes her head. I was invited to speak before the annual dinner hosted by the National Press Club. Of course, I didn't know it at the time, but this is a major event on the Capitol calendar, attended by everybody who is anybody: Supreme Court justices, leading business people, major politicians, celebrities, and, of course, all the Washington media. Four new members of Congress, including me, had been invited to speak.

But they wanted more than a speech. We were expected to be funny, too. It was supposed to be a lighthearted and amusing evening, with everyone guaranteed a good time. I had three problems with the event. First, I have no talent for stand-up comedy before hundreds of strangers with whom I have nothing in common. Second, I was in no mood for jokes when a war which I vigorously opposed had just broken out. And third, this was a black tie affair and I didn't have a tuxedo or a black tie (and I had no intention of ever buying either).

For those reasons and a few more, I called the organizers and told them that, on reflection, I didn't think I should attend. They strongly disagreed. The invitations had already gone out with my name as one of the speakers: everybody would be *terribly* disappointed. I just *had* to be there.

The upshot was that I allowed myself to be talked into going. The evening was a disaster. There I was, morose, telling lame jokes that a few of us in the office had cooked up minutes before I left for the event, my performance beamed by C-Span back to Vermont and across the country. The only consolation was that Senator Paul Wellstone, another invited speaker, was equally bad. This was a miserable night for me during a miserable period.

☞

Y esterday, the *Burlington Free Press* published a story analyzing Vermonters' opinions on whether Barbara Snelling should con-

On the picket line in the 1981 mayoral race. I am on the right.

My first inaugural speech in 1981.

We win by ten votes. Election night, 1981.

Good election results for Burlington Progressives in 1982.

The "men's caucus" and Carina. (left to right) Co-author Huck Gutman, daughter Carina Driscoll, son Dave Driscoll, brother Larry Sanders, son Levi Sanders, friend Richard Sugarman.

My last meeting as Mayor, 1989.

The bike path that we built on Burlington's beautiful waterfront.

The "People's Republic of Burlington" takes on the business community in a softball game. We won.

Representative Peter Smith and I disagree in a 1990 TV debate.

We make history in 1990. The first Independent elected to Congress in forty years. My wife Jane is at my side.

Campaigning with Jesse Jackson in 1988, and Vermont Rainbow Coalition activist Ellen David Friedman.

Okay, now you know. I wasn't raised on a dairy farm.

Going door to door in the 1986 governor's race.

Attending Nelson Mandela's inauguration in South
Africa with other members of Congress.

Welcoming Jean Bertrand Aristide to Vermont at
a ceremony at St. Michael's College.

Meeting with President Daniel Ortega in Nicaragua.

Chatting with Hillary Clinton on a plane trip.

President Clinton meeting with the Independent Caucus in the Oval Office.

(Above) Michael Moore comes to Burlington in the 1996 campaign.

(Above right) Gloria Steinem drew a great crowd at a 1996 Sanders for Congress rally at the University of Vermont.

(Right) Jane, me, and some friends marching in a Vermont parade.

Jack Long, Democrat, Susan Sweetser, Republican, and I debate on Vermont Educational Television.

(Above) The family playing for the camera in the snow. Top row: (left to right) Levi, Carina, Jane, and me. Bottom row: Dave, my son-in-law Andreas, Heather.
(Above right) Toasting the legislative victory of the Northeast Dairy Compact with (center) Vermont Agricultural Commissioner Leon Graves and (right) U.S. Senator Patrick Leahy.

Chairing a meeting of the House Progressive Caucus with Rep. Lynn Woolsey and Rep. Maurice Hinchey.

Progressives meeting with President Clinton. (Left to Right) Clinton, Ron Dellums, Barney Frank, George Miller, Charlie Rangel, aide Pat Griffen, Leon Panetta, and me.

tinue her candidacy for governor. Snelling, an old friend who is currently the Republican lieutenant governor, suffered a massive stroke a month ago. What that tells me is that the *Free Press* conducted a poll, and that means they asked more than one question. So I assume that in today's paper there will be a poll on the congressional race. That worries me, because it will undoubtedly show that the gap is closing. We're not going to win this election by the twenty-one points predicted in their last poll. Sweetser will then roll out the patter used by all challengers: "We're closing the gap, we're gathering momentum, the Sanders camp is panicking"—the usual stuff.

I hate polls. If you're the incumbent and better known, you're supposed to be ahead. If the race gets closer, as it invariably does when the challenger becomes better known, then you're "in trouble." It is a no-win situation for a well-known incumbent. But what is particularly amazing about the *Free Press* poll is that I am so preoccupied with it. I even wake up in the middle of the night thinking about the damn poll. Yet, tomorrow I will have surgery on my vocal cords. Here I am, having surgery for the first time in my life, and I don't think about that at all. No nightmares. No anxiety attacks. Instead, I'm worried about a stupid poll five months before the election.

The operation is intended to correct a problem I've had with my voice. It's a scary business. I assume the doctors know what they're doing and they seem to think it's a minor procedure. Still, if they make a mistake, it's my voice for the rest of my life.

The idea of surgery has plagued me for months in a low-key, persistent way. The problem with my voice began a year and a half ago, toward the end of the 1994 campaign, when I developed a cold and was hoarse for a few days. In the midst of a campaign, you do what you have to do, so I continued giving speeches. Eventually the cold went away, but the hoarseness remained. Since then, I have had problems speaking: my voice sounds gravelly at best, and there are times when it rasps so much I have difficulty finishing a sentence.

The truth is that I've handled this voice situation stupidly. I've been a healthy person all my life: I was a mayor for eight years and have been in Congress for six, and in all that period I have missed less than five days of work. When I get a flu, I still go to work. Being sick is not part of my life. So when my throat became hoarse, I thought it would take care of itself. It didn't.

After a number of months without my voice improving, I consulted a specialist at Bethesda Naval Hospital. He told me I had a benign nodule on my vocal cords, and recommended an operation to remove it. I hoped there might be an alternative treatment, so I tried all sorts of nonsurgical remedies: throat lozenges, resting my voice, herb teas. Although my voice is marginally better than it was a year ago, it is still far from normal. All sorts of advisers, from my wife to close friends, tell me that my voice is the major point of discussion about me in the state. There's even some speculation that I have throat cancer.

The condition doesn't cause me any physical discomfort and I can forget about it most of the time. But no one else seems to be able to. On the radio last week, the last question on a call-in show was, "So, Bernie, how's your voice doing?" By now each Vermont newspaper has published several articles on the subject, including front-page stories. My medical condition is making Vermont's throat specialists famous. There has been more coverage of my vocal cords than any of the work I've been doing in Congress.

A month ago I went back to Bethesda and then to the medical center at Georgetown University. After sticking a tube down my throat and looking at my vocal cords on a TV monitor, the Georgetown doctor agreed that I could not escape surgery. The next day, I made an appointment for the operation at Bethesda. One has to remain silent for four days after the surgery, so we scheduled it for a time when it would be least inconvenient.

Naturally, I have fears about the operation, with so much at risk. It is through the voice that each of us communicates to our fellow human beings, be they wives or children or political constituents. Further, for me, an activist and a politician, speaking is an essential tool for what I need to do.

I hope to God this guy doesn't make a mistake. He seems to think it is a routine operation, no big deal. He tells me they do it all the time. I asked him, "What rate of failure do you have?" He told me there is success the overwhelming majority of times. We'll see.

Two weeks later: The operation is a success. For the first time in fifty-four years—my entire life—I have had surgery. I was very well behaved. They told me not to talk for three to five days afterward so, breaking the habit of a lifetime, I didn't. I fear, though, now that almost two weeks have passed, with all the demands on me, I am probably overdoing it. I shouldn't have given that speech to the regional United Electrical Workers convention a few days ago. So I am going to be cautious again. I've got to be very disciplined, because the worst thing I can do is to blow it now, which is what Governor Pete Wilson of California did when he had similar surgery. I do not want to go through this again, the voice I can't control, the fears, yet more surgery.

Jane thinks I am more relaxed now, which is probably true. Not knowing what sound was going to pop out of my mouth was nerve-racking. In order to compensate for the hoarseness, I had a natural tendency to raise the decibel level. On one occasion on the floor of the House, my voice went completely dead and only a glass of water brought to me by a colleague enabled me to finish my remarks.

Consequently, it is a strange experience to go to the podium for the first time following surgery. For a year and half I have had to shout into the microphone but this time, coming forward to speak for an amendment, I am astonished. My voice is so clear and smooth that as I begin to speak, I actually *lower* it, and for the first time I appreciate the quality of the sound system in the House chamber. My voice resounds all over the hall, without any need to shout. Only now do I realize what a strain it has been.

Every year Burlington restaurants sponsor a remarkable festival called the Green Mountain Choo-Choo, bringing out thousands of Vermonters interested in sampling the wealth of dishes that the restaurants provide for the occasion. A large crowd always attracts my campaigner's instincts, so here I am, shaking hands and saying hello. Over and over again people tell me that my voice sounds great, that they are glad to see me back to my old self. I'm astonished that this matter attracts so much attention—more than any political issue I've ever worked on. But it's gratifying to find out how many Vermonters are concerned about my well being.

Meanwhile, there have been some major developments in the campaign. Jack Long, a Democrat, will be entering the race. Long is the former state commissioner of environmental protection. Instead of a two-way race between Sweetser and me, there will now be a three-way campaign. Sweetser is delighted. She and many others believe that Long's candidacy will draw votes away from me. I'm not so sure. If he does well, he will hurt me. If he doesn't get many votes, Sweetser will probably lose as much as me. The Democratic candidate only received 3 percent of the vote in 1990 and 6 percent in 1992. In 1994 there was no Democrat.

Long, a lawyer and former state administrator, is more credible than past Democratic candidates. Governor Dean is supporting him, but states publicly that he doesn't think Long will get more than 10 percent of the vote. Clearly, I will lose some votes to Long from Democrats who would have voted for me because they dislike Sweetser. But Sweetser will lose votes from moderate Republicans who think she's too conservative and would never support me. Who knows how it will all shake out?

Long is staking out the "moderate" position. He says: "I think if I decide to run I will easily differentiate myself from Mr. Sanders and Ms. Sweetser. They are on the extreme ends, extreme right and left. There is no moderate candidate representing the views of moderate Vermonters."

Another troubling development: a new *Burlington Free Press* poll shows that Sweetser has narrowed the gap. In March, according to their poll, I was ahead by 45 to 26 percent. By late May, my lead is down to 41 to 25. It's not good news. At this stage an incumbent should be doing better. We've got a lot of work to do.

☞

The struggle never ends. If it's not one fight, it's another. If it's not the perversity of those who represent the wealthy, it's the absurdity of congressional politics. Right now, for instance, I am fighting very hard to maintain the Northeast Dairy Compact. The Compact is an attempt to save dairy farms in Vermont and throughout the Northeast.

I was born in Brooklyn, and did not know one end of a cow from the other when I arrived in Vermont twenty-seven years later. Today, while I am by no means an expert on agricultural economics or dairy farming, I do know it is absolutely imperative that we save the family farms. They are a vital part of our state's economy, they protect our environment, and they connect us to our heritage. Vermont can be many things without its farms, but it would not be what any of us know as "Vermont."

Over the years I have developed an almost emotional attachment to the state's dairy farmers and have fought hard for them against overwhelming odds. Today there are fewer than 2,000 dairy farms in the state, a number that declines annually. The work is not attractive to young people, since the hours are long and the work week usually runs seven days. No wonder our farm population is aging.

Most people who see lovely red barns and cows grazing in pastures do not understand the economy behind the pastoral vista. Farmers have a great deal in common with workers in urban areas. Like low-wage workers everywhere, many are able to survive only because of food stamps and other programs for low-income families. And like both unionized and nonunionized workers, farmers are at the mercy of huge corporations. Agribusiness dominates the feed industry and is rapidly taking over milk production and processing. Now it is even trying to turn cows into an extension of the corporate production process.

Several years ago I led the effort in Congress against Monsanto's bovine growth hormone (BGH), which treats cows as if they were chemical factories for producing milk. The last thing that Vermont farmers need is the production of *more* milk to drive prices even lower, and the addition of new costs, not for hay or equipment but for genetically engineered chemicals. The last thing that consumers need is milk produced with artificial stimulants that make cows sick. But Monsanto, a multibillion dollar corporation, has enormous political influence with the Food and Drug Administration as well as in Congress. There was very little support in Congress for my efforts to stop the introduction of BGH.

Each of New England's six states passed legislation to create the Northeast Dairy Compact. Briefly, the Compact would enable representatives from the six states to set a fair price to farmers for the milk sold within the region. Because it is an interstate compact, it requires the approval of the United States Congress. Vermont's two senators, Patrick Leahy and James Jeffords, have worked hard and effectively on the issue, as have a number of us in the House. Finally, against great odds, the legislation has been passed. It is now awaiting the signature of the secretary of agriculture, Dan Glickman, whom I knew from his days in the House. Glickman has to decide whether the legislation meets the criteria of "compelling public interest."

The Northeast Dairy Compact legislation is on his desk and we are waiting for him to sign it ... and waiting, and waiting. I am worried. There is strong political opposition from midwestern Representatives who mistakenly believe that the Compact will hurt their dairy farmers. There is also opposition from the powerful forces that want cheap milk—the chocolate companies, the food processing industry, and the milk processors—whose profits go up when milk prices go down. On several occasions, I have spoken to President Clinton about the legislation. He appeared supportive, but certain people in his administration were defi-

nitely unsympathetic. I also spoke to his chief of staff, Leon
Panetta, and to Glickman himself.

Clearly, the Northeast Dairy Compact was more than an agricultural issue. Politics were involved. There's a presidential election coming up. Vermont has three electoral votes. Wisconsin,
Minnesota, and other midwestern states have a lot more. I wonder
if Clinton's folks will abandon us in the end. Glickman reassures
me that the Compact will be signed. Still, I worry.

Now, right at the end of this enormously convoluted legislative process, one of those ironies that are so commonplace in politics occurs: Wisconsin's David Obey, a friend and a fellow
progressive, offers an amendment in the Appropriations
Committee to kill the prospective legislation. Obey represents
Wisconsin, and they're opposed to the Compact. But here is
another twist that underlines the strangeness of congressional
politics: Bob Livingston, a Louisiana conservative and Gingrichite,
chairs the Appropriations Committee. His job is to push through
the Agriculture Appropriations bill, which contains the
Compact. The Republican leadership is nervous that, because the
legislation contains so many compromises, it could easily
unravel. They want to keep the bill whole, and, at that late date, it
doesn't matter any longer what is in it.

In theory, the Compact—which allows heavy government
regulation of the price of milk in the Northeast—runs directly
counter to all that Livingston, a free-market conservative, stands
for. On the other hand, it is consistent with Dave Obey's general
outlook. Dave is a progressive, who has long advocated a strong
role for the federal government to protect working people.

Fortunately for us, on this one, Livingston wins and Obey
loses. The Northeast Dairy Compact, as part of a major agricultural bill, is shepherded to victory by an antigovernment conservative. We take it any way we can get it.

The Scapegoating Congress

The last couple of weeks in Congress have been particularly depressing and ugly. After all the fine-sounding intellectual rhetoric about "philosophy" and "contracts," after all the books, conferences, and position papers by Republican think tanks, the Gingrich political strategy which we see on the floor of the House as we head into the election comes down to gay bashing, immigrant bashing, racism, sexism, and attacks on the poor.

Nothing new here. A slight variation on very old themes. The same garbage that the right wing always rolls out. If you have no rational analysis of the causation of social problems, if you represent the rich and powerful and *can't* address the needs of ordinary people, then the surefire route to political success is to manipulate peoples' fear and ignorance, to play off one group against another—to *scapegoat*.

For a hundred years, the white workers of the South were the most exploited white workers in America. They were paid the lowest wages, they endured the worst working conditions, their housing was abysmal, their kids went to the most backward schools, and very few could send their children to college. But what *did* they have? They were given "niggers" to hate and look down on, "niggers" who couldn't vote, drink at their water fountains, use the same bathrooms, or sit up front in the buses or movie theaters.

The political, economic, social, and educational systems of the South enforced those divisions and continually fed the antagonisms. Above all things, white workers were encouraged to despise, and protect themselves from, their black neighbors, or face losing what little they had. The rich folks in the South—the bankers, the manufacturers, the cottonfield owners—laughed all the way to the bank.

During that period, some of the bravest people in the history of America risked their lives fighting the system that perpetuated racism. In illegal meetings throughout the South (it was against the law for blacks and whites to sit in a room together), these political activists and union organizers brought black and white workers together to fight for justice. They did this not only because they believed in civil rights and equal opportunity but also because they understood that real economic and political transformation would never be achieved as long as whites and blacks were busy fighting each other—rather than their common oppressors.

Some things never change. Some struggles never end.

Today, the Republicans understand that tax breaks for the rich, cuts in Medicare, Medicaid, education, and environmental protection, and support of NAFTA, GATT, and other disastrous trade policies are not exactly a winning ticket.

Of course, it *is* the agenda of rich folks and corporate leaders, and what the Republicans are paid to deliver. But there are only so many millionaire voters, and Republicans know that this agenda is not going to win points among middle-class and working people—the people who determine the outcome of elections. Slashing Medicaid and allowing corporations to pollute our drinking water are not the kind of achievements that can be celebrated in thirty-second campaign ads for all the world to see.

Given that their real ideology—not the sham philosophy of "states' rights" or "personal responsibility" created for public consumption—reflects the interests of a tiny and very privileged seg-ment of the population, Republicans are faced with the same dilemmas that vexed the ruling elites of the South: How to con-vince working people and the middle class to vote *against* their own best interests. Or, equally important, how to get them not to vote at all. Further, how to deflect attention *away* from the issues that affect the vast majority of people and around which they could *unite*.

Sound strange? It may to you, but I see it every day of the week. That's what the politics of scapegoating and "wedge issues" is all about. White against black and Hispanic. Straight against gay. Working class against the poor and welfare recipients. Men against women. Native born against immigrant. People on the outside against jail inmates. On and on it goes.

The Republicans of 1996, who undertake massive polling, understand very well the legitimate fears and anxieties that mil-lions of Americans feel. And they are prepared to spend huge sums of money to exploit those anxieties, to divide working peo-ple and set them at each other's throats, to blind working people to the fact that instead of justice they are getting scraps from the rich man's table.

Most importantly, the Republican strategy is designed to keep working people from looking at the *real* causes of their prob-lems, from examining who owns and controls the system and who benefits from current policies, and from seriously consider-ing how the current political and economic structure can be changed. The Republicans pit people with little power against those with no power. Meanwhile, scarcely anyone looks at who's pulling the strings.

For the last twenty years, the average American has been working longer hours for lower wages. As real wages have dropped by 16 percent, millions of workers are now stressed out because they are working 160 hours a year more than they did just two decades ago.

And millions of Americans say, "When will it end? How hard do I have to work to pay the bills? Saturdays, Sundays, overtime?

Two jobs? Three jobs? Surely I'm entitled to some vacation time. Surely I'm entitled to some fun—to see a movie, to hunt, fish, read, enjoy my children."

All over this country, women who would prefer to stay home with their children have been forced into the workplace because families now need two paychecks in order to survive. Millions of single people are fighting desperately to support themselves and to raise families alone.

And throughout the country Americans are wondering, "Am I a good parent? How can I plan for a family when my job will not allow me to take a leave? Has my boss ever had to get up ten times a night and feed a baby? Haven't his kids ever been sick? How do I get decent and affordable child care? Why was it that my father alone was able to bring home enough money to support the family?"

Most of the new jobs that are being created are low-wage jobs, paying $5.00 or $6.00 an hour. Many of these jobs are part-time or temporary. Parents know that if their kids are going to become self-sufficient, they will need a college degree, but they also know that there is little chance they can afford to pay for college fees out of wage rates that are so low.

And millions of Americans say, "But how do we send the kids to college when it costs $15,000 or $20,000 a year and we only earn $25,000? How do we save money for education when we can barely pay the mortgage or the interest on the credit card? No. We can't go $50,000 into debt. What are we supposed to do?"

More and more Americans have no health insurance or are underinsured. *Medical debt is the primary cause of personal bankruptcy in this country.* Despite Medicare, a large number of senior citizens are unable to afford the prescription drugs that they need.

And millions of Americans are asking, "Who can afford $5,000 a year for adequate health coverage? Who can go to the doctor when the deductible is so high? Three thousand dollars a day in the hospital, when you're making $20,000 a year. It might as well be a million bucks a day. Let's hope no one in the family gets sick this year."

For the self-employed, small business person, payroll taxes are often higher than income taxes. And then there are property taxes for schools and municipal government, and state taxes. Taxes. Taxes. Taxes.

And millions of American's say, "Doesn't anyone understand? I can't afford to pay more taxes. I can barely survive on what I earn today. Why doesn't the government stop spending so much of my money? Why do these politicians always want more and more from me in taxes?"

Every night on television, we see reports of horrible crimes. Murder, rape, assault, robbery. Some of them are so utterly senseless. Drive-by shootings, kids killing each other for a pair of sneakers, parents doing unspeakable things to their own children.

And millions of Americans demand an explanation. "I obey the law. I play by the rules. Why do I have to live in fear when I walk down the street? Why can't my kid be safe when she goes to school? Why is it costing me a fortune in taxes to pay for extra police or to send these people to jail? Why can't they get a job, and be decent citizens? And why does the government want to take away my guns at the very moment when I most need them to defend and protect my family?"

In summary, many Americans are thinking: "This world is changing very fast. I am confused, I am frustrated, and I am *angry*—and I'm frightened about the future."

Well, relax. Newt Gingrich, his pollsters, and his colleagues hear you. And they are prepared to *act*—boldly, forcefully, and swiftly on the floor of the House.

No, there will be no rational discussion in Congress of the *cause* of your problems and concerns. There will be no serious debate as to why the middle class has collapsed, why the gap between the rich and the poor has grown and is now wider than in any other industrialized country, why two-thirds of the increase in family wealth goes to the richest one percent, or why that same one percent now own more wealth than the bottom 90 percent.

There will be no serious debate as to why the United States has gone from first in the world in terms of wages and benefits to thirteenth, why CEOs of large corporations now make almost 200 times what their workers earn, or why we now lag behind every major industrialized country on earth in the amount of paid vacation time and parental leave our workers receive.

Nor will there be any serious discussion as to why we have record-breaking trade deficits, why our industrial base has suffered a major decline, and why the United States has lost millions of decent-paying jobs as profitable corporations close down plants here and move to countries where they pay their employees twenty or thirty cents an hour.

There will be no serious debate about tax policy that has significantly lowered taxes for the rich and large corporations, and raised taxes for the middle class, or why company after company threatens states and local communities with job loss if they don't get tax breaks which result in higher local taxes for individuals and homeowners.

There will be no serious debate as to why the United States continues to have the most expensive and wasteful health care system in the world, and is the only major nation on earth that does not guarantee health care as a right of citizenship.

There will be no serious debate as to why the United States now has, by far, the highest rate of childhood poverty in the industrialized world, and how that poverty is translated into the highest per capita rate of incarceration of any major nation; or why two-thirds of the inmates in jail are functionally illiterate, or why more people are shot to death in two days in this country than in a year in Japan.

No. These and similar issues will not be discussed by Gingrich and his colleagues. If they were, they might bring people *together* to find solutions that would benefit the vast majority of Americans. Imagine. Black and white, Hispanic and Asian, straight and gay, middle class and low income, native and immigrant coming together to create an economy that worked well for the majority, not just the rich; a health care system that guaranteed health care for all, not huge profits for insurance and pharmaceutical companies; federal funding for education, not B-2 bombers; a tax system that favored workers, not the wealthy and multinational corporations. People coming together for the common good. Newt Gingrich's nightmare.

No. Gingrich, his colleagues and corporate sponsors can't discuss or resolve the real problems facing the average American, but they can certainly deflect attention from them. They can pass legislation that will make some us feel better, by making others feel worse. They can divide the middle class from the poor, and all of us by race, gender, national origin, and sexual orientation. They can beat the hell out of the weak and the powerless. It's a mean, ugly kind of politics. But it's a kind of politics that wins elections.

And I see the fallout in Vermont. At a town meeting in Addison County, a woman says, "Bernie, I'm working hard and I can't afford health insurance. Why is it that my kids don't have health care, but the children of welfare recipients do? It's not right. What are you going to do about it?"

And I reply that I'm going to fight so that everyone in this country has quality health care through a national health insurance program. And she says, "No. I'm not asking you to provide health insurance for my family. I just want you to take it away from those welfare people."

Similarly, at a festival in Orleans County, a woman says, "I work at a grocery store. I'm disgusted. I see these people with food stamps come in and buy steak and better food than I can afford. Do something about it."

I hear comments like this all over the state.

As Congress winds down and prepares for the November 1996 elections, the Republican leadership introduces wedge-issue legislation, bills designed to divide the American people against each other, and so win votes for the Republicans.

On July 12, 1996, the so-called Defense of Marriage Act is brought to the floor of the House. It's a "good" issue for the

Republicans. Gays constitute a small percentage of the population, and most of them do not vote Republican. Tapping into
homophobia and the sexual insecurity of Americans is an effective, time-tested, vote-getting strategy.

In the early days of the Clinton administration, there was a
very divisive discussion about gays in the military. While tens of
thousands of gay men and women have served this country with
honor and dignity and many have died defending it, President
Clinton's attempt to bring the issue out into the open—and
acknowledge what already existed—created an uproar. The
Republicans, as well as conservative Democrats like Senator Sam
Nunn, had "done well" by exploiting the issue, and Clinton suffered a serious political setback. If gay bashing worked well in the
past, why not revive it?

Homophobia is a very serious problem in this country—even
within the ranks of Congress. Representative Bob Dornan
(R–Calif.) spends much of his time on the floor delivering
homophobic diatribes and, while his extremist views are atypical,
he is rarely rebuked or controlled by the Republican leadership.
Last year, Dick Armey, the Republican Majority Leader, referred
to openly gay congressman Barney Frank as "Barney Fag" during
a press conference. He later simulated an apology. Just a "slip of
the tongue," he explained. During a debate on the floor totally
unrelated to any issue concerning sexual orientation, I was
stunned when Representative Duke Cunningham of California
made a gratuitous comment about "homos" in the military. I
demanded that he withdraw his remarks. Shouting ensued. "Sit
down, you socialist," he yelled. The next day, after gay rights
groups convened a press conference to condemn his remarks, he
apologized, promising never to use the term "homo" on the
House floor again.

These flagrant displays of homophobia have a political ratio-
nale. Dornan and Company are playing to a particular constituency. Gay bashing has become a cornerstone of the agenda
advanced by the Christian Coalition, a powerful element in the

Republican "revolution." During the 1994 election, the Coalition distributed millions of pieces of literature ranking candidates on their "family values" yardstick. Homosexuality is, by their definition, "antifamily," and so is support for gay rights.

Again, I see the alarming results in my home state. Peter Clavelle, who followed me as mayor of Burlington, did a courageous thing in 1992 when he approved the provision of health benefits for domestic partners of city workers, including gay couples. This was one of the reasons Clavelle lost his reelection bid that year—and that was in the liberal city of Burlington.

The Defense of Marriage Act is a preemptive response to the Hawaii State Supreme Court's anticipated decision in favor of the right of gays to be legally married. The proposed federal legislation would make gay spouses ineligible for federal benefits and would allow a state to refuse recognition of gay marriages legally performed elsewhere. The bill is introduced by Representative Bob Barr (R–Ga.), who personally has a great deal of experience with the institution of marriage. He has been wed three times. Representative Enid Waldholtz (R–Utah), Acting Speaker in this debate, is also well versed in the intricacies of marriage. She is currently pressing charges against her former husband, Joe Waldholtz, who is cooling his heels in the slammer. And Mr. Gingrich himself is no slacker when it comes to marriage. His former wife, whom he divorced after her cancer operation, turned to the local church for help when Gingrich refused to pay child support. These are some of the main defenders of marriage taking the floor in the debate.

The Defense of Marriage Act is supported by *every* Republican except Wisconsin's Steve Gunderson, who is openly gay. In fact, Gunderson provides some of the strongest and most emotional arguments on the floor against this absurd piece of legislation, as does Barney Frank. Conservative Republican Jim Kolbe from Arizona votes for the bill. Several weeks later, because of anger against his vote by members of the gay community, Kolbe is about to be "outed." This rather quiet, fifty-four-year-old Vietnam veteran who served in the House for twelve years, suddenly announces to his Arizona constituents that he is gay.

After much sanctimonious breastbeating, the Defense of Marriage Act carries on the floor by a vote of 342 to 67. One hundred eighteen Democrats vote for the bill. Sixty-five Democrats and one Independent vote against it. Many people in the House are speculating about the TV ads that the Republicans will develop for use in the upcoming election against anyone who offers support for gay marriage. So does President Clinton. He endorses the legislation.

On August 1, 1996, the Republicans bring their "English Only" bill before the House. This legislation is just one part of their ongoing anti-immigrant strategy, which capitalizes on racial bigotry and general ignorance about immigration. Needless to say, most anti-immigrant prejudice is not directed at British, French, or Canadian individuals who want to become American citizens.

Unfortunately, many Americans don't know the difference between legal and illegal immigrants and, as in other countries with economic problems, xenophobia is intensifying. The issue for some can be summarized by the writing I recently saw on a T-shirt: "If you can't speak English, get the fuck out of the United States." In California, *Time* magazine reported on a nurse from Woodland Hills who "was pelted with rocks and anti-Hispanic epithets at a high school she has walked by for 10 years without incident."

The "English Only" bill mandates that all official communication by the federal government be in English. This means that members of Congress from a heavily Hispanic or Polish district, for instance, would be prohibited from communicating with their constituents in Spanish or Polish. Election, tax, and other information needed by millions of citizens would be available only in English. President Clinton indicates that he will veto this legislation, and the bill will not go anywhere—not even to the Senate. But it passes in the House by a vote of 259 to 169. Eight Republicans, 160 Democrats, and I vote against the bill.

The major scapegoating effort of the Republican leadership, however, is not gay bashing or immigrant bashing. It is not the attack on affirmative action or the bills limiting women's access to abortion.

The crown jewel of the Republican agenda is their so-called welfare reform proposal. The bill, which combines an assault on the poor, women and children, minorities, and immigrants, is the grand slam of scapegoating legislation, and appeals to the frustrations and ignorance of the American people along a wide spectrum of prejudices.

Tired of high taxes and spending huge sums of money on people too lazy to work? Tired of paying black teenagers to stay home all day and have babies while you work your butt off? Tired of providing an incentive for Mexicans to skip over the border in the middle of the night? Welfare reform is for you!

The legislation is a real political winner for the Republicans, and has caused a dramatic and fundamental change in the philosophical underpinnings of the Democratic Party.

The legislation approved by the House and Senate is monumental because, after sixty years, it withdraws federal protection from the weakest and most vulnerable members of our society. The United States of America will no longer guarantee minimal support for hungry and disabled children or for the poor. Instead, there will be a massive cut in funds and responsibility will be transferred to the states.

Here is what "reform" will actually accomplish:

- Benefits will be limited to a lifetime maximum of five years. All recipients must find work within two years or lose their benefits. These regulations take effect regardless of economic conditions in a community or the availability of jobs.

- Seventy percent of recipients of Aid to Families with Dependent Children (AFDC) are children, including, at any given moment, about a third of all black children.

At a time when 20 percent of all kids in the United States live in poverty, "reform" will push one million more children over the edge.

- Three hundred thousand children with disabilities will be denied Supplemental Security Income (SSI). The bill substantially narrows the definition of disability for poor children with tuberculosis, autism, serious mental illness, head injuries, arthritis, and mental retardation.

- Benefits for legal immigrants will be cut by $23 billion over six years. People who play by the rules, come to the United States legally, and work and pay taxes, will be denied Medicaid, SSI, AFDC, and other resources because they were born in another country.

There was a lot of uncertainty in Washington about whether or not Clinton would support this Republican legislation. Some people pointed out that he had vetoed two previous pieces of similar legislation as being too harsh on kids. But I saw a harbinger of his ultimate decision in the administration's rejection of a request to study the actual impact of the provisions on the nation's children. Clearly, they chose not to do the study because it would confirm the fact that large numbers of children would descend into poverty. So my bet all along was that Clinton would acquiesce. A few hours before the vote, Clinton held a press conference to announce that, while he had certain reservations about the bill, he would sign it. The legislation is a step forward, he asserted.

What was especially noteworthy about these past few weeks, especially in terms of so-called welfare reform, was the historic collapse not only of the president, but of much of the Democratic Party in Congress in supporting draconian cuts which five years ago nobody in the party would have seriously discussed, let alone voted for.

That collapse indicates the enormous success that Newt Gingrich, Rush Limbaugh, corporate America, and the far right have had in changing the political and social landscape of America. It also makes clear that there is now *no* major political party that represents the poor and the vulnerable.

There is no question about it. Beating up on the poor is now "good politics." As Rush Limbaugh has told us: "The poor in this country are the biggest piglets at the mother pig and her nipples ... They're the ones who get all the benefits in this country. They're the ones that are always pandered to." Congress and the president have heard Limbaugh's message, studied the polls, and clambered aboard.

It is astonishing how little fanfare accompanies such an historic event. Here is the Democratic Party, a party which prided itself for sixty years on defending the interests of working people and the poor, making a radical shift to the right, and accepting policy which Richard Nixon would have summarily rejected. If, five years before, someone had suggested that a Democratic president and the vast majority of Democrats in Congress would have supported legislation that cut food stamps by over $20 billion, viciously attacked legal immigrants, and terminated a child's right to minimal economic support, they would have been laughed at. But that's exactly what happened. And where was the great debate in the party? Where were the attacks on the president, the demonstrations, the mass resignations from the administration?

The speed of the collapse is breathtaking. Only two years before, in 1994, the Democrats brought forward a welfare reform bill sponsored by Representative Nathan Deal of Georgia. It was the most conservative welfare bill ever supported by the Democratic leadership. (Mr. Deal, by the way, subsequently left the Democratic Party and became a Republican.)

But compared to the welfare bill that the Democrats supported in 1996, introduced by Representative John Tanner of Tennessee, the Deal legislation was a model of humane concern. Despite its many defects, it was based on the assumption that if the federal government wanted to get people off welfare, it would have to provide the education, job training, and child care necessary for people to make the transition and at the same time protect their children. It actually *increased* funding for food stamps, child care, and other programs. Although I had very serious concerns about the Deal bill, I ultimately voted for it, as did most House Democrats, because it maintained federal support for the rights and needs of poor children and their parents, and was clearly the best welfare bill with a chance of passing.

Two years came and went. Gingrich became Speaker, and Rush Limbaugh's brutal attitude toward the poor had permeated both parties. Now the Democrats have lent their weight to the Tanner bill, a far more punitive "reform" than the Deal proposal, which calls for $20 billion in cuts in food stamps and in most respects is a miniature of Republican proposals. It accepts the brilliant proposition that poverty is caused by the poor, and advances as a solution an end to government support for the most vulnerable people in the country. This bill, which is not quite reactionary enough for the Republicans, wins the support of 159 out of 195 Democrats. Eventually, 98 Democrats support the Republican bill, which is passed by a vote of 328 to 101. Significantly, relatively few *white* Democrats vote against the Tanner bill—only ten. Most of the opposition comes from minority members.

In passing this legislation, the Republicans have been successful not only in playing on people's fears but also in exploiting voters' lack of knowledge. The degree to which the American people are alienated and uninformed about the political process is hard to appreciate. In January 1996, a poll conducted by the *Washington Post* revealed that only 40 percent of Americans were able to name the vice president of the United States, 66 percent did not know the name of their member of Congress, and 75 percent could not name their two U.S. senators. Further, 40 percent of the respondents believed that either welfare or foreign aid constituted the largest single expenditure of the federal government. This, at a time when the budget for AFDC was $14 billion—one percent of the federal budget—and foreign aid was slightly less.

So here we have millions of Americans who believe that cuts in welfare are necessary to move the country toward a balanced budget, while they are unaware of the fact that at exactly the same time the Republican leadership is increasing military spending by about $60 billion over a six-year period, an increase *larger* than the savings produced by cuts in welfare.

The Republicans have succeeded in convincing Americans that poor people are responsible for the federal deficit, rather than a series of policies over the last twenty years which have given huge tax breaks to the rich and thrown billions of dollars at defense contractors. Not only that. They have also successfully propagated the view that compassion and human sympathy are not the province of government. For the federal government to reach out and provide assistance to those in need is bad and harmful.

And what is the right thing to do? Cut welfare. Cut food stamps and nutrition programs. Cut affordable housing. Cut health care. Cut education. Cut fuel assistance. Are these things not harmful acts? Is this not selfish, cruel, and immoral? No. Increasing hunger, homelessness, and human misery is how we *help* the poor.

The Republicans get away with this absurd argument, the Democrats collapse before it, and the American people swallow it because there is virtually no organized opposition. The Children's Defense Fund, the National Council of Catholic Bishops, and a few other organizations stand up for kids and the poor. But overall, the silence is deafening.

A further reason that the Republicans can mount this assault on the poor is because they understand an obvious social fact: the vast majority of poor people do not make campaign contributions, do not vote, and do not participate in the political process. In fact, the poor are almost totally irrelevant to contemporary politics, except when being using as scapegoats.

Poor people are a good target for the Republicans. Exhausted by an increasingly difficult struggle for survival, they are not organized and can't fight back. Seventy percent of welfare recipients are children, a constituency that cannot vote and has few civil rights. What a target. It's like shooting fish in a barrel. You can't miss.

Here is the great catch-22 of American politics: as long as low-income people do not vote or participate politically, they will be scapegoated. But as long as both major parties continue to ignore the problems of low-income citizens, the poor will see politics as irrelevant and won't vote or join the political process. The politicians who get elected will continue to ignore their needs.

How many times have I knocked on doors at low-income housing projects and heard people say, with pride in their voice, "I don't vote. What difference does it make? Nobody's going to represent my interests."

Let me digress here to share a few observations.

When I was mayor of Burlington, we came close to *doubling* voter turnout. Why? Because we made it clear that we would stand up and fight for low- and moderate-income people—and we did. Many low-income people understood that and, as a result, they supported us. If poor people believe that voting will make a difference, they will vote.

The ruling class of this country knows perfectly well how important it is for them to keep voter turnout *down*. The United States has, by far, the lowest rate of electoral participation in the industrialized world. In 1994, when Gingrich and friends took power, only 38 percent of Americans voted. The vast majority of poor people stayed away from the polls. For the Republicans it was a great election. Almost nobody voted, and rich people contributed huge amounts of money. This is the kind of "democracy" the ruling class likes.

In Third World countries, when political organizations want to protest against what they consider an illegitimate government, they organize voter boycotts. In this country, it would be impossible to *organize* a voter boycott, because we already have an *unorganized* one. In the 1994 elections, 62 percent of the people boycotted.

In 1993, President Clinton signed the Motor Voter bill, which makes voter registration easier for low-income people. Registration forms can be filled out when applying for a driver's license, at the welfare office, at the unemployment office, at the public library, at various government office buildings. It's a good bill, but only a tiny step forward in terms of where we ought to go in improving people's access to the voting booth. Nonetheless, the Republicans went berserk at the passage of the bill, and a number of Republican governors flatly refused to implement the law. How terrible! Imagine that. Poor people are registering to vote. What next?

Yet, when the next war comes, who will be returning home in body bags, or without legs or arms? Who, as a result of their wartime experience, will be unemployed and end up sleeping in the streets? It will be the sons and daughters of the people who don't vote, and who the Republicans don't want to vote ever.

If voter turnout in this country reached the levels of Canada or Europe—70 to 80 percent—American society would change substantially. Most importantly, if poor people would utilize their leverage at the polls, they would realize the great principle that in a democratic society they, as much as anyone else, have the right to determine the future of this country and shape its social contract. That sense of empowerment, in itself, would transform the lives of millions of people and, ultimately, the entire nation.

If poor people voted, the government would pay far more attention to economic injustice, health care, education, and other issues largely ignored today. At the very least, legislation like the recently passed welfare "reform" bill would never be enacted, would just be a dim dream of the far right fringe. The Republicans agree with me on this point. They fully understand the implications of expanded participation by low-income citizens in the electoral and political process. That is why they work so hard, in so many ways, to prevent it from happening.

W elfare, gay and immigrant bashing, increasing military expenditures, and cuts in Medicaid and education are scarcely all I have to deal with. Back in Vermont I have to juggle these painful realities with trying to figure out what to do with the campaign. On that front, I'm not sure where things are heading.

It's May 21, and I'm in Washington. Jane gives me the bad news that Susan Sweetser has begun her television advertising. This is an unexpected development which catches us completely by surprise. By Vermont standards, going on television in May is almost unprecedented. In the last three elections, we began our TV advertising in October. Her ad is a high-quality, thirty-second spot. In the trade, it's called an "intro piece," designed to familiarize viewers with her life and her views. The ad has been produced by Dresner and Wickers, a big-time Republican media company.

While we try to figure out how we should respond to this major campaign development, one thing is clear—if Sweetser is already putting substantial sums into TV, she must be confident of raising a very significant amount of money. Could she raise a million dollars? Is corporate America that anxious to get rid of me? And what about the additional help that she will almost certainly get via "independent expenditures" from the NRA and other organizations? My first thought concerning Sweetser's TV ads is that we'd better accelerate our own fundraising efforts. We're in for a tough and expensive race, and we'd better get moving.

Should we go on television early ourselves or just wait? It's a big question. In the 1994 campaign, my Republican opponent, John Carroll, went on TV in late August, which we considered "early," and we made a mistake by not responding. We gave him a full month to get his message out without any reply from our side. I don't intend to make that mistake again, but it's strange to think about going on TV with the election five months away. Not only did we have no intention of going on the air this early, but we are not financially prepared to do so.

The question of how we should respond to Sweetser's TV campaign is largely answered by a "baseline" poll that we have commissioned. This year, for the first time in my life, and with great reluctance, we hired a professional Washington polling firm, Bennett, Petts & Blumenthal, to conduct an in-depth survey of my strengths and weaknesses among Vermont voters. For most politicians, this is pretty standard fare, but although we have done lots of polling within our progressive movement, we have never done anything this thorough before. The poll costs us $15,000, which seems to me a staggering amount.

We work with the pollster in helping to design questions for a thirty-minute interview with respondents. You are supposed to throw out all of the arguments your opponent will use against you, and see how people respond. In that way you learn where you're vulnerable and what your strengths are. We also include a "horserace" in the poll, to see how we are doing against Sweetser.

To make a long story short, the results of the baseline poll are very reassuring to us. In fact, the consultants who analyze the results with Dave Petts say they have never seen anything quite like it—and they have been looking at polls for many years. The bottom line is that Vermonters know me very well. Some of them agree with my views, and some do not, but they all know where I stand. The pollsters are surprised at the enormous numbers of respondents who believe that I am honest and straightforward with voters, and who see me as someone who fights for what I believe to be right. Few Vermonters, it turns out, regard me as a typical politician.

What most interested me was that the poll indicated that very few of the arguments and attacks that we anticipate Sweetser using against me will have a major impact on changing the views of voters. In the head-to-head "horserace," we are ahead by 27 points. Although her feel-good television ads have been on the air for two months, Sweetser's negatives are unexpectedly high.

Frankly, I think the poll is too good to be true, even if these pollsters are professionals and come highly recommended. But it does convince me of one thing. We don't have to spend money putting ads on television yet. We'll husband our resources, and save them for the end of the campaign when we'll really need them.

At around this time the Becker Poll comes out, a major statewide poll commissioned by the business community and Vermont's largest television station. This poll has us up by 20 points, and also finds Sweetser's negatives to be high. No one quite knows why Sweetser seems not to be doing well. Even though she is pouring $80,000 into television ads, my lead remains wide and her negatives continue to go up. It's very strange, but we're not complaining.

Our immediate strategy is to keep things reasonably quiet, try not to make too many stupid mistakes, and then sprint hard toward the end of the campaign. It's likely that Sweetser will receive a huge amount of money from her wealthy supporters and buy up the airwaves, but there's not a lot that we can do about that. Everything being equal, I am now feeling more confident than I expected to be two or three months ago.

At the outset of the campaign I identified three areas in which we had to improve over past efforts. The first grew out of my dream of seeing a thousand politically knowledgeable people, part of our movement, canvassing all over Vermont. If a thousand people each knocked on two hundred doors, we would knock on every door in the state. Frankly, that ain't gonna happen now—and I know it. But it's a dream worth having.

Many people don't pay much attention to TV news, don't read the papers or listen to the radio. They are not actively involved in the political process—especially in trailer parks and low-income areas. The goal of a canvassing effort is to bring political ideas right to the front doors and, if possible, into the living rooms of thousands of Vermonters through face-to-face contact. In my view, all the TV ads in the world are not as effective as an intelligent and personable canvasser who is able to discuss the issues and listen to voters' concerns. I refuse to give up on the idea that a campaign in a democratic society should include a significant educational dimension.

A few months ago two young people, Peter Baker and Ashley Moore, walked into our campaign office looking for jobs. Both of them had extensive canvassing experience working for environmental organizations in Oregon. They were bright and energetic—just the sort of people I wanted. In the beginning, the two of them would just go to a town that we had selected and knock on doors by themselves. But after a while, Phil Fiermonte and Tom Smith were able to organize local volunteers in the various towns to go out with Peter and Ashley.

The canvassers take campaign material to every door in a community. If no one is home, they leave a leaflet. When they come across a supporter, they give him or her a "Bernie 96" bumper sticker—these are beginning to show up in large numbers on cars all over the state. They take addresses for lawn signs—we have over a thousand people who have indicated they want to put these up, a remarkable achievement for a campaign many months from election day. They are also signing up supporters to volunteer and are registering people to vote as well as bringing back questions from constituents to which we try to respond.

The canvassers have also asked supporters to write to newspapers, resulting in more letters supporting me on editorial pages than ever before. Occasionally, they even manage to sell a "Bernie for Congress" T-shirt. An added bonus is that some of our supporters are making campaign contributions. Five dollars here, twenty dollars there. It all adds up. Further, and very importantly, by knocking on doors every evening we are getting firsthand impressions of how people are feeling about the campaign and the issues.

In St. Albans last night, four local volunteers who know the community well went with Peter and Ashley and another staff person: that meant there were seven people canvassing for the evening in a small city. That gives you a real presence. The people of St. Albans will know that the Sanders campaign was in their town—and that's great. Tonight, five or six people will be going to the suburban community of Williston. Every day the effort continues in another city or town. In some of the smaller towns, three or four people can knock on every door in one night.

Canvassing gives people a chance to interact with the Sanders campaign in new ways. Even though I return from Washington each week to spend three or four days in the state and I make a concerted effort to visit every area of Vermont, tens of thousands of people have never met me personally. So while we are handing out literature, registering voters, giving out bumper stickers, obtaining signatures to get on the ballot, raising money, we are doing what is most important of all: talking directly with people. If you are serious about building a movement, you have to go out and talk politics. We haven't done enough of that in the past, but we are doing better now. The canvassing effort is something I am very excited about.

Perhaps the high point of the campaign for me so far has been the meeting Phil Fiermonte put together a few weeks ago in Montpelier, the state capital. The goal was to bring volunteers together to discuss the role they could play in the campaign. Seventy-five people turned out to learn how they could be effective campaign workers—a great turnout.

One of the challenges that any serious campaign faces is how to deal effectively with volunteers. If you give them "make work" that is not useful or challenging, they're not going to come back. Nobody wants to waste their time. If you ask people who hate making phone calls to use the phone, they're gone. A good campaign is successful when it matches volunteers with the work they enjoy and are interested in. We need people to canvass and to maintain booths at the state fairs and on street corners. We need volunteers to hand out literature and to make phone calls, to work in the office in Burlington, to get out the mailings, and to run our computers. In the fall, we'll need supporters to help out in our regional offices. We have a lot of work to do, and this meeting is to get volunteers to do it.

I was surprised and gratified by the number of low-income

people who attended. For these folks, Gingrich's policies are not issues for intellectual debate. They are life-and-death matters of food on the table, health care, education, and Medicare premiums. When Phil first suggested the idea of the meeting, I had my doubts, because it took a lot of work to organize it. But I was wrong. We were bringing some great people into the campaign.

While we seem to be attracting more working-class and low-income volunteers, we're not generating quite as much enthusiasm and support as we have in the past among progressives, who, historically, have been the backbone of our movement. I'm not complaining. The new volunteers are hard workers and know their communities very well.

The second goal I set was to do better with direct mail in Vermont. While this is an area where being an Independent places me at a real disadvantage compared to the Democrats and Republicans, there is no question that we should be able to improve greatly on our past performance.

Direct mail is an expensive proposition when you're talking about 250,000 voters. In the last campaign we sent out about 35,000 pieces targeted mostly to hunters, to deal with the gun issue and to counter the NRA's vehement opposition to my candidacy. Historically, the Republicans mail to every household in the state, and the Democrats are not far behind. They usually push their entire ticket, so the state or national parties can pick up the cost. For us, everything has to be paid for out of my campaign funds.

This year we got smart and started early. We took advantage of resources that have always been there. Many professional and occupational groups in Vermont must register with the state, and these lists are available to the public for free, often on computer disks. Using them has enabled us by mid-August to send mail to 95,000 Vermonters.

Our plan of action is not complicated. We get people who are well known within the various professions to write letters of support, we enclose our standard literature and a return envelope with a contribution form, and we mail out bulk rate—about eighteen cents a letter. And we are making an exciting discovery: these mailings have almost paid for themselves; in fact, some of them have actually made money. In other words, we're able to do mass mailings to Vermonters at no cost to the campaign. So far, we have sent out letters to doctors, lawyers, and every teacher, nurse, physical therapist, chiropractor, farmer, and university professor in the state. Now we are buying lists of senior citizens and environmentalists.

Our success with bulk mailing encouraged us to come up with an even bolder plan. What would happen, we brainstormed, if we picked a district in which we did well in the last election, and sent a mailing to every single household? Well, the results of the first few tries are in, and we did well, getting the one percent response necessary to cover our costs. An advantage of this kind of mailing is we can use a "postal patron" address (which means mail goes to *every* residential address, instead of to a named addressee), which is the cheapest form of mail. The disadvantage is that a number of the people you are sending mail to don't vote. But frankly, for us, this is not so much of a problem. We want to communicate with those folks, too.

In general, then, our mailing efforts are going far better than ever before. We're communicating with more people, we're raising more money, and we're drawing more supporters into the campaign. I'm very excited about this aspect of our work.

When you run a campaign you have to become an expert in all kinds of things: mail solicitation, direct mail, postal rates, buying drive-time slots for radio advertising, writing campaign brochures and laying them out, estimating printing costs, purchasing buttons and bumper stickers, scripting radio ads, and editing television slots. Believe me, a campaign is more than just giving speeches and turning up at debates.

Our third goal was to do a better job using the telephone. Yes. I apologize. We also engage in that activity hostile to human sentiment, telephone canvassing. Generally, most congressional candidates and political parties hire professional telemarketing organizations that are located in South Dakota or some other far-away place. I think that the geographical location of the company is dependent upon the callers being "accent free"—Vermonters would not appreciate callers with an Alabama accent—and the cost of labor being cheap. These companies have hundreds of workers who do nothing else but dial phones automatically, give the same spiel over and over again, and type the results into a computer. "Yes. I intend to vote for Congressman Jones no matter what happens." Strong supporter. "No. I haven't a clue as to who is running for office. Is there an election coming up this year?" Undecided.

For years, we have argued among ourselves about the advantages and disadvantages of making calls in-state or out of state. The clear advantage of making the calls through a professional telemarketing company is that they'll get made. You put down your money, and they can make fifty or one hundred thousand calls—whatever you want to pay for. And you'll get voter ID responses back nice and clean, done by professionals. It's expensive, but it's simple.

The disadvantage of this approach is that the people who are making the calls couldn't care less about what they're doing. They don't know Vermont, they don't know Bernie Sanders, and some of that will surely come through. Also, when it works well, telephoning is an excellent activity for our volunteers. It is very effective for a supporter in Hinesburg, Vermont, to call a neighbor and talk about the campaign. You can't beat that. But it's very hard to get the number of volunteers that you need to make any sizeable number of calls. A lot of folks, quite understandably, do not like calling up strangers. Also, given the fact that our callers are not professionals, and that they're not working on computers, some of the results come back a bit jumbled.

Once again, after a lot of discussion, we decided to do our telephoning in-state. We have to get lists of registered voters and phone numbers to our volunteers, order a bunch of telephones for our office—and do the best we can. Although Tom Smith is doing an excellent job in coordinating this, and we're doing better than in the last campaign, we're still struggling. On any given night we only have three or four people on the phones. People say they'll come in, and don't. I have my doubts as to how successful our overall telephone campaign will be. It will be better than last campaign, but still won't be very good.

Y ou don't have to be a political genius to know that if you function alone, there are real limits to what you can accomplish. The Democrats have their party, the Republicans have theirs. As an Independent, functioning outside the two-party system, I have worked hard throughout my political career to bring people together into the progressive movement in the fight for social justice.

When I was first elected mayor of Burlington, I knew that a progressive agenda could never be implemented without the efforts of a strong and successful political movement. Working with other progressives in Burlington, we created the Burlington Progressive Coalition, which, in the city, has been a de facto political party for the last fifteen years. During that time, the Progressive Coalition has elected two mayors, dozens of city councilors and school board members, and four representatives to the state legislature.

Statewide, we have not developed a formal third party. I have, however, been active with many others in creating a strong Vermont progressive movement which over the years has, among other activities, run a number of candidates for state legislature.

Obviously, when I took office in Congress in 1991, the dynamics were very different than those in Vermont. I was the only Independent in Congress, the only person outside the two-party system. There was no way that was going to change in the next two years. In Congress, there were Republicans, Democrats, and me—and that was that. Given that reality, I thought hard about the political role I could play.

After a short time in Congress, I decided to try to bring

together the most progressive members so that we could more effectively fight for economic justice. There were already a number of caucuses in Congress, some of them doing excellent work, but there was no group explicitly fighting for a progressive agenda to address the needs of America's working people.

I was aware that, over the years, the most progressive positions in Congress had been articulated by the Black Caucus. For decades it had done an excellent job in fighting not only for the needs of the black community, but for the needs of low- and moderate-income people of all races.

When I was mayor, I became aware of the "alternative budget" introduced by the Black Caucus every year. In this document, they showed how we could increase funding for affordable housing, community and urban development, health care, education, and the general needs of low- and moderate-income Americans by shifting the funding priorities of Congress. In a very simple and effective manner, their "alternative budget" exposed the moral bankruptcy of congressional priorities. It was a terrific initiative and was widely used by political activists all over the country. For years the Black Caucus had been, in effect, *the* progressive caucus in Congress.

But not every progressive in Congress is black, and so it seemed to me an important step forward to develop a caucus which brought *all* progressives together—white, black, Hispanic, Asian, male, and female—so that we could stand together in fighting for rational priorities.

Obviously, the Black Caucus will always focus its attention on the particular needs of the black community, the Hispanic Caucus on the particular needs of Hispanics, the Women's Caucus on the particular needs of women. A Progressive Caucus, however, would try, on an ideological and class basis, to represent *all* Americans who were struggling to obtain a decent standard of living. I bounced the idea of a progressive caucus off some of my friends.

One of the first members I talked to was Ron Dellums of California. Ron is one of the great heroes in the United States

Congress. For twenty years he has been a leading voice in the
struggle for a world of peace and social justice. He entered
Congress from the Berkeley area and was already well known for
his opposition to the war in Vietnam, and for his struggles against
racism. He has continued to fight for justice, year after year.

I also talked to Peter DeFazio of Oregon, who was one of two
members of Congress to endorse me when I ran in 1990. (Barney
Frank was the other.) I didn't know Peter well then but he has
since become a very close friend. He represents a rural district in
Oregon which, in many ways, is similar to Vermont. We end up
approaching many issues with a similar outlook. Peter has been
especially strong in the fight against corporate welfare, and on
trade and the environment.

Then there was Lane Evans, a Vietnam-era veteran from
Illinois who had one of the strongest anti-Reagan voting records
in Congress. Lane received national recognition for leading the
effort to expose the Pentagon's cover-up of the Agent Orange
fiasco, and has been a leading voice for veterans throughout his
tenure. (He is also a good landlord. I live in the basement apartment of his house.)

Finally, I approached Maxine Waters of California, who came
into Congress the same time as I did and sits next to me on the
Banking Committee. Maxine was well known as a powerful progressive voice in the California State Assembly, and firebrand
advocate for low-income people. She was born in a low-income
housing development, and did not forget where she came from.

We five got together and formed the Progressive Caucus.
Over the years the group grew slowly and steadily, so that by the
time our largest battle took place—against Newt Gingrich and
his reactionary "Contract with America"—we were fifty-two
members strong. I was elected chairman of the Caucus in 1991
and have held that position since.

In addition to the founders, other members of Congress who
have been active in the Progressive Caucus include Major Owens,
Maurice Hinchey, Cynthia McKinney, Nydia Valazques, Lynn

Woolsey, Bob Filner, Jerry Nadler, Eleanor Holmes Norton, Barney Frank, Marcy Kaptur, and Jesse Jackson, Jr.

In October 1992 I got my first major piece of legislation through the Congress when the National Cancer Registries Act was signed into law by President Bush. Every so often, Congress actually works the way it is supposed to: ordinary citizens see the need for new legislation to tackle a problem, approach their elected representatives, and their proposal gets translated into law. This was the genesis of the National Cancer Registries Act.

In 1991, a number of Vermont women became concerned that the mortality rate for breast cancer in Vermont was extremely high, and significantly higher than in the rest of the country. Why was this and what could be done about it? Led by three breast cancer survivors—Joann Rathgeb, who eventually died after a courageous battle with cancer, Patricia Barr, and Virginia Soffa—these Vermont women mounted a strong educational campaign in the state and a petition drive which secured thousands of names. Their demand was the establishment of a national cancer registry.

I learned from these women that the United States was far behind most major countries in keeping uniform statistics on who was contracting cancer, their place of residence, their occupation, the types of treatment they were receiving, and the effectiveness of the treatment. Clearly, if researchers are going to get a better handle on the causes of cancer, and the most effective ways of dealing with it, we need more information.

What does it mean that certain types of cancer are more prevalent in Vermont than in California? What is the relationship between environmental degradation and cancer? Are people working at certain types of jobs more likely to come down with particular types of cancer than people working at other jobs? Are people living near land fills or incinerators more likely to develop cancer?

If we had uniform national statistics, would we learn more about the connection between diet and cancer, and life style and cancer? Would we discover more geographical "clusters" of certain types of cancer? Are there reliable national statistics about the rate of cure for one type of procedure as opposed to another?

Given the fact that one American in three is expected to develop some type of cancer in his or her lifetime, these issues are of enormous consequence. I learned about the problem not only from women in Vermont, but from trade unionists in the Oil, Chemical and Atomic Workers Union. The people in their union do work which exposes them to a lot of unhealthy substances, and they have great difficulty in getting information from their employers about the rate and kinds of cancer workers in their union are developing. Workers all over the country face similar obstacles.

This issue is especially important to me because I have long been interested in preventive health care measures. This country spends $1 trillion a year on health care, and almost all of it goes into treatment. We spend relatively little trying to prevent disease—whether it is cancer, heart disease, or the common cold. In the long run we can eliminate much human suffering, and great cost, if we better understand the *causation* of disease.

After undertaking some research, we found that only ten states in the country had effective cancer registries. And while some national statistics were being tabulated by the National Cancer Institute, they ignored 90 percent of the population. In early 1992, I introduced the Cancer Registries Amendment Act. The bill was later introduced in the Senate by my Vermont colleague, Senator Patrick Leahy. As a result of some excellent work by my staff member Katie Clarke, we picked up strong support from physicians and health care organizations all across the country. Then we had a stroke of good fortune.

In their June 1992 issue, *Reader's Digest* ran a lead article by Dr. John H. Healey, of the Sloan-Kettering Cancer Center, titled "The Cancer Weapon America Needs Most." And what was that weapon? The passage of the Cancer Registries Amendment Act of 1992. The *Reader's Digest* also ran full-page ads in the *New York Times* and other papers discussing that article. We could not have asked for better publicity. Soon, letters of support for the legislation began flooding the Capitol.

The legislation wound its way through the committee process, winning support as it proceeded. Unfortunately, we were heading into the very end of the session, and it was likely that time would run out before we got a vote on the floor of the House. If that were the case, I would have to start all over again—assuming I was reelected.

The cancer weapon America needs most

There we were on the very last night of the session, with Congress rushing toward adjournment. At this point in the legislative process, the only legislation passed is through "unanimous consent." There is no time for debate or vote taking. The only bills that pass have got to win support from the floor leaders of both parties, with no opposition from any member, even one who only wants to see the bill debated. If there is any objection to "unanimous consent," the bill is dead.

At four o'clock in the morning, I was desperately trying to figure out how I could get my bill on the floor and secure unanimous consent. The Democrats were amenable to bringing it up, but the Republican floor leader was William Dannemeyer of California, one of the most right-wing members of the Congress. He only had to say "I object," and it was all over for the session. Frankly, I thought I would do the bill more harm than good if I approached Dannemeyer alone. He and I did not see eye to eye on most things.

My heroine of the hour, the person who saved the day (or rather the night), was Representative Mary Rose Oakar of Ohio.

Mary Rose, who served with me on the Banking Committee, literally took me by the hand and led me to the Republican offices off the floor where we discussed the issue with the Republican staff. She personally intervened with Dannemeyer and other Republicans and, I believe, even tried to call Dannemeyer's wife. (I don't remember if she ever got through.) In any case, on the morning of the last day of the session, the legislation was approved by voice vote with no objections. I was a sleepy but happy congressman. I believe that the National Cancer Registries Amendment was the second-to-last piece of legislation passed in the House in the 102nd Congress. Today, as a result of that legislation, and some $50 million in appropriations, almost every state in America now has an effective cancer registry and researchers are gaining valuable information from the data.

In 1992, two Republicans were vying for the right to oppose me in the general election: Tim Philbin, a right-wing Christian Coalition type, and Jeff Wennberg, the conservative mayor of Rutland, the state's second largest city. No strong Democrat entered the race. A relatively unknown candidate from Brattleboro, Lew Young, put his name into the Democratic primary.

Both Philbin and Wennberg had their strengths. Philbin was a dynamic speaker and had strong, conservative grassroots support. Wennberg, on the other hand, was an experienced politician and, as the Establishment candidate, would receive substantial funding from the monied interests.

Philbin won the Republican primary. Consistent with his ideology, he opposed a woman's right to abortion, even in the case of incest and rape. In Vermont, every statewide officeholder was pro-choice. It was very definitely the prevailing opinion in the state. Moreover, on a variety of issues Philbin was out of touch with the Vermont Republican Establishment, and he got little support from them.

On November 3, I was reelected as Vermont's congressman. The results were Sanders 58 percent, Philbin 31 percent, and Young 8 percent.

Getting Around Vermont

Last month, the *Rutland Herald* ran a detailed article by Diane Derby contrasting my views on abortion with Sweetser's. My position is that a woman's decision whether to have an abortion is a private one, and that this principle must hold true for all women, regardless of income. Susan Sweetser is a "moderate" Republican and describes herself as pro-choice. On the surface, our positions appear similar. But there is one significant difference: Sweetser opposes the use of Medicaid funds for abortion. She supports a woman's right to an abortion, but only if that woman can afford to pay for one. So, while our positions seem similar, there is a very real difference between us. The *Herald* article made that clear.

Unfortunately, serious articles which explore, in detail, the difference in positions between the candidates are few and far between. We need more of that kind of writing, and less emphasis on campaign gossip.

On the subject of women's issues, one of the more gratifying aspects of the campaign so far is that we are winning very strong support from women and women's organizations—despite my running against a female candidate who has been active in victim's rights activities. Poll after poll shows the "gender gap" to be enormous. We're ahead with women by as much as two to one, while we're barely winning among men. We have also been endorsed by the National Organization of Women (NOW), the National Abortion Rights Action League (NARAL), and the Business and Professional Women's Association. Sweetser has won the backing of the National Women's Political Caucus, which only endorses women candidates.

Over the years my office has played a very strong role in the fight for women's rights. I not only have a 100 percent voting record on women's issues, but have worked hard and successfully on women's health matters and against domestic violence. The women of Vermont know that. Furthermore, most women understand that it is hard for a candidate to be "pro-woman" while supporting a political party that wants a constitutional amendment to ban abortion and is waging war against low-income workers and Medicare recipients, who are mostly women, as well as single mothers and their kids.

Yipes. I'm the subject of a major editorial in the *Wall Street Journal*. I'm pissed. Not only is the content absurd, but the picture they run of me stinks. Now why is the *Wall Street Journal*, the voice of corporate America, worried about the congressional race in little old Vermont? Don't they have bigger things to worry about? Well, in truth, they're really not too concerned about me, they *are* on to bigger things.

In an editorial which refers to me "as the nation's highest-ranking socialist elected official," the *Journal* is despondent over the fact that the national Democratic Party and President Clinton are not supporting Jack Long—the Democratic candidate for Congress. See, we told you all along, suggest these perceptive editorial writers. That Clinton, those Democrats, they say they're "moderates," but when given a choice between a moderate Democrat and a socialist, whom do they choose?

Yup. The Democrats are backing an incumbent, favored to win, who helped lead the opposition to Gingrich rather than a candidate nobody's ever heard of who is running 6 percent in the polls. Big surprise. Clinton and his friends may not be too progressive, but they ain't dumb. Interestingly, this was the exact theme used in an editorial in the extreme right-wing Moonie newspaper, the *Washington Times*, a few weeks earlier. I wonder. Is this the prelude to a national Republican redbaiting ad campaign? Are we going to see thirty-second TV ads all over America on how Clinton is supporting a socialist?

Of course, I have been winning the support of Vermont progressive Democrats for years, and have worked on a number of important issues with Democrats in the legislature like Cheryl Rivers, Liz Ready, and Dick McCormick. We have our differences but we've found it mutually advantageous, and in the best interests of Vermont, to work together when we can.

Generally speaking, what appears in the *Wall Street Journal* is of no concern to me. I'd estimate that over 98 percent of the people in Vermont do not read the *Journal*—and most of those who do aren't going to vote for me in any case. So the editorial by itself doesn't mean much. But what happens is that this sort of attention from the national press can become a focus for political gossip in Vermont. The very fact of the *Wall Street Journal* carrying a story on a Vermont issue may well become news in the state.

Shortly after its appearance, the *Journal*'s analysis gets picked up by the Vermont media, and my office receives umpteen calls on the now-famous "Jack Long story": "How come Sanders has the support of many leading Democrats in Vermont while Jack Long, a Democrat, doesn't?" (To the best of my knowledge, Governor Dean is the only major Democrat to come out for him.) The fact that I won widespread support from Democrats in 1988, 1990, 1992, and 1994 is now forgotten, and we're starting this discussion all over again.

And what a strange discussion it is. Here is a man who has yet to hold a press conference explaining his position on any issue since he announced his candidacy, a man who has raised almost no money, a man who is between 4 and 8 percent in the polls— and yet the great unexplained point of interest turns out to be— remarkably—why Democrats will not support him. The recirculation of superficial punditry never stops. Story after story appears in the *Burlington Free Press* and elsewhere, and the issue attracts the attention of the largest television station in the state.

WCAX-TV calls for a comment on the *Journal*. I'm not particularly interested in discussing political gossip. What do I have to say that hasn't been said ten times before? But I'm ready to deal. I'll give them a response if I'm also allowed to say a few words about something substantive—something that might actually be of interest to someone. "If you allow me to discuss a recent press release I just sent out," I say, "I'll talk about the editorial." My press release was critical of a Pentagon policy which is farming out billions in Defense Department contract work to countries abroad, work that should be done in this country by American workers. At a time when the defense industry is laying off tens of thousands of American workers, it's an issue of real concern—especially in a state with several defense plants. The reporter calls back and we have a deal. They get their comment on the absurd *Wall Street Journal* editorial and I get a decent story about something relevant.

Not only did we make the *Journal* last week, but we also made the *New York Times*. The *Times*, covering "all the news that's fit to print" got the scoop. As careful as they are perceptive, the paper calls me to confirm the story. Their details are accurate. "Yes, it was me. I did it. I really was the back half of the tiger in the Bread and Puppet Circus that took place in Glover, Vermont a week ago." I had been asked, not for the first time, to participate in the huge outdoor drama/celebration, and had been cast in the role of the hind end of a large tiger puppet. (It's better than being a horse's ass.) I told the writer the whole story, and he wrote a few lines about it in the Chronicle column. He also quoted me accurately: "As for the conventions, Mr. Sanders said: 'I'm the luckiest man in the U.S. Congress. I'm not in Chicago, and I didn't go to San Diego.'"

There was a story here, but it is not about me. The Bread and Puppet Domestic Resurrection Circus, an annual two-day gathering in August is put on by a radical theatrical troupe which, traveling from its base in Vermont, performs street theater all over the globe. On this occasion it brought out between twenty and thirty thousand people to Glover—a beautiful town in the north of the state. The Bread and Puppet theater—founded by Peter Schumann—is a political company whose accomplished theatrical productions are truly radical. They are especially well known for their huge masks and the performers who wear them while walking on stilts. Bread and Puppet does a tremendous job, and we in Vermont are very proud of them.

While there are many out-of-staters at the festival, the number of Vermonters who attend the Bread and Puppet Circus always amazes me. In the week since my appearance as the back end of a tiger I have been stopped a dozen times by people who told me that they saw me there. I'm not sure how many of them actually heard my fourteen-second speech about the dangers of Newt Gingrich, given when I stepped out of my tiger costume. (The Bread and Puppet Circus is performed without electricity or microphones.) Still, it was great to be there.

My son Levi was with me at the event. Levi works full time for the Chittenden County Emergency Food Shelf but whenever he can get a free weekend, he travels with me around the state. I enjoy his company a lot, and he helps me by doing most of the driving and by working the crowds: handing out buttons and bumper stickers while I shake hands. With the enormous crowd in Glover, we had four other campaign workers there. It's a great place to campaign.

One of the fun aspects of being a congressman is the different kinds of people that I meet. After we left Glover, Levi and I took a beautiful drive across the width of the state to Swanton, which is located in northwest Vermont, just south of the Canadian border. I often think how lucky I am not only to live in Vermont, but to campaign there. Driving along beautiful Vermont country roads in August, as the sun goes down, just ain't hard work. It's exactly the kind of thing I would do if I never ran for office. In the back of the car I always have a bathing suit, and it's not uncommon for us to stop midday on the campaign trail and jump into a nearby lake or river.

My business in Swanton that Saturday night was to address members of the Mississquoi Valley Emergency Rescue Service. The contrast between the huge crowd of the afternoon and the dinner event of the evening, attended by forty or so members of the rescue service, was striking, from radical theatrics to community-based service. (Interestingly, the differences strike me as more superficial than deep: both the rescue workers and the drama troupe are focused on giving, on giving of themselves to build community.) The rescue workers are all volunteers. Their work is difficult and emotionally traumatic. Since Interstate 89 passes right through Swanton, serious highway accidents are not uncommon. These men and women are often the first people to arrive at the scene of an accident. They deal with life and death in the course of their work. At the dinner, person after person talked about the trauma of seeing people die and the joy of saving people's lives.

They were an impressive group of working people—young and old, men and women, with a strong pride and attachment to their community. Being among these people reminds me, once again, of why Vermont is such a good place to live: here is an organization whose members are not paid a nickel but serve the community because they care. There are hundreds of organizations like this one in the state.

While I have been going to county fairs, parades, "circuses," banquets, picnics, and shopping centers all over Vermont, on the national scene something far more visible—and scripted—has been taking place. The last couple of weeks have witnessed both the Republican and Democratic conventions.

What was most noticeable about the Republican convention—I held a press conference on this—was the degree to which the Republicans were running away from who they are. They spent almost a week on prime-time TV erasing recent history and substituting image for actuality. The Republican Party established a record in the Congress over the last two years. Newt Gingrich and Dick Armey led what I believe is the most reactionary Congress in the modern history of the United States. Yet, when it came to the convention, these people, and the issues they advocated, disappeared entirely. I couldn't find them on CBS, NBC, ABC, or PBS. Puff. They were gone.

Two years previously, the Republicans were pushing large photos of hundreds of their candidates signing the "Contract with America." Now, that term was never mentioned. Newt Gingrich was sidelined. Dick Armey was barely noticeable. Everything the two of them had fought for with the almost unanimous support of the Republican House was pushed into the hinterlands. It was as if two years of Republican legislative activity never existed. Even the Republican Party platform, which a majority of the delegates had just approved, was ignored. Golly. Bob Dole just didn't get around to reading it.

Instead, on center stage were people like Colin Powell—a black, pro-choice, pro–gun control, pro–affirmative action, moderate Republican. His views are not shared by more than 5 percent of the Republicans in Congress, but it was he and not the "revolutionary" Speaker of the House Newt Gingrich who gave the major speech. The keynote speaker was a pro-choice woman, Susan Molinari of New York.

As the selection of speakers and the entire tone of the GOP convention revealed, when the Republicans have to go beyond the narrow confines of congressional committees and $1,000-a-plate fundraisers and speak to tens of millions of ordinary Americans, they choose to hide who they are. In a five-day period, on prime-time TV, the Republicans went from a party of right-wing extremists to the center of the political spectrum.

The convention also showcased my opponent. In her ninety seconds on national TV, Sweetser said, "This will be an historic election. Why? Because we have the opportunity to replace the most liberal, most out-of-touch member of Congress. Bernie Sanders." According to the Associated Press, "after mentioning his name, the crowd erupted in boos." I must be doing something right. Sweetser got a lot of Vermont media coverage from her appearance in San Diego.

It was deeply depressing to see the Republican ticket go up fifteen points in the polls in the course of the convention—for no other reason than that the American people happened to see them on their television sets every night. It does make one think: What could happen, what would happen, in this country if progressives were allowed to have four or five nights of prime-time television and front-page newspaper coverage? What would happen if we could present a point of view that most Americans are unfamiliar with? Would we suddenly become the dominant political force in America? No. Would millions of Americans develop a much more sympathetic attitude toward democratic socialism? Yes.

Predictably, the rise of Dole and Kemp in the polls was ephemeral. Two weeks later, when the Democrats got their four or five days in the limelight, the Dole-Kemp surge evaporated. Clinton is now back to where he was before the conventions—fifteen points ahead.

At both conventions there was a general acknowledgment on the part of the Republican and Democratic leaders alike that it was not in their best interests to allow serious discussion on the most important issues facing the American people. Both parties put on well-produced TV shows. Each had a different focus, but both were in complete agreement that debate on the problems facing America was not something they were going to get into.

The Democratic convention was heavily scripted and entirely poll-driven. They made emotional appeals on several issues where the polls showed they had significant support. Seventy-five percent of the people support the ban on assault weapons. So they focused on the tragedy of Jim Brady, and support for gun control.

Christopher Reeves is a very popular actor, handsome and articulate, so his accident and paralysis became a major focus of their convention. So, too, did the issue of cigarette smoking, especially among the young. This *is* a serious health concern, and

Clinton and Gore deserve credit for addressing it—although how far they will really go in taking on the tobacco industry remains to be seen. But it is only one small part of the health care crisis in America. The fact that it is a relatively easy one politically—you lose the votes of a few thousand tobacco farmers in return for those of millions of parents—made it *the* central health care issue the Democrats addressed.

Perhaps more remarkable were the issues *not* talked about. There was virtually no discussion of class, despite the fact that we have the most unequal distribution of wealth and income in the industrialized world, and real wages of workers continue to fall. There was no discussion of our huge trade deficit, nor of corporate investment in China, Mexico, and other Third World countries, which is causing the loss of millions of decent-paying jobs. There was no mention of the fragility of a democracy in which half the people no longer vote and have given up on the political process.

And what about health care? Three years before, Clinton and the Democrats had raised the banner high for a universal health care system that covers all Americans. At the time, I disagreed with the details of their proposal, but the Democrats deserved credit for at least addressing this issue of critical importance to tens of millions of Americans. The health care crisis is now *worse* than it was three years ago. More people are uninsured or underinsured. More people have less choice of providers as medicine becomes more and more corporatized. During the convention the best the Democrats were willing to allow was that at some undetermined time, in some undetermined way, we should try to provide coverage for children. That was the sum total of their commitment.

In a convention that focused on gun control, smoking, and the personal tragedy of a popular actor, most of the important issues facing the American people were ignored. The vast majority of Americans reject the right-wing extremism of the Republican Party. The Democrats held a convention that refused to address the most important issues facing the middle class and working families of the country. Is it any wonder that most people don't vote and have lost interest in politics? Is it any wonder that the United States faces a major crisis regarding the viability of our democracy?

Watching the convention coverage, it was hard to decide which was worse—the speeches on the floor or the "analysis" by the media pundits. David Brinkley, for instance, complained that President Clinton's acceptance speech dragged on too long, lasting more than an hour. Imagine—at a time when the average American watches forty hours of television a week, fifty-two weeks a year, Brinkley's main concern was that the president of the United States, and candidate for reelection, spoke for more than an hour on the future of the nation. What a profound analysis. And they pay him for saying things like that.

Although I agree with his critique of American trade policy and his opposition to NAFTA, I am no great fan of Ross Perot. There's no way he would be a major political leader if he weren't a billionaire. But I think that he is getting a bum rap from the media when they refer to his half-hour speeches as "infomercials" and make fun of his use of charts. Instead of putting thirty-second attack ads on the air, he is trying to seriously discuss some of the most important issues facing the country. You may not agree with his analysis or his conclusions, but at least he's treating the American people with some respect. What's wrong with that?

☞❘

During the summer and fall, there are a large number of parades in Vermont—from one end of the state to the other. Fortunately for me, I love parades—I always have, even as a kid. I try to participate in as many as possible. Not only is it good politics, because you get to see and talk to a lot of people, but it's a helluva lot of fun. Parents and their kids lining the streets. The high school and military bands. The fife-and-drum corps. The Scottish bagpipes. The country-music dancers. The Girl Scouts and the Little

Leagues. The fire trucks. The antique cars. People dressed in Civil War outfits.The Shriners driving around in their tiny go-carts.

From the town of Brattleboro, to Middlebury, to Vergennes, to Essex Junction, to Lyndonville, to St. Johnsbury, to Windsor, to Burlington, to Rutland, to Swanton, to Waitsfield, to Barre, to Montpelier, to Bellows Falls, to Bradford, to Irasburg, to Springfield, to Woodstock, to Newport, to Brandon, to Enosburg Falls, to White River Junction, to St. Albans—I've marched in all their parades, and dozens more. And I enjoy it every time.

Yesterday was Labor Day. I went, as I almost always do, to the Labor Day Parade in Northfield, Vermont. It is one of the larger parades in the state, and certainly the largest on this holiday commemorating workers and their labor. Some 10,000 people are there, either participating in the parade or lining the streets to watch.

Over the past few years, progressives and union activists have made a concerted effort to involve workers and labor unions in the Labor Day parade. Just a few years ago there was virtually no union involvement. But yesterday several hundred workers from Vermont's unions joined in. That may not seem like a large number, but Vermont isn't a major union state, and for us it was a terrific presence.

It was nice to see a whole lot of kids and spouses there. That's how you construct a movement, build a political presence: one step at a time, adding person to person until you have involved enough people to make a difference on the political landscape.

It gave me a strong feeling of solidarity, that most important of all political emotions, as I marched together with them. After the parade, the Vermont Association of Letter Carriers sponsored a roast beef dinner on the green. We ate, played some football with the kids, and had a great time.

There was very strong support for my candidacy among the thousands who lined the sidewalk. Our campaign supporters were getting rid of buttons and bumper stickers as fast as they could get them into their hands. Parades are a pretty good indicator of what's happening politically. And the response at

Northfield was strong and positive—with almost no negativity.

Labor Day weekend is not only a time for parades, it is a time for the largest fair in Vermont. Throughout August I have been attending county fairs all over the state, and talking to thousands of Vermonters. In addition to my presence, "Sanders for Congress" has booths manned by volunteers at almost all the fairs—and we are giving away large amounts of literature and campaign paraphernalia. Fairs are probably the best places to make contact with Vermonters.

County fairs have been going on in Vermont for well over a hundred years. Originally, they were large agricultural exhibitions, an opportunity for farmers to learn about new products and techniques. Today, obviously, they are much changed and more commercialized and entertainment-oriented, but the agriculture component remains strong in a number of them. At the Barton Fair, at the Rutland Fair, and at most other fairs, boys and girls still exhibit their prize cows. The 4-H clubs are out in full strength. New tractors and other farm equipment are on display. At the Champlain Valley Fair, Huck Gutman has won a number of blue ribbons for his outstanding tomatoes.

Depending on the fair, there are also ox-pulling contests, balloon rides, demolition derbies, horse racing, pig races, spitting contests, professional wrestling, parades, exhibition halls, bingo and other games of chance.

The most "notorious" fair in the state, and the last major fair of the season, is the "Tunbridge World's Fair." Well, what can I say about the Tunbridge World's Fair? Let's just mention that, among other exciting activities, they have a beer hall. I believe that I'm one of the few politicians in the state to campaign *inside* that beer hall. Or at least who lived to talk about it.

This year the Tunbridge World's Fair celebrated its now famous hometown movie star, Fred Tuttle. Fred, now seventy-eight, milked cows in Tunbridge for most of his life before being discovered by his neighbor, filmmaker John O'Brien. (John's dad, Bob O'Brien, was a friend of mine who was a state senator from

Orange County in the 1970s.) John made a hysterically funny (fictional) film about Fred and his run for Congress called *Man with a Plan*. It played for months in Vermont's movie theaters and is being shown around the country. Now that Fred has been featured on the front page of the *New York Times*, appeared on the "Late Night with Conan O'Brien" TV show, and was fêted by the congressional delegation in Washington, the local folks don't know what to do with him anymore. In fact, Fred was at the first congressional debate of the campaign between Sweetser, Long, and me. Guess who got all the attention?

The largest fair in the state is the Champlain Valley Fair, in Essex Junction, which in a little over a week draws close to 300,000 people (although obviously some of these are repeat visitors) in this state of less than 600,000. It is far and away the largest single attraction for Vermonters each year. During several nights at the fair, some of the best known names in country music perform— before huge crowds. There are also all kinds of rides and games for the kids.

At the fair, which is in my home county and only five miles from Burlington, I walk around, shake hands, and talk to people who freely offer opinions on every conceivable issue. Interestingly, much of what I hear about has nothing to do with Congress, but concerns over high property taxes, a state issue.

Our booth is fully staffed with volunteers—senior citizens and long-haired young people, veterans and peace activists, trade unionists and women's advocates—reflecting the diversity of our coalition. The heart of our campaign is in that booth, and they do a terrific job.

Perhaps the most active volunteer at the fair is Ed Walton, a disabled Vietnam veteran. I met Ed last year at a conference for veterans organized by my congressional office. Ed lives in Bristol, about an hour away from Essex Junction, and stays with relatives in Essex during the fair. Every day, first thing in the morning, he helps set up the booth, and makes certain that it is covered throughout the day. When no one else can take a shift, Ed does. It makes me extremely proud that people like Ed are supporting my candidacy.

As I walk around the fair, I can sense that our support is strong. While this is a different part of the state, it reinforces the feeling I got from the Labor Day parade in Northfield—there is a lot of good feeling out there, and things appear to be going well.

Any good politician develops that extra sense. You can look into people's eyes, shake hands, say hello, and after a few hours, develop a real feeling about how things are going politically. At a fair, or other public place, when people bump into you unexpectedly, their feelings are transparent—right on their sleeves. There you are, right in front of them, and they don't have time to hide their emotions. If they like you and what you're doing, they smile and are happy to meet you. If they're not feeling good about you, their eyes don't meet yours, and they look away. Sometimes people are rude and overtly hostile. But that's very rare in Vermont. Most people in Vermont are very civil, even when they don't agree with you.

And let me tell you. The feelings out there this time are much different than they were two years ago, in 1994—when I only won by three points in the midst of the Republican tidal wave. Why is that? I don't know. The economy is better. The anti-Clinton hysteria has died down. The NRA is quieter. Most importantly, I think, people are concerned about the Gingrich agenda and the right-wing extremism he represents. I believe that they appreciate my willingness to stand up for them, and against the savage cuts that the Republicans are proposing.

My sense that things are going well is borne out by a more "objective" measure. Recently, a new poll appeared in the *Burlington Free Press*, the largest paper in the state. It had us at 47 percent, Sweetser 24 percent, Long 8 percent. (The rest are undecided or are supporting another candidate. There are a total of seven candidates in the race.) That's a very good poll for us because it suggests not only that we have a large lead, but that we're going up and Sweetser is going nowhere. While 47 percent is not necessarily a great number for a well-known incumbent like me, 24 percent is a poor number for an establishment Republican at this time of the campaign—especially one who has spent big bucks on TV ads.

For whatever reason, the Sweetser campaign is not clicking. Peter Freyne, not an infrequent critic of mine, is an astute and long-time observer of the Vermont political scene. He offered a few observations in the September 11 issue of *Seven Days*:

> The GOP's best political minds were absolutely certain a woman like Susie Creamcheese would be Ol' Bernardo's worst nightmare. After all, none of the three Republican notches on Congressman Bernie's gun belt (Peter Smith, Tim Philbin and John Carroll) were female. Aha! they thought—the key is to match him up against a woman! "Bernie can't handle a strong woman," they crowed. Susan Sweetser had all the necessary credentials and then some.
>
> Sweetser signed up one of the top political consulting firms going: Dresner & Wickers. Dick Dresner worked for Jim Jeffords for years ... and just upped his fee by pulling off the upset of the century in getting Russia's Boris Yeltsin reelected. Knocking off the only political aberration on Capitol Hill surely would be child's play for these political heavyweights, right?
>
> The plan was simple. Hit the airwaves early to build up statewide name recognition, and with it garner a bump in the polls. Take that bump to the bank and close in for the kill. Keep Sanders on the defensive. Attack his contributors. Portray him as out of touch, a fringe-type who consorts with out-of-state left-wing extremists.
>
> But in life, things don't always go the way you plan. Susie's TV blitz in June did build up her name recognition statewide. Unfortunately, a whole lot of Vermonters who began to recognize her also began to get a bad taste in their mouth. Her commercials were too slick, too New York. A clear gender gap developed. Women didn't like her. Too brassy, too bitchy, too loud-mouthed. The bump in the

polls never came. Instead, her unfavorable rating doubled. Oops. Iceberg, dead ahead!

The campaign is going well. But the last thing in the world that we need now is to become overconfident. It's still two months to polling day and in a political campaign that can be a lifetime. Anything can, and probably will, happen.

In early August 1993, seven months after Bill Clinton became president, I voted for the Clinton budget. It passed by two votes, 218 to 216. As the only non-Democrat to vote for it, you could say my vote was the decisive one for the passage of that important piece of legislation. (On the other hand you could also say that *anyone* who voted for it cast the winning vote.) No Republicans supported it, and forty-one Democrats voted against it. In the Senate it won by one vote.

As the vote on the budget approached, the president and his cabinet scrambled for support. There was an enormous amount of jockeying for votes. The conservatives in the Democratic Party wanted more cuts in social spending, and a smaller tax increase. The Progressive Caucus worked hard to make certain that the legislation remained as responsive to low- and moderate-income people as possible. We expressed our concerns to Leon Panetta, who was then head of the Office of Management and Budget (OMB). We met with Speaker Tom Foley, and told him not to count on our support if the Democratic leadership caved in to the conservatives and cut back on children's programs, health care, and other needs. And we eventually met with the president.

While the bill contained some regressive elements, it was the most progressive budget that Congress had voted on for many years. It increased funding for children's programs, lowered taxes on the working poor by expanding the earned income tax credit, and raised taxes on the rich and corporate America.

For as far back as I can remember, I have always been a proponent of a national health care system. It just seemed eminently fair and right. How can we call this a civilized society when some Americans have access to the best medical care in the world and others are unable to walk into a doctor's office because they lack money? How can we tolerate a situation where the children or parents of the rich get the medical attention they need in order to stay alive, while members of working-class families, who lack health insurance, have to die or needlessly suffer—or go hopelessly into debt to get the care they need? This is an outrageous injustice and it cannot be rationally defended.

Wherever I go in Vermont, people talk to me about health care. Old people tell me about the difficulty they have paying for their expensive prescription drugs. Young people tell me that the jobs they have do not provide health insurance. Union workers tell me that their bosses are attempting, at every contract negotiation, to cut back on the health insurance benefits they provide. And people of all income levels tell me that various kinds of alternative treatments they want to use are not covered by their insurance plans.

People from almost all income levels are growing increasingly concerned about the depersonalization of medicine and the quality of care they are receiving. They often no longer have a personal physician and believe that the care they receive is dictated more by the financial needs of their HMO or managed care provider than by their illness.

The fight for a national health care system today is not basically different than the struggle for universal public education which took place in this country over a hundred years ago. At that time, children of the well-to-do received an education, and a tremendous advantage in life. Most of the children of working people and the poor did not. Finally, after enormous struggle, our society concluded that all children, regardless of income, were entitled to at least a high school education. Some day we will also accept that all people, regardless of income, are entitled to health care.

The fact that the United States continues to be the only major nation in the industrialized world without a national health care system should be a source of national shame. Canada, Great Britain, France, Germany, and Scandinavia all have one. Alone, among the great nations of the earth, we do not guarantee health care for all people.

Despite the fact that 40 million Americans lack any health insurance, and many more are underinsured, we spend a far greater amount per capita on health care than any other nation. Increasingly, the function of the health care industry in this country is not to make sick people well, or to prevent disease, but to make huge profits for insurance and pharmaceutical companies and some well-paid professionals.

In my first year in Congress in 1991, I worked with Doctors David Himmelstein and Steffie Woolhandler on legislation to create a state-administered, single-payer national health care system. A husband-and-wife team, David and Steffie are two of the most knowledgeable and effective proponents of national health care in the country. They have produced an enormous amount of writing on the subject, both technical and popular, and have appeared often in the mass media.

Steffie received a grant to intern in my office and drafted legislation for me, HR 2530, which set out the creation of a national health care system. Simply put, this bill created a single-payer, comprehensive, universal health care delivery system, to be administered by the states. It had many advantages over the system in place then, and over the strange hybrid—corporate-run managed care—which emerged in the period following the collapse of Clinton's health care reform initiative.

The legislation would have created a health care delivery system that covered *every* American. It was a "single-payer" plan— which means there would have been only one state-administered insurance agency paying the bills, creating a far more efficient delivery system. About one-quarter of American health care costs go to cover bureaucracy, billing, and administrative over-head. Canadians spend half that much on administration; the British, one-quarter!

Under this proposed single-payer plan, any American, upon presentation of a health care card much like a credit card, would have been able to get *all* the health care he or she needed, from the doctor of his or her choice. The coverage would have been portable—not connected to a particular job or employer. And, because it would have been administered by the states, citizens would have had more control over their own plan. No distant Washington bureaucracy would have been responsible for health care. While the major single-payer bill that session was intro-duced by Representative Marty Russo of Illinois, my bill won sup-port from those who preferred to see the program administered by the states, rather than from Washington. In that sense, my bill was closer to the Canadian health care system than Russo's.

Two years later, Bill and Hillary Clinton raised the health care debate to the highest level that it had ever reached in this coun-try. They deserve credit for that. They also deserve credit for pro-claiming that all Americans are entitled to health care. Unfortunately, the complicated and compromised bill which they brought forth was not something that I could support.

Throughout that congressional debate—a debate ulti-mately decided by the millions of dollars that the insurance companies put into "Harry and Louise" ads and a massive lobby-ing effort—a number of us, led by Representative Jim McDermott of Washington, worked hard for the single-payer system in Congress.

At the same time, as an adherent of addressing health care concerns on the state level, I also fought to implement health care reform in Vermont. It seemed to me then, and now, that a small state like Vermont could become a model for the rest of the country in health care. I was also mindful that national health care did not come to Canada until it had first been implemented in one of the provinces. Vermont has two major tertiary hospitals in the area, eleven regional hospitals, a medical school, and very competent physicians and health care workers. If there is any state in this country where a single-payer system could be implemented quickly and successfully, it is Vermont.

In 1993, a number of health care reform advocates began working together to gather political support for a single-payer system in Vermont. My office was an active part of that coalition. Among other activities, I appointed a task force to develop a single-payer model for Vermont. It was easy to talk about the benefits of a single-payer system in general, it was harder to be specific as to how it would work in Vermont.

How much would it cost to provide comprehensive health care to all of our people? What would be the mechanics of the delivery system? How could we finance it? Bob Brand, a former health care analyst for the Service Employees International Union, and John Franco, a long-time associate who had worked with me when I was mayor and in my first year in Congress, did an extremely thorough job in leading the task force, and their work generated much discussion. Their conclusion was that, under a single-payer system, we could provide health care to every man, woman, and child in Vermont—without spending any more than we were currently spending.

As part of our health care educational campaign, we held well-attended town meetings all over the state. Sometimes these meetings included state representatives like Cheryl Rivers and Dean Corren who were active in the fight for a single-payer plan in the legislature. Sometimes they included Vermont physicians like Dr. Jason Kelley and Dr. Leigh LoPresti, advocates of the single-payer system.

Needless to say, our efforts were not successful in Vermont or in Congress. The insurance companies and the medical establishment poured tens of millions of dollars into massive and effective lobbying and advertising campaigns against any kind of real health care reform. And they won.

Let's be clear. The debate over health care in this country is *not* a debate about medical treatment or the best way to prevent disease. It is a debate about economics and class politics. Either we maintain a profit-driven health care system whose main function is to enrich certain individuals and institutions, or we develop a nonprofit, cost-effective system that provides quality health care for all people as a right of citizenship.

Health care reform in America will not come without radical political change and the growth of a strong progressive movement.

While I strongly disagreed with Clinton's health care proposal, I respected his willingness to raise the issue and fight for the right of all Americans to have some form of health insurance. But at the very same time as health care was on the congressional agenda, Clinton pushed another issue to the forefront. And on this major initiative, Clinton was just plain wrong—very wrong. His support for the North American Free Trade Agreement (NAFTA) was a sellout to corporate America. Pure and simple, it was a disaster for the working people of this country.

Consider the following: The United States has a federal deficit problem and the Republicans, President Clinton and many Democrats, and the corporate media have made it the focus of their attention. Over and over again we hear about the federal deficit and its implication for the future of this country. Their way of dealing with this has been to come down heavy on low- and moderate-income people and cut programs that currently benefit tens of millions of Americans.

Now, the United States has a major trade deficit problem. In fact, the deficit is at record-breaking levels. For most Republicans, President Clinton and many Democrats, and the corporate media the trade deficit is no cause for alarm. We hear very little about proposals to eliminate *that* deficit. No one suggests that we hold corporate America responsible or demand that they rebuild the manufacturing base in this country rather than invest tens of billions of dollars in China, Mexico, or other impoverished Third World countries.

The United States currently has a trade deficit of $114 billion. Economists tell us that $1 billion of investment equates to about 18,000 (often decent-paying) jobs. Connect the dots. Our current trade deficit is causing the loss of over 2 million jobs. Over the last twenty years, while the United States has run up over a trillion dollars in trade deficits, millions of American workers have been thrown into the streets. During that period our industrial base has declined and real wages for American workers have plummeted. While corporate America shuts down factories in the United States and invests in low-wage countries abroad, young Americans can expect to earn the minimum wage flipping hamburgers at McDonald's, with no benefits or opportunities to advance.

The function of trade agreements like NAFTA is to make it easier for American companies to move abroad, and to force our workers to compete against desperate people in the Third World. But our workers cannot compete, and should not be asked to do so, against people who are forced to work for incredibly low wages, as they do in Mexico.

It is absurd to merge the economy of a modern industrial nation like the United States with a Third World economy like Mexico's. It is absurd to merge the economy of a democratic society with a country whose president at the time of the passage of NAFTA, Carlos Salinas, was elected through massive electoral fraud. It is absurd to merge the economy of the United States with a country where workers are unable to join free trade unions. The result of such a merger will only make the wealthy in both countries richer, cause massive dislocation, and hurt both Mexican and American workers. That's precisely what's happening.

In 1993, I traveled through Mexico with a congressional delegation led by my friend, Representative John Conyers of Michigan. It was an eye-opening experience. In one maquiladora area I toured a modern factory owned by Delco Battery. The workers, almost all women, were earning a dollar an hour. Later, a few of us walked a half-mile up the road to the homes of some of these workers: wooden shacks, without electricity or running water. Not so long ago workers in the United States were earning a living wage producing the same product.

At a meeting with Mexican workers we heard firsthand about their atrocious working conditions. One woman described the chemical vapors that permeated the work space. A number of the workers had experienced miscarriages.

We also went to an agricultural region. There, we heard from small farmers who believed that they would lose their farms and be forced into the cities if they had to compete with American agribusiness. They predicted massive dislocation if NAFTA passed.

During the course of the NAFTA debate, various congressional members expounded on the need for American workers to become more competitive in the global economy. I was so impressed by their arguments that I introduced legislation that would make the president and members of Congress competitive with their Mexican counterparts. My office discovered that members of the Mexican Congress earned about $35,410 a year. If American workers were going to have to compete against Mexicans who were forced to live on $1.00 an hour, I thought that members of Congress should lead by example and lower their $133,644 salaries to the Mexican level. I didn't get many cosponsors for this legislation.

In late October, my office organized a large meeting in Montpelier in opposition to NAFTA. About 300 Vermonters showed up, mostly workers, farmers, and environmentalists, to protest the agreement. Dave Bonior of Michigan, the Democratic Whip in the House, who, along with Marcy Kaptur of Ohio, was helping to lead the anti-NAFTA effort in Congress, gave the major speech.

During the NAFTA debate, every editorial page in the state of Vermont opposed my position—over and over and over again. As the only statewide official who opposed NAFTA I was called a "protectionist," an "anachronism," a "tool of big labor." Some of my political opponents even suggested that I was a racist and anti-Mexican.

But the media support for NAFTA went far beyond Vermont.

In fact, in a nation which polls said was divided pretty evenly on this legislation, *every* major newspaper in America supported NAFTA. Every one. It was an incredible display of the power and unity of corporate America defending its interests. The *Washington Post* was running editorial after editorial, column after column, in support of NAFTA—and printing virtually nothing in opposition. Toward the end of the debate, the paper ran a huge story that showed how much in campaign contributions members of Congress who opposed NAFTA received from trade unions. Somehow, they forgot to run the story about the money that pro-NAFTA members were getting from corporate America.

The class divisions in the NAFTA debate were very apparent. Virtually every major corporation in America supported it, while opposition came from unions, many environmental groups, family farm organizations, and working people throughout the country. The political divisions created some strange alliances. On the pro-NAFTA side were the corporatist elements of both the Democratic and Republican parties, including liberals, moderates, and conservatives. Bill Clinton, George Bush, Jimmy Carter, Ronald Reagan, and Jerry Ford stood together with moderate Speaker of the House Tom Foley and the arch right-winger Newt Gingrich.

In opposition to NAFTA were progressives like Jesse Jackson and Ralph Nader, centrists like Ross Perot, and right wingers like Pat Buchanan. In the House, the most vocal opposition came from a left-right coalition. On November 17, 1993, NAFTA won approval in the House by a vote of 234 to 200. One hundred fifty-six Democrats, 43 Republicans, and I voted against it. It is one of the great political ironies of the NAFTA debate that if George Bush had been reelected in 1992, NAFTA would not have passed. A number of Democrats who voted for NAFTA did so because they wanted to support a Democratic president.

Three years have come and gone since NAFTA was passed and the results are clear: a soaring trade deficit with Mexico and the loss of over 260,000 jobs. Polls now show a sizeable majority of

Americans are opposed to NAFTA, as are an increasing number of congressional members.

In 1993 I spent a great deal of time fighting the carpet industry. What? The carpet industry? Let me explain: In 1992 a woman from Montpelier, Mrs. Linda Sands, called my office. She had an unusual story to tell. Seven years earlier a new carpet had been installed in her house. After the installation, the air in her home became heavy with a strong chemical smell. A short time later, she and several of her children became ill with body tremors, chronic headaches, dizziness, and respiratory problems. They went through hell.

Frankly, I had real doubts about this story. A congressman receives a lot of strange phone calls. But a member of my staff, Anthony Pollina, who had been talking with Mrs. Sands, urged me to take this seriously and so I paid her a visit. This was my introduction to the very serious problem of indoor air pollution, and a disorder called "multiple chemical sensitivity." Mrs. Sands, it turned out, was not alone in having been made ill by certain carpets. During one stretch, over 6,000 people telephoned the Consumer Product Safety Commission wanting information about the problem, and twenty-six state attorneys general across the country had petitioned this agency to have the carpet industry issue warning labels on their products. Both the industry and the agency were stonewalling the attorneys general.

In the course of my investigation I met a researcher in Massachusetts, Dr. Rosalind Anderson, who had developed a test with mice to measure the toxicity of carpets. A lot of her mice were dying.

I met with three workers in northern Georgia who had worked in a factory that produced carpets, and they told me about the serious health problems experienced by the employees.

I heard from physicians around the country who were treating people who had been made ill from certain carpets. For instance, Dr. Doris Rapp recounted her experience with school children: "Over the years I have treated a large number of children from all over the United States, many of whom could no longer attend school after new carpets were placed in their school." Dr. William J. Rea wrote, "My colleagues and I have seen over 20,000 chemically sensitive patients over the last 20 years. Many of these patients have been made ill by the fumes emanating from new carpet." And Dr.

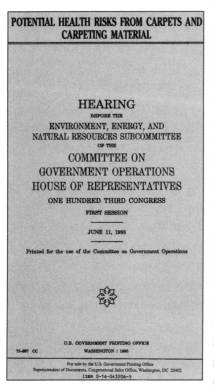

Aubrey Worrell, Jr., wrote, "I have seen many patients who have become chemically sensitive and completely disabled because of exposure to toxic carpet in their home or their workplace. It is my feeling that the chemicals coming from carpets, in many instances, cause severe illness."

I discovered that, irony of ironies, the Environmental Protection Agency itself had removed over 20,000 feet of new carpet from its *own* headquarters in Washington after several hundred workers there suffered health problems caused by toxic carpets.

At my request, Representative Mike Synar, chairman of the Subcommittee on Environment, Energy, and Natural Resources of the Government Operation's Committee, held a very well-attended hearing on the health problems associated with carpets. The media picked up on the issue and it received wide coverage in newspapers and magazines, and on national television.

And my phone was bopping off the hook from people all across the country who had been made sick by carpets.

Throughout this entire process, we had been pleading with the people at the Consumer Safety Products Commission and

the Environmental Protection Agency to do something.
There's a problem here. Address it. Meeting followed meeting.
Letter followed letter. Nothing happened. They were worse
than pathetic.

Finally, after extensive negotiations with the Carpet and Rug
Institute, the attorneys general, Mike Synar, and I reached an
agreement with the industry. The manufacturers agreed to put a
warning label on all carpets, place a counter display of the label in
the stores, and commit substantial sums to researching the problem in order to produce a safer product.

In 1994, I faced my toughest campaign since winning political
office in 1981. I barely survived.

I knew we were in for an interesting race when my conservative Republican opponent, State Senator John Carroll, opened his
campaign by expressing concern about the growing gap between
the rich and the poor. How come I always run against the only
Republicans in the country who want to tax the rich and are worried about income inequality?

Carroll ran a very smart race. Overnight he went from a conservative to a moderate, and spent most of his campaign appealing to Democrats. He also benefitted from the strong anti-
incumbent, anti-Washington sentiment that was blowing across
America which gave the Republicans their first majority in the
House in forty years.

I assisted his efforts by running a very stupid campaign—the
worst of my political career. I allowed Carroll to define me, and
didn't at all go on the offensive. He had been the leader of the state
senate during a disastrous, unproductive, and unpopular session,
but I barely discussed his record. When he put some slick ads on
television and attacked me and my record, I allowed them to go
unanswered for a whole month. In addition, my voice failed me
over the final several weeks—making me sound tired and sick. My
whole campaign was overly cautious and poorly executed.

At 11 p.m. on election night, political pundits thought Carroll
would win. But overcoming historical trends, we did better than

expected in small, rural towns that usually vote Republican. At 1 a.m. the Associated Press declared me the winner and at 10 a.m. the next morning, Carroll called me to concede.

☞❧

Susan Sweetser has hired a private investigator to dig up dirt on me. Cathy Riggs is the wife of right-wing California congressman Frank Riggs, a former police officer, a lawyer, and a well-known GOP operative. She has been listed on two consecutive Sweetser Federal Election Commission (FEC) financial reports as a consultant.

We first learned about Riggs when we were formally contacted by the official House of Representatives bureaucracy that she was examining all of the bulk mailings that my office sent out. There was nothing improper or surprising about that. If a member of Congress sends a mailing to hundreds or thousands of constituents, an opponent has every right to research those mailings. They are a matter of public record, an expression of the candidate's position on the issues, and worthy of political scrutiny.

Riggs, however, went a lot further than that. She contacted my ex-wife, Deborah Messing, from whom I've been divorced for over twenty-five years. Deborah contacted her friend and neighbor, Anthony Pollina, who used to work with me, and Anthony contacted me. Deborah and I then talked.

Clearly, Riggs was hoping to find a disgruntled ex-wife who would spill the beans on her former husband. But that was not going to happen with Deborah, who has been remarried for over twenty years. While we don't see each other very often, we remain good friends, so Deborah told Riggs where to get off. Her sentiments were reflected all over Vermont. Christopher Graff, the long-time bureau chief for the Vermont Associated Press, captured the feeling in the state in a September 19th article under the headline "Vermonters Hold Their Own View on Fair Play in Politics":

Vermonters, grasping sometimes desperately to the belief and hope their state is different, have a unique criteria to judge people, places, and proposals. "That's just not Vermont," is the oft-heard refrain, with the variation "That's so un-Vermont-like."

Things and ways that fit well elsewhere just seem inappropriate for Vermont. It may be as concrete as a Wal-Mart or as ambiguous as a neighbor's airs. The judgment is very subjective, but the verdict always deeply felt.

This is especially true in politics. What may be considered fair and proper in other states leaves Vermonters apoplectic. Campaign ads that even hint of criticism of an opponent are harshly condemned as mudslinging in Vermont, while they would be considered upliftingly positive in most other states.

It is against this background that Vermonters viewed Susan Sweetser's hiring of a private eye to probe Sanders' background. Such a hiring would not even gain a passing mention in most states these days. It is accepted practice. Cathy Riggs is a rising star in the ranks of Republican "opposition researchers."

She says her background as an ex-cop, a law school graduate and wife of a congressman gives her an edge in political probing. And she said in a newspaper interview this past week that she checks everything. "I'm very thorough. I do a total, complete package," she said. "Contacting an ex-wife is just something on my checklist."

But clearly it is not on the checklist of Vermonters. Riggs' call to Sanders' ex-wife was viewed in Vermont as crossing the line. It's not fair play. It's not Vermont-like.

And what was especially un-Vermont-like was the reaction of the Sweetser campaign. Instead of talking to their own investigator to find out whether she had called Sanders' ex-wife, the campaign officials put the burden of proof on the ex-wife, a woman who had worked for 25 years to maintain her privacy.

The story of the hiring of Riggs came out on Wednesday. The Sweetser campaign spent most of Wednesday night and all day Thursday denouncing the story, calling it a fabrication and saying it was merely hearsay.

The campaign kept insisting that since the only source of the fact Riggs had called Sanders' ex-wife was Sanders, the story was suspect. The campaign spokeswoman spent Thursday saying, "All of this is innuendo and hearsay. We would like Bernie's ex-wife to come forward."

Deborah Messing of Middlesex, who was divorced from Sanders more than 25 years ago, was reluctant to talk to the media on Wednesday, but when contacted again on Thursday, as the Sweetser campaign was casting doubt on the story, she agreed to be interviewed and have her name used.

It was a few hours later that Sweetser finally talked to Riggs and found out the telephone call had been made. Sweetser said she could not condone such a call. But by then, Deborah Messing had been dragged into the spotlight.

My campaign always does research on our opponent's public record. Needless to say, however, we have never hired a private detective to dig up dirt. It is a sad comment on the tenor of national politics that Cathy Riggs, responding to a piece about our refusal to probe my opponent's private life, "scoffed at Sanders' claim. 'Everyone does research,' she said. 'He's full of it.'"

The second Tuesday in September is primary day in Vermont. Voters select the Democratic and Republican representatives they want to represent their parties. This year, except for the Republican nomination for lieutenant governor, there's not a whole lot of excitement. Sweetser is unopposed for the Republican nomination. Long is unopposed for the Democrats.

Some Democrats are urging a write-in vote for me. They are strongly anti-Gingrich and are afraid that Long's presence on the ballot could take away enough votes from me to elect Sweetser. As in the past when this same situation arose, I announce that if, by chance, I win the Democratic nomination I will respectfully decline. I am an Independent, and proud of it. On September 10, Long wins the Democratic nomination. With his name on the ballot he receives 9,291 votes. I receive 4,037 write-ins.

Two years before, when the Democrats had no name on their primary ballot for U.S. Congress, the primary turned out to be very serious business. I announced that I would not accept the Democratic nomination and would certainly not campaign for it. John Carroll, the Republican candidate, waged a last-minute stealth write-in campaign to become the Democratic candidate. Fortunately, with no activity on our part, we managed to get a few more votes than he received. If we hadn't, he would have been on the ballot as both the Republican and Democratic candidate. As a result of my victory, there was no Democratic name on the ballot in 1994. That was just as well—in an election which I won by three points, a bipartisan designation could have resulted in a Carroll victory.

In letters to Vermont newspapers, and even in the left-wing national press, I am sometimes criticized as not being a true Independent because I almost always vote with the Democrats. Some reporters view me as a "quasi-Democrat." People who believe this miss the point. I am not an Independent because my views fall somewhere between the Democrats and Republicans. It's not my goal to vote with the Democrats half the time, and the Republicans half the time. I am an Independent because neither of the two major parties represents the interests of the middle class and working people of this country.

In Congress, you're given three choices on a vote—yes, no, present. I almost always vote with the Democrats because, of the choices available to me, their position is usually better than the Republican's. That's the reality I live with in Congress.

I read with amusement how some of my congressional colleagues engage in two or three debates during a campaign—sometimes even fewer. That Rose Garden strategy wouldn't work in Vermont and it shouldn't work anywhere else. If you want people to reelect you, you should be prepared to debate your opponents. In a typical campaign, I participate in between ten and fifteen debates all over the state.

Obviously, the most important debates are those that are televised and are broadcast on statewide radio. In the past, all five of the state's major television stations, WCAX, WPTZ, WVNY, WNNE, and VT.ETV have held debates. Surprisingly, this time around, Vermont Public Television (VT.ETV) is the only major station sponsoring debates—two of them (although Vermont public access TV stations are also holding one). The first is on September 29, at the Statehouse in Montpelier. The second will be held at the very end of the campaign.

The debate at the Statehouse turned out to be controversial—but not because of anything the candidates said. VT.ETV decided to invite only three candidates—the Republican, the Democrat, and myself. They did not invite those running for the Libertarian, Grass Roots, Liberty Union, or Natural Law parties. When the format of the debate was explained to me, I urged VT.ETV to invite everyone who was running. As someone who ran on four occasions on the Liberty Union slate, I knew what it was like to be left out—and I didn't like it. VT.ETV's response was that everybody would be invited to the second debate but, because this event was part of a national public television event, it could only feature the "major" candidates.

I was in a no-win position. If I refused to attend the event on the grounds that all candidates should have been invited, I would have been criticized for running away from the most watched debate of the campaign. If I attended, I would be criticized for participating in an unfair, undemocratic event. In the end I chose to participate. Mr. Diamondstone of the Liberty Union Party staged a nonviolent attempt to enter the hall, and was arrested. His arrest generated more media coverage than the debate.

I was not overly impressed with my performance that night, in any case. I did alright, but was not in top form. Sweetser, I thought, gave an articulate presentation of her views. She is bright—and got her positions across. Perhaps the big surprise of the night was Jack Long, who demonstrated a keen sense of humor and effectively played the role of the moderate against the "extremists" of the right and left.

One of the key components of Sweetser's campaign is to show that she is a serious candidate who has the full support of the national Republican Party. The clear implication is that, if elected, she will have clout with the powers that be, especially if the Republicans continue to control Congress. On the other hand, Bernie Sanders, as an Independent, will always be out of the loop and unable to deliver anything for the state.

To prove how well connected she is, Sweetser brings a long and impressive list of Republican heavyweights to campaign for her in Vermont: Representative Dick Armey, majority leader of the House; Representative Bill Paxon, chairman of the Republican National Congressional Campaign Committee; Steve Forbes, former Republican presidential candidate; Haley Barbour, national chairman of the Republican Party; Representative John Kasich, chairman of the House Budget Committee; Representative Susan Molinari, keynote speaker at the Republican convention; and Representative Deborah Pryce. There is a Republican invasion of the state.

The goal of these visits is not only to show Sweetser's clout within the party, but to raise money at big-dollar fundraising events and to generate news coverage. Armey raises $30,000, Paxon $40,000, and Kasich $25,000. The others raise lesser amounts. Representative Bill Paxon, on his visit, tells the party faithful that the national GOP will kick in the maximum amount allowed by law—$123,600. He expresses the sentiments of his national party when he states, "We're going to pull out all the stops" to defeat "that god-awful Bernie Sanders."

Will all of these endorsements by big-name Republicans have an impact on the campaign? I have my doubts. While they generate a great deal of publicity for Sweetser, I don't think endorsements mean a whole lot in Vermont, where people know more about the candidates than in most other states.

(I speak here from experience. In the past I've endorsed candidates who've ended up doing terribly.) Also, I think Vermonters may resent all of this heavy hitting coming from Washington. I note with interest that when John Kasich endorses Sweetser he doesn't criticize me. John and I have worked together on some issues regarding corporate welfare.

One Republican endorsement does bother me, however. I'm not surprised that Jim Jeffords, Vermont's Republican junior senator, came out in support of Sweetser. He had signed a fundraising letter for her early in the campaign and, as the leading Republican in the state, it would have been odd if he had not endorsed her. What disturbs me, however, is the tone of some of his comments. Frankly, I had knocked my brains out to see that the Northeast Dairy Compact, legislation vital for Vermont farmers, was passed. And Jeffords knew that. Our staffs frequently communicated on the issue. While almost all of the action took place in the Senate, and Leahy and Jeffords did an excellent job there, I did all that I could in the House to see the Compact pass, and helped lead the effort there. I really do not appreciate Jeffords's assertion that I am claiming credit for something I didn't do. It is a cheap shot.

The Final Push

One month remains before the election. According to various statewide polls and our own polling, we are now ahead by fifteen to twenty points. Further, Sweetser's negative ratings are quite high. As they say in the trade, this is our election to lose.

At this point in the campaign, the most important thing we can do is go back to the basics—and try to avoid any stupid mistakes. We have our game plan and must play it out effectively: focus on our issues, respond strongly to inaccurate statements about my positions in either the free or paid media, get around the state as much as we can, motivate our volunteers, be well prepared for the debates, keep raising money, and make certain that our advertising campaign—TV, radio, newspaper, and tabloid—is effective. All this is a lot easier said than done.

We are operating now with a major gap in our campaign staff. In August, my wife Jane left the campaign to become provost of Goddard College in Plainfield, Vermont. The president of the college had resigned amid a great deal of on-campus controversy. Jane, who had been chair of the Goddard board of trustees for the past five years, had been asked to replace him.

Before making a decision about this, Jane and I talked at great length. She had been the nonpaid chief of staff at the congressional office, and had then moved over to a key position in the campaign. She has a very good sense of practical politics, is excellent with details, and does a much better job than me in communicating with the media. But it was clear that this was an opportunity of a lifetime for her. In 1980, she had graduated from Goddard as a single mother with three kids and no money, and the college had always remained an important part of her life. She is great with young people, enthusiastic about education. It is an offer we cannot refuse but the job will be more than full-time. While Jane can still play some role in the campaign, Phil Fiermonte and Tom Smith will have to pick up a lot of the responsibilities she is leaving. I will have to spend more time on the administrative end of things.

I have no intention of trying to compete with Sweetser in bringing "big names" to Vermont for the campaign. But we do bring some people up. In August, Representative Barney Frank of Massachusetts joins me in Burlington and Brattleboro. In Washington, Barney serves with me on the Banking Committee. While we have some political differences, he is a good friend and one of the smartest members of Congress. He is also very funny—his acid wit has sent many a Republican running for cover during debates on the House floor.

Barney is here not only to campaign for me but also for Ed Flanagan, Vermont's auditor of accounts. Ed has recently announced that he is gay, and he is now the only openly gay statewide-elected official in the country. Barney, who is also gay, is one of the leading gay rights advocates in Congress and has acted very courageously in forcing some of our colleagues to act with a modicum of decency in this area. The turnout for the Frank event was terrific in Burlington, but not good in Brattleboro. The media coverage in both areas was excellent. I am also talking to Representative Pete DeFazio about coming up. If his schedule allows he will make the visit, but it's a long way from Oregon to Vermont.

Bad news. What we had feared and anticipated has now begun.

Sweetser is running negative TV commercials—big time. In politics, media consultants have a tried-and-true formula. It's ugly, but sometimes it works. When your candidate is behind with high negative ratings and is going nowhere in a hurry, your best chance of success is to try to destroy the credibility of your opponent. That way, you leave voters with what is perceived as two bad choices, and you have a shot at winning in a lesser-of-two-evils contest. That's what they're trying to do now.

The ad that they're running is a blatant lie. In the past, I would probably have shrugged my shoulders, assumed nobody would believe it, and left it at that. Not now. Early in this campaign I decided that I would respond vigorously when people distorted my record. Sweetser and I have strong philosophical differences. There is more than enough room for her to distinguish her views from mine without distorting my record.

The ad states: "After raising our taxes ... on gasoline ... small businesses ... and on farm families ... In 1993 Sanders cast the deciding vote for the largest tax increase in history." An accompanying chart suggests that every Vermonter now pays $5,178 in federal taxes, compared to $4,209 in 1993. The ad continues: "The result: a higher per capita tax burden of almost $1,000 for every Vermonter. Thanks a lot, Bernie."

Well, if I had raised taxes for "every Vermonter" by almost $1,000, as the ad implies, I wouldn't vote for me either. But what are they talking about?

Obviously, they are referring to the Clinton budget of 1993, which passed the House by a vote of 218 to 216. Of course, they don't mention Clinton's name in the ad because he is now twenty-five points ahead of Dole in the last Vermont poll.

The big lie that the Republicans are peddling here, and all over the country, is that Clinton's 1993 budget resulted in a large tax increase for all Americans. What they have done is simply added up the total increase in taxes in the 1993 budget, and divided it by the population. Mr. Jones pays $1 million in taxes. Ms. Smith pays zero in taxes. On average, per capita, they are paying a half million

in taxes, say the Republicans. But, clearly, the *impact* of the tax burden is a little bit different.

The truth is that Clinton's 1993 budget included a largely *progressive* tax proposal which fell disproportionately on the wealthiest people in the country. Ninety percent of the total tax increase
fell on the *upper* 4 percent, those people then earning $100,000 a
year or more. Only the top 1.2 percent saw an increase in income
taxes. In fact, as a result of a substantial increase in the earned
income tax credit included in that budget, 20 million low-income
families, including 26,000 families in Vermont, saw a *decrease* in
their federal income taxes. For the middle class, and the vast
majority of Vermonters, there was almost no tax increase at all,
certainly not $1,000 a head as the ad implies.

Unfortunately, there *were* elements of regressive taxation in
that proposal, including a 4.3 cent increase in the gas tax. That's
about $30 a year for the average Vermonter, not much but still
regressive in that it hits the average working stiff who travels a
hundred miles a day to and from work. Clinton also increased the
amount of taxable Social Security income. That hike affected the
upper 13 percent of Social Security recipients, many of whom live
on only $44,000 a year. I opposed these aspects of the legislation
when it was debated because I have always been a strong proponent of fair taxation. I also knew that the opponents of that budget would sooner or later exploit the issue, which is precisely what
they are doing now.

There is a lesson here: if you raise taxes on the rich, raise taxes
on the rich. Keep it simple. And if your opponents want to oppose
taxes on the rich, let them do it. But don't include *any* taxes on
working people, even if it's only a tiny amount, because your
opponents will distort the reality of the situation.

When I met with Clinton in the Oval Office in the summer of
1993, I told him about an experience I had the day before at the
Washington County Fair in central Vermont. The media in
Vermont and nationally was then playing right into the
Republican Party's hands. They were talking over and over again

about the aggregate sum of the tax increase that Clinton was proposing, the so-called "largest tax increase in history," but no one was talking about *who* would be paying the increase in taxes. I asked person after person at that fair if they understood what was in the tax proposal, and only one out of twenty people did.

Clinton acknowledged to me that he was having a very difficult time getting the information out. Shortly afterwards, he organized what I thought was a successful press conference with low-income workers who would be getting a *reduction* in their taxes. Meanwhile, I had to actually raise my voice to a reporter in Vermont just to get him to identify in his story who would actually foot the bill for the tax increase.

This is an issue of enormous consequence, well beyond the ad that is currently being thrown at me. If the media refuses to differentiate between a progressive tax proposal which hits the wealthy and a regressive tax increase which hits working people, and simply defines the proposal as a "tax increase," no president is ever going to raise taxes—no matter how appropriate that may be. No member of Congress is ever going to support a tax increase. In order to balance a budget it will always be easier for elected officials to cut back on Medicare, Medicaid, education, the environment, and other important social programs.

But the truth of the matter is that the vast majority of the people do not stay up nights worrying about tax increases on the rich. By and large, given the unfair distribution of income and wealth in this country, and the fact that tax rates for the wealthy have declined dramatically over the last twenty years, most people think it's quite reasonable to ask upper-income people to pay their fair share of taxes. Several years ago, my campaign did a poll and we asked Vermonters if they would prefer Congress to increase taxes on the rich or cut Medicare. Eighty percent replied, TAX THE RICH.

In any case, one day after Sweetser's negative ad was aired, I hold a press conference refuting its bogus allegations and demanding that she take it off. "Susan Sweetser is a tax lawyer," I say, "and she knows full well that 90 percent of the tax increase fell on the upper 4 percent of income recipients, those people in 1993 who were earning $100,000 or more." Sweetser responds, "I'm not going to take off ads that I believe are truthful, that I believe are comparative, that I believe are depictions of his record. The fact is, Bernie raised taxes on Vermonters." She then issues a long press release attacking the TV ad that *I* had just put on the air as "misleading and unsubstantiated," containing a "disingenuous" statement that is "not accurate."

Now, for all of you readers who are interested in seeking political office and don't want to pay media consultants huge sums of money for advice on how to do it, let me explain how you proceed. The first thing is that before you go negative, attack your opponent for running a negative campaign—then, after your ads are on the air, and your opponent responds in righteous indignation, you can expect that much of the media will describe how both sides are attacking each other for negative campaigning. That's sleazy politics 101. And it works quite often because the media wants to be "evenhanded." For example, after my press conference, the large headline in the *Burlington Free Press* reads, "Sanders, Sweetser attack TV ads." Needless to say, the issue is far too involved and complicated for the thirty-second TV coverage it receives.

Fortunately, however, this approach isn't working for Sweetser because reporters at the Vermont Press Bureau (who write for the second and third largest papers in the state, the *Rutland Herald* and the *Montpelier Times-Argus*) actually checked the facts, concluded that Sweetser's ads were dishonest and misleading, and wrote intelligent articles on the subject. Diane Derby of the Press Bureau wrote, "Smulson [Sweetser's press secretary] conceded that Sanders' vote on the deficit reduction bill did not result in a $1,000 tax increase for every Vermonter, as the ad's chart says. But he said the ad's narrative use of the words 'per capita' was intended to *clarify* for viewers that the figure represented only an average." Clarify? Right!

Jack Hoffman, wrote a long Sunday column for the *Herald* entitled, "Sweetser's New Ad Doesn't Let Facts Get in the Way," dissecting the ads contents: "The $1,000 figure is absurd on its face, and the ad is another example of how far political candidates are willing to distort the truth to try to make an opponent look bad." The *Rutland Herald* also ran a front-page story titled "GOP's Figures On Tax Off Base," which noted, "The Vermont Republican Party and congressional candidate Susan Sweetser are using incorrect figures to describe the effects of 1993 tax law changes on Vermonters, according to a spokesman for the organization that prepared the information being used by the Republicans."

I won't let up either. In virtually every public appearance I hammer away at the dishonest ads saturating the airwaves. Even at a speech before 500 people at a conference on mental health, I talk about the ads. This is something I never would have done in the past. Obviously, there is self-interest in my actions, but I honestly believe that if candidates can get away with blatant lies in TV ads, then the political process in America is in very deep trouble.

In January 1994, the Republican Party took control of the House of Representatives for the first time in forty years. Newt Gingrich, a brilliant, articulate political strategist and right-wing ideologue, was elected Speaker of the House and, in a very bitter moment for the Democrats, Dick Gephardt handed the Speaker's gavel over to him. I disagree with everything that Gingrich stands for, but I was impressed by the scope of his vision. He thinks big.

The Democratic loss in 1994 was devastating. In an election in which 38 percent of the people voted, thirty-five incumbent Democrats lost their seats in the House. Not one Republican incumbent was defeated. The Republicans went from a minority of 176 members in 1992 to a majority of 230 members in 1994. Seventy-four new Republicans were sworn in, a huge freshman class. Gingrich became the darling of the media, on the front pages every day. As the leader of the new American revolution, he proclaimed, as had Franklin Delano Roosevelt sixty-two years before, a period of "one hundred days" in which Congress would enact landmark legislation on its way toward fulfilling his "Contract with America."

The Democrats were in a tailspin. Early in the session they held their first caucus. Although I am welcome to attend these meetings, I usually go only when the president is speaking. But I went to this meeting and the shock and confusion were palpable. There did not appear to be a clear analysis of why the Democrats were beaten so badly, nor agreement as to how they should go forward. They were angry and demoralized by their new status as the minor party, symbolically represented by their "banishment" to the House Ways and Means Committee room. From now on, Republicans would meet on the House floor.

Veteran Democrats who had chaired powerful committees, sometimes for years, were now consigned to the position of ranking members, that is, leaders of the opposition. Many of them had to lay off large numbers of loyal staff who had worked for them for years. It was not a happy time for Democrats.

While most Democrats responded with confusion and paralysis to the Republican victory, the members of the Progressive Caucus immediately mobilized to fight back—both in Congress and back home at the grassroots level. We were not confused or hesitant. We knew exactly what we had to do. Intellectually, we had to expose the Contract with America for exactly what it was: a vicious assault on working people and the poor, orchestrated at the behest of the most affluent and powerful people in America. Politically, we had to rally public opinion in opposition to the Gingrich agenda, and bring our constituent groups together into an effective counterforce.

Moreover, if the stated purpose of the Contract was balancing the budget in six years, we decided we would accept that challenge. While there was some disagreement among us as to how much emphasis we should give to the importance of a balanced budget in a specified time frame, most of us agreed that we could expose the bankrupt vision behind the Contract by demonstrating that the budget could be balanced in a way that was fair and did not wreak havoc on the lives of millions of low- and moderate-income Americans.

There was an enormous amount of work to be done and Bill Goold, Elizabeth Mundinger, and Eric Olson in my office, along with the staff in other progressive offices, undertook the responsibility of providing the members with the information they needed. It was an example of the vital role that staff play in the United States Congress, where there are so many issues and so many functions that no congressperson can get a handle on them without back-up.

We launched our anti-Contract campaign with a press conference in the House Radio-Television Gallery. We notified the media and waited. That day, the room was so mobbed with reporters and TV cameras, we had to fight our way in. They had come to hear some of the first voices of opposition against the Republican agenda in the Capitol.

Yes. We had all heard that the Gingrich vision was supposed to be sweeping America, and that Americans were no longer concerned about the needs of the elderly, children, and the poor. Yes. We had been told for months that what we believed in was "old-fashioned," "outdated," "1930s-style" government, and that social justice and human dignity should no longer be issues of concern for Congress.

But we disagreed—strongly, and began the long hard fight against the legislation that Gingrich and his corporate sponsors were beginning to introduce. We used every tool at our disposal to educate Americans on the content of the Contract, from press conferences to "special orders" at the end of each legislative day that enabled us to communicate with C-Span's growing audience. We introduced "one-minutes" before legislative business began in the morning and we vigorously debated the specific pieces of legislation as they came to the floor. Clearly, we didn't have the votes to defeat the Republicans, but we fought them tooth and nail and in the process helped to illuminate the dirty business behind the high-flying rhetoric.

What we soon realized was that most Americans didn't have a clue as to what was in the Contract. It *sounded* good, but the more they learned about it, the less they liked it.

Do you want to see Congress move the country toward a balanced budget? "Yes," the American people responded overwhelmingly. Do you want to cut Medicare by $270 billion and increase Medicare premiums by $500 a year while providing lower quality service to senior citizens? "Hell, no," the American people shouted back. And it turned out that the American people really did not want to cut health insurance for millions of low-income children or eliminate the guarantee that low-income senior citizens would have access to nursing homes. They didn't want to cut loans and grants for college students. They didn't want to eviscerate environmental legislation. They didn't want a constitutional amendment to ban abortions. They didn't want to cut back on school lunch programs and increase funding for B-2 bombers.

In the midst of all of this, the American people surely didn't want to give huge tax breaks to the rich and the largest corporations in America, while cutting back on the earned income tax credit—which would have resulted in higher taxes for the working poor. The more that people learned about the Contract with America, the stronger the opposition became.

Members of the Progressive Caucus were not the only people in Congress in opposition to the Contract. As the new session progressed, Dick Gephardt, Dave Bonior, John Lewis, and the other Democratic leaders became stronger, more focused, and more confident. After forty years in the majority, they were beginning to learn how to function effectively as the minority opposition. Gephardt's office did an excellent job in sending out clearly written, digestible information about various aspects of the Contract.

I was especially impressed by my friend Rosa DeLauro of Connecticut, who is not a member of the Progressive Caucus. Rosa never stopped. It seemed that every day, morning, noon, or late at night, she was on the floor talking about the devastating impact that the Republican cuts in Medicare would have on senior citizens. She was relentless.

Gradually, as people learned more about the Gingrich agenda, the fight against it spread all across America. Trade unionists began to respond as they learned about the impact of pending legislation on workers' rights; senior citizens were getting organized as they began to realize how devastating the cuts in Medicare, Medicaid, and other senior programs would be; women were fighting back against the horrendous attacks on abortion rights; and students began organizing on college campuses against the cuts in student loans and grants.

And then Gingrich and the Republicans shut down the government in the winter of 1995. They showed the American people that not only were they prepared to make savage cuts in desperately needed programs, but they were unwilling to respect basic constitutional divisions of power. These right-wing extremists lacked the votes to override President Clinton's vetoes, so they just stopped appropriating money and brought government to a halt.

And support for Gingrich and the Contract with America eroded even further.

In early 1995, I decided that the major effort my office would make in Vermont over the next two years was to help lead the opposition to the Gingrich agenda. In that regard we held twenty-five town meetings throughout the state—in our larger cities and our smallest towns. Sometimes hundreds of people showed up and sometimes a few dozen. In general, the turnouts were excellent.

Meanwhile, grassroots organizations throughout the state organized a demonstration against the Contract, timed to coincide with the National Governor's Conference in July 1995 in Burlington. The turnout for the demonstration was huge. Progressives also distributed 50,000 copies of a well-produced newspaper which showed the Contract's impact on Vermonters.

During the 1995–96 session we held six major conferences in Vermont, involving thousands of people. Some of them dealt specifically with aspects of the Contract with America, and some did not. All of them were based, however, on the belief that in a democratic society the government has a major role to play in protecting the rights and economic well being of ordinary people. It has long been my view that one of the important roles of a congressional office is citizen education—bringing in some of the most knowledgeable people in the country to discuss issues that they are concerned with. All of these conferences were free and open to the public, and almost all were held on Saturdays—when working people could attend. They were also videotaped and broadcast on public access television throughout the state.

In March 1995 we held a conference for senior citizens, and 400 seniors from all over the state turned out. Our keynote speakers were Eugene Lehrmann, national president of the American Association of Retired Persons, and Max Richtman, vice president of the National Committee to Preserve Social Security and Medicare. In my helter-skelter life as a congressman, I sometimes forget how important education is as part of human life. At the senior citizen conference, which was held at Montpelier High School, I was very moved to see seniors, in workshop after workshop, taking careful notes and intelligently discussing issues of concern to them. They wanted to know not only about what was going on in Washington but also about health and nutrition and how they could play a more active role in their communities.

We held an excellent conference on economic and social justice in conjunction with many of the antipoverty groups in the state. Frances Fox Piven, one of the outstanding experts in the country on social welfare policy, explained the implications of right-wing "welfare reform" to a large audience.

Then there was the conference we held on veterans' affairs— an area of growing importance to my office. This event was organized with the help of the Veterans' Council, which advises my office on veterans' matters. I am an antiwar congressman, but I am strongly pro-veteran, as all antiwar activists should be.

The young working-class men and women who fight our

wars, who lose their limbs in our wars, who come home sick or traumatized by our wars—*do not make the wars they fight in.* Wars are made by politicians. It is an outrage that these men and women, who put their lives on the line for their government, often find that this same government turns its back on them in their times of need. This conference brought to Vermont Jesse Brown, the former head of Disabled American Veterans (DAV) and Clinton's secretary of veterans' affairs. The many veterans who attended the conference were especially pleased to see Brown's staff sympathetically and immediately responding to their personal concerns.

Another conference that brought out a surprisingly large crowd, despite a snowy January day, was an all-day event on alternative health. Wow! Is there interest in that issue.

I am a fierce proponent of a national health care system which guarantees health care for all people. I am also a firm proponent of a much stronger approach toward disease prevention. We spend huge sums of money treating disease, and relatively little trying to prevent it. Further, in the midst of the explosion of modern medical technology, we too often ignore traditional, low-tech medical treatments which have cured diseases for thousands of years in different cultures throughout the world.

The conference, held in conjunction with alternative health care providers throughout the state, included fifteen workshops dealing with topics ranging from diet to acupuncture to massage. Dr. Wayne Jonas, director of the National Institute of Health's Office of Alternative Medicine, and Dr. Herbert Benson, of Harvard University's Mind/Body Medical Institute, contributed their expertise.

The last major conference was a labor conference, which featured Richard Trumka, the secretary-treasurer of the AFL-CIO. It was organized by the Vermont AFL-CIO, the Vermont National Education Association, the Vermont State Employees Association, the United Electrical Workers, and other unions, and was the most successful labor meeting in the state in many years. Trumka, the former president of the United Mine Workers and now part of the AFL-CIO's progressive new leadership, is a very forceful speaker. When working people come together and stand up for their rights, it is amazing how politicians suddenly become interested in labor issues. The governor of Vermont, Howard Dean, and the junior senator from Vermont, Jim Jeffords, both asked for time to address the conference.

In late spring of 1996 we held our last conference, on women's health. Dr. Susan J. Blumenthal, the deputy assistant secretary for women's health, outlined women's health care needs and her department's efforts to address this long-neglected area in a very effective speech. That conference was held in conjunction with many of the women's health organizations in the state, who provided a number of workshops.

Meanwhile, back in Washington, members of the Progressive Caucus were expending a great deal of energy focusing on corporate welfare—the massive government tax breaks and subsidies which are given to some of the largest corporations in the country. We focused on this issue for two reasons. First, it is absurd that working people should provide handouts to multinational corporations that are earning billions in profits and paying their CEOs astronomical salaries. Second, we were able to use the corporate welfare issue to contrast our priorities with those of the Gingrich agenda. Newt and his friends proposed to balance the budget on the backs of the poor and working class, slashing Medicare, Medicaid, education, environmental protection, veterans' benefits, school lunches, and other programs. Meanwhile, they were leaving untouched approximately $125 billion a year in corporate welfare. This exposed not only the vulgarity of the Gingrich agenda, but also its hypocrisy. If Gingrich's supporters were serious about balancing the budget, they could do it without savaging programs essential to the most vulnerable members of our society. Of course, this would require them to stand up to their corporate sponsors—something they were not likely to do.

But could *we*, the progressives in Congress, balance the budget in seven years in a way that was fair and would not hurt the kids, the elderly, the sick, or the poor? Damn right we could! In an article I wrote for the *Burlington Free Press*, I showed how we could save more than $800 billion over seven years by dealing with *some* of the giveaways in corporate welfare and tax breaks for the rich. This illustrative list gives some details:

LOOPHOLES

- Change how income of multinational corporations is allocated between nations: increased income—$143.5 billion.
- Eliminate foreign tax credit for multinational corporations and subsidiary income exemption: increased income—$82.5 billion.
- End U.S. firms' delay of tax on income of foreign subsidiaries: increased income—$5.7 billion.
- Close loopholes for foreign-owned firms in the United States, including bond-interest exemptions: increased income—$1.9 billion.
- Repeal housing and wage exemptions for U.S. citizens working abroad: increased income—$7.2 billion.
- Eliminate the Overseas Private Investment Corporation (OPIC): increased income—$.560 billion.
- Subject major foreign stockholders in U.S. companies to capital gains tax: increased income—$7 billion.
- Reduce Export-Import Bank subsidies to foreign purchases of U.S. products, increase fees based on credit risk and direct loans to worthy firms in growing countries: increased income—$1.4 billion.
- Tax capital gains at regular rate: increased income—$49 billion.
- Repeal exemption on income earned by U.S. firms in Puerto Rico and other U.S. possessions: increased income—$19.7 billion.

SUBSIDIES

- Cap the home mortgage interest deduction at $300,000: increased income—$34.8 billion.
- Reform standards allowing corporations to deduct equipment faster than it wears out: increased income—$160 billion.
- Cap deductions for CEO pay, counting excess salary/stock options/perks as taxable profit: increased income—$50 billion.
- End deduction of advertising costs, instead depreciating 20 percent as a capital cost to build recognition: increased income—$18.3 billion.
- End nuclear weapons production and test site costs: increased income—$3.06 billion.
- Terminate the Advanced Neutron Source Project, Tokomak experiment and Gas Cooled Reactor: increased income—$9.1 billion.
- Phase out grants for fossil and nuclear energy development: increased income—$2.3 billion.
- Suspend purchases for Naval Petroleum, Oil Shale Reserve, Strategic Petroleum Reserve: increased income—$1.4 billion.
- End funding for Clean Coal Technology research: increased income—$.330 billion.
- End 1872 Mining Act's patent provision and set an 8 percent royalty on minerals recovered from public lands:

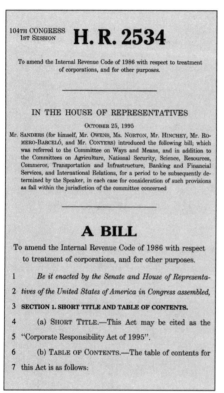

104TH CONGRESS
1ST SESSION

H. R. 2534

To amend the Internal Revenue Code of 1986 with respect to treatment of corporations, and for other purposes.

IN THE HOUSE OF REPRESENTATIVES

OCTOBER 25, 1995

Mr. SANDERS (for himself, Mr. OWENS, Ms. NORTON, Mr. HINCHEY, Mr. ROMERO-BARCELÓ, and Mr. CONYERS) introduced the following bill; which was referred to the Committee on Ways and Means, and in addition to the Committees on Agriculture, National Security, Science, Resources, Commerce, Transportation and Infrastructure, Banking and Financial Services, and International Relations, for a period to be subsequently determined by the Speaker, in each case for consideration of such provisions as fall within the jurisdiction of the committee concerned

---

A BILL

To amend the Internal Revenue Code of 1986 with respect to treatment of corporations, and for other purposes.

1   *Be it enacted by the Senate and House of Representa-*
2 *tives of the United States of America in Congress assembled,*
3   SECTION 1. SHORT TITLE AND TABLE OF CONTENTS.
4   (a) SHORT TITLE.—This Act may be cited as the
5 "Corporate Responsibility Act of 1995".
6   (b) TABLE OF CONTENTS.—The table of contents for
7 this Act is as follows:

increased income—$.300 billion.
- Phase out Senatech and Technology Reinvestment Project subsidies: increased income—$1.5 billion.
- End NASA's subsidy of U.S. aerospace firms: increased income—$1.8 billion.
- Discontinue subsidies to foreign purchasers of U.S. defense products: increased income—$2.5 billion.
- Raise fees to cover Securities and Exchange Commission and commodity market operation costs: increased income— $.4 billion.
- Reduce subsidy of wealthy farmers by limiting payments to $50,000 per person: increased income—$.76 billion.
- End subsidy of produce purchased by foreign consumers: increased income—$4.2 billion.
- End subsidy of overseas advertising campaigns and trade shows for U.S. firms: increased income—$.5 billion.
- End tobacco subsidies: increased income—$287 million.
- Raise fees for grazing on public lands: increased income— $.28 billion.
- Rescind new funding for highway projects that do not qualify under state transportation plans or highway grant programs: increased income—$2.6 billion.
- Conduct competitive bidding for operating concessions at National Parks: increased income—$.280 billion.

DEFENSE
- Stop funding for 20 additional B-2 bombers: increased income—$30 billion.
- Stop funding for Star Wars and space stations: increased income—$35 billion.

The total seven-year savings for such a budget deficit program is over $800 billion—enough to balance the budget in the year 2002. And these are only *some* of the savings that I, and other members of the Progressive Caucus, came up with. There was no question that we could move this country forward to a balanced budget without decimating the safety net on which tens of millions of Americans depend.

In October 1995, I introduced HR 2534, the Corporate Responsibility Act, which contained many of these provisions. While the fight against corporate welfare has been led by progressives in Congress, we've also had support from honest conservatives who are rightfully appalled at this waste of taxpayer dollars. As a result, the concept of corporate welfare is now filtering into the mainstream, and some legislation has been passed which is beginning to chip away at this outrageous waste of money.

I may not have the majority leader of the U.S. House campaigning for me, but I do have some of the funniest people in America lending a hand. In Washington, Al Franken, a star of "Saturday Night Live," and author of *Rush Limbaugh Is a Big Fat Idiot and Other Observations*, does a fundraiser for us at the Eastern Marketplace and about 100 people show up, including a number of long-lost Vermonters. I had met Al during our joint appearance on the show "Politically Incorrect" with Bill Maher. (Although why I went on that show I will never know.) Al Franken is one of the funniest people in America, and he does not like Newt Gingrich and right-wing Republicans. He gives a hilarious performance.

Back in Burlington, Michael Moore, the filmmaker, television producer, and writer, is here to help the campaign, and I'm proud to have his support. His film *Roger and Me* is one of my favorites, and the most successful documentaries in American history. Moore is one of the very few media people in America with serious politics, a great sense of humor, and an ability to utilize the media effectively.

We only charge seven dollars for admission, so this is not going to raise a lot of money, but that's not the purpose. We want to bring out and politically energize a lot of young people who might have been familiar with Moore through his program "TV Nation." Three hundred people turn out to see Moore in his now legendary baseball cap. There is no front to this man—he is exactly what he appears to be. Whether he's up on the stage, writing inscriptions in his bestselling book, *Downsize This! Random Threats of an Unarmed American*, or having dinner with Jane and me, he *is* unassuming, down to earth, and very funny. Moore is a big hit in Burlington. Unfortunately, there is almost no interest in his presence on the part of the local media.

But despite all of the lively fundraisers that we're having, I'm getting nervous. Sweetser now has not one but two negative ads on the air attacking me. How should we respond? (On a personal level, it is the damnedest thing to be lying in bed, watching TV, and out of nowhere comes an ad attacking you. If I live to be 500, I will never get used to that.)

In my view, and in the view of people who talked to me, the ads we're running are very good. Produced by Shrum, Devine and Donilon, they are straightforward and positive—addressing themes that I have long been associated with. I'm not sure how they did it, but they've even managed to make me look cheerful, optimistic, and friendly.

They show me with Vermont workers, senior citizens, and young people. They talk of my opposition to the Gingrich agenda. The ads speak to my concerns and effectiveness. One of them is sixty seconds, the rest thirty seconds. The *Burlington Free Press* conducted a focus group comparing Sweetser's ads to mine. The almost unanimous opinion of the group was that our ads were much better. But that was before the recent bombardment of Sweetser's negative spots. What impact are they having?

I have never run a negative TV ad in my life. I have never run a TV ad for the express purpose of attacking an opponent. I don't believe that Vermonters want to be subjected to a mudslinging campaign nor do I want to participate in one. But how do we respond to all of the dishonest ads that are now flooding the airwaves. Can we afford to ignore them? Should we respond? If so, how?

Our consultants tell us that their general rule is that you don't allow a deceptive ad to go unanswered, in one way or another you must respond. I discuss the options with my campaign advisers. Should we go negative on Sweetser? Nobody thinks we should. We decide to respond by exposing her inaccurate premises, and we ask our media people to produce an ad that corrects the record but does not attack Sweetser personally.

On October 22, we have a great event at the University of Vermont. Gloria Steinem is here to campaign for me, and over 500 students and community people overflow a large auditorium to hear her. I'm stunned and delighted by the size of the crowd, which is our largest of the campaign. Over and over we are being told that college students and Generation X are politically apathetic and concerned only about themselves. Well, not today. It's a beautiful sight.

Gloria is introduced by some of the most active people in the Vermont women's movement, Sally Conrad, Martha Abbott, and Judy Murphy. Her message is both analytic and deeply radical. She tells the students that it is no accident that there is a feeling of discouragement and disillusionment in America today. The Republicans, the right wing, the press with its insistence on sensationalism are all powerful forces that are changing the nature of politics.

The strategy of corporate America, Steinem tells the young people, is no longer to convince people to vote Republican or conservative. The new strategy is to convince them that there is no reason to vote at all, that everyone is crooked, nothing works right, that politics is corrupt and inefficient. But don't get discouraged, she tells them: progressives must fight *for* democracy or democracy will be eroded from under our feet. It is self-destructive for progressives to allow themselves to become disillusioned by the current political process. If the left does not participate, the right wing will only grow stronger.

The young audience listens intently and is very responsive to her message. Gloria makes me an "honorary woman," and congratulates me "for having survived the 104th Congress." It is one of the nicest moments of the campaign.

Sally Conrad, a popular former state senator from Chittenden County, is also very supportive. She says, "As we know, to be a feminist a person does not have to be a woman. A feminist is a person who challenges the power structure of our country. Bernie Sanders is that kind of feminist."

Susan Sweetser, on the other hand, is not quite so kind regarding Steinem's visit: "What is really interesting to me is this is somebody who is supposed to be an outspoken advocate for women, and she comes here to campaign against the only woman who is running for statewide office here in Vermont."

The new thirty-second spot responding to Sweetser's ad has come back from Tad Devine, the very talented media consultant with whom we're working. It's not quite what we had in mind. Jane and I talk to Tad on the phone. While the ad is by no means a "negative" ad, we still think it's too hard, and we ask him to soften it.

Now a group calling itself The Coalition: Americans Working for Real Change has started spending tens of thousands of dollars in "independent expenditures" and is flooding the airwaves with more negative TV ads against me. This group was formed by the U.S. Chamber of Commerce, the National Association of Manufacturers, and the National Federation of Independent Businesses, and is part of a coalition of thirty-three big business organizations. These wonderful folks, representing some of the biggest money interests in the country, have opposed raising the minimum wage and the Family and Medical Leave Act. They are down the line in support of the Gingrich right-wing agenda. And now they're spending a fortune trying to defeat me.

I read in a Washington newspaper that I am one of twelve members of Congress—two senators and ten members of the House—to be targeted by this group. Between their ads and Sweetser's there are now *four* different negative spots attacking me. Sweetser is also running positive ads. It is clear that big money is now rolling into her campaign. Her recent FEC report indicates that she has raised $26,000 in large contributions in the last week. Also, we learn that the NRA is making automated phone calls to their members in Vermont and has called for my defeat in its publication. The National Right to Work Organization, the major anti-union group in America, is sending an ugly letter around the state to the owners of small businesses.

Interestingly, WCAX-TV, the most Republican station, is refusing to accept the ads from "The Coalition." WCAX has a longstanding policy against "independent expenditure" advocacy ads. From a civil liberties point of view, I have mixed feelings about this because groups advocating causes and positions are denied access to the airwaves, even when they are prepared to pay the going ad rates. For the moment, however, I must confess that "intellectual consistency" is taking a back seat to political reality. I'm delighted that corporate America cannot flood the largest station in the state with negative ads against me. I do *not* call up WCAX protesting their policy.

We get another version of the response ad back from Tad, our media consultant. It's more appropriate than their first try, and we discuss among ourselves whether we should air it. It is delivered to all of the TV stations—and is ready to go.

Meanwhile, we have now begun our radio advertising, which, given the dozens of radio stations in the state, takes an enormous amount of time to coordinate. Angela McDonald, Peter Timponey, and other campaign workers help to drive the ads to those stations where we want them to air immediately. We are running five separate radio ads. One is a soundtrack of our TV ad, another is a very funny ad done by my good friend, the great Vermont storyteller Mac Parker, and one is an ad on the environment featuring Robert Redford, which was arranged for me by the League of Conservation Voters. The others are straightforward statements by me of my views on the major issues of the campaign. I write the ads in the morning and record them in the afternoon.

During the last week or two of the campaign, many of the newspapers release their endorsements. Predictably, the two major Republican papers in the state, the *Caledonia Record* in St. Johnsbury and the *St. Albans Messenger*, endorse Sweetser. The big surprise, however, is that the largest paper in the state, the *Burlington Free Press*, endorses Jack Long. I had an unpleasant interview with their editorial board, and am not surprised by their endorsement. For many years, and up until the early 1980s, the paper's editorial page was very right wing. In the mid-eighties it became more balanced and moderate, but is now moving back to a position as defender of the state's monied interests.

The good news is that we received very strong endorsements from the *Bennington Banner* and the *Brattleboro Reformer*, as well as editorial support from some weeklies. For the second campaign in a row the *Rutland Herald* refuses to make an endorsement in the congressional race—despite going through the endorsement interview process.

On October 30, a new poll comes out from the *Rutland Herald*. It has us ahead by only 13 points, which is significantly less than other polls had indicated. The poll's results are Sanders 50, Sweetser 37, and Long 4. Are we losing ground? Does Sweetser have some momentum which could carry her over the top? We think not. For whatever reason, throughout the entire campaign, the *Rutland Herald* poll has Sweetser doing much better than the other polls, including our own polls. In fact, this poll shows exactly the same thirteen-point spread as the last poll they did a month before. The *Herald* itself concludes that there does not appear to be much movement in the race.

We have finally decided *not* to use the new ad that Tad has sent us. It is well crafted and balanced, and given the fact that there are now four negative ads on the air attacking me, it would be a very useful antidote. But we have gone this far in the campaign using our TV ads in a strictly positive way—talking about our ideas and our vision. We think that's what Vermonters want. And that's the way we'll end the campaign.

Finally. It is November 5, Election Day. Thank God. The campaign is over. This has been a very, very long campaign.

On Election Day, I follow a pretty established routine. In the morning Jane and I vote at St. Mark's Church. David votes with us. (Levi votes at another polling station, and Heather and Carina have already sent in their absentee ballots.) The media knows what time I will be voting, and I say a few words to the TV cameras. I am surprised at how nervous I am. My remarks are forced.

I then drive around alone to all of the other six polling stations in Burlington, an old habit from when I was mayor. I say hello to the candidates and campaign workers who are assembled outside the stations, check on the voter turnout, and do a little campaigning for the Progressive candidates—four of whom are running for the legislature from Burlington. I then go to the campaign office, where Phil, Tom, Martha, David, and others are coordinating what seems to be a very smooth get-out-the-vote effort.

In the afternoon, Jane and I drive thirty miles up to St. Albans where John Gallagher, our Franklin County coordinator, tells us that things look good. He feels more optimistic than he did two years ago, when he also coordinated the campaign there. I say hello to some folks, learn about the local races, and shake a few hands.

We return to the house. I rest up, and do some reflecting on the campaign. I think I'm going to win, but I'm not 100 percent sure. I thought I would win the last election easily, and only squeezed home by three points. Could I lose tonight? Absolutely. I don't think I will, but it's certainly possible. Maybe Vermonters will believe that barrage of negative TV advertising and that glossy piece of literature that the corporate interests have sent to what appears to be every household in the state, including a couple to my own home. During the last few days I've told my family and co-workers not to be too disappointed if we lose. We worked hard and ran a damn good campaign. We should win, but we could lose.

I make some phone calls, and then head out again to Burlington's polling stations. I spend some time at the Barnes School, in the heart of Burlington's Old North End. This is a strong working-class area, and has lent more support to me over the years than any other district in Vermont. They gave me over-whelming victories when I was mayor, and have continued to back me strongly in the congressional races. As the campaign comes to an end, win or lose, it's nice to be with friends.

The weather is not good. There's a steady drizzle. And I'm concerned about this. We do best when the voter turnout is high.

I stay out until the polls close at 7 p.m., and then head home. Our election night gathering is at Mona's restaurant, on the waterfront, but I won't be going there until I know for sure if we've won. I'll get the results at home with family and a few friends. Phil and some other people will be calling them in as soon as they hear from our campaign workers around the state. In the house, we have the TV and a few radios on. People are munching on cold cuts.

Where Do We Go From Here?

January 7, 1997. I am sworn in for my fourth term as Vermont's representative. Still the only Independent in Congress. Still an outsider in the House. There is much to do, and for an Independent there is no established trail to follow.

But after three terms in Congress, I know what my job is. Vermont is a small state with only one representative: me. Like every one of my colleagues, I must first represent my state. So I'll be looking out for the particular needs and concerns of Vermont and the Vermonters who elected me. I'm going to fight for everything to which my beautiful state is entitled.

I have a second responsibility. I must continue to defend the rights of all working people when the issues affecting them come before the Congress. I must continue to stand up for the needs of the great majority of Americans: workers, the middle class, the poor, the elderly, the nation's children. All Americans are entitled to live lives of decency and dignity, and I will not abandon that struggle.

The longer I have been in Washington, the more clear a third responsibility has become. As the only Independent, I must do my best to force discussion of matters that the entrenched powers and big money interests do not want discussed. I must insist that we address these issues even though commitment to these concerns is not on the agenda of official Washington. Many of these problems are complicated, and I'm not so smart that I have all the solutions. But I do know this: these difficult questions will not be resolved until millions of Americans, as well as the United States Congress, join in the debate. That's what democracy is supposed to be about.

Honest people have differences of opinion as to what they believe are the most important problems facing this country. Let me tell you straight out the way I see it. Here they are: the unfair distribution of wealth, the decline of decent-paying jobs, the erosion of our democracy, the unchecked power of the corporate media, the insufficiency of our health care system, the inadequacies of American education. Obviously, there are other enormously serious problems facing this nation, but these are the ones at the top of my list. In my view, if we could address these problems forthrightly, our nation would become the great society it has always had the promise of becoming.

Why don't we just roll up our shirtsleeves and start addressing these concerns.

Let me begin by presenting two rather startling facts, and then posing a few questions. Fact 1: in 1993, Michael Eisner, the president of Walt Disney Corporation, earned $200 million. Fact 2: 20 percent of America's children live in poverty. Now, why is neither of these facts—the outrageous vulgarity of Eisner's salary or the unjust condemnation of almost a quarter of our children to a life of poverty—at the forefront of public dialogue? Why do we hear more about O. J. Simpson or the Superbowl or a plane crash than we do about the fact that in a period of declining wages for working people the average CEO of a major American corporation makes more than $3 million a year? Could there be any relation between what we see on the *ABC Evening News* and the fact that Michael Eisner runs Disney and that Disney in turn owns ABC?

I'm not trying to sell you a conspiracy theory. I doubt that Michael Eisner (or Rupert Murdoch or Ted Turner) decides what specific items will be aired on an evening news broadcast. Still, there *is* a convergence. Big money interests own the media. The media plays an enormous role in shaping our view of reality. Our view of reality too often turns out to be that the nation's problems are insoluble. And because these problems are insoluble, democracy is no longer relevant.

Let's take a hard look at some of America's major problems.

WHILE THE RICH GET RICHER, ALMOST EVERYONE ELSE GETS POORER

THE STANDARD OF LIVING OF MOST AMERICANS IS IN DECLINE

DEMOCRACY IS IN CRISIS, AND OLIGARCHY LOOMS

WHAT WE KNOW IS DETERMINED BY THE CORPORATE MEDIA

OUR HEALTH CARE SYSTEM IS IN SHAMBLES

OUR EDUCATIONAL SYSTEM IS FACING A CRISIS

The picture looks grim. In America we have the most inequitable distribution of wealth in the entire industrialized world. The middle class is shrinking, the working class is scraping by, and the poor are ever more deeply mired in poverty. Our democratic institutions are so endangered that a clear-eyed observer might well conclude that we live not in a democracy but an oligarchy. The media, which informs and shapes our perceptions of social problems, is owned by a very small number of powerful corporations with deeply vested special interests. Millions of Americans are uninsured, while the quality of health care delivery has declined dramatically just in the past few years. Our democratic system of education, once the gateway to economic and political equality, often fails to provide children with even the rudimentary skills and may soon be dismantled.

But in spite of the magnitude of these problems, *each of them can be addressed and solved*. This, and not a vindictive scapegoating campaign like Newt Gingrich's Contract with America, should form the basis of our nation's legislative agenda.

NO INDUSTRIALIZED NATION HAS AS GREAT A GAP BETWEEN RICH AND POOR AS THE UNITED STATES

The richest one percent of Americans now own 42 percent of the nation's wealth, compared with 19 percent in 1976. That top one percent own more than the bottom *90 percent*. Between 1983 and 1989, 62 percent of the increased wealth of this country went to the top one percent, and 99 percent of the increased wealth went to the top 20 percent. The CEOs of major American corporations now earn 170 times what their workers make, the largest gap between CEO and worker of any major nation. In 1982 there were twelve billionaires in the United States. Today there are 135.

Meanwhile, the past twenty years have seen declining or stagnant income for *80 percent* of all American families. In fact, adjusted for inflation, the average pay of four-fifths of American workers plummeted 16 percent in twenty years. The inflation-adjusted median income for young families with children— headed by persons younger than thirty—plunged 32 percent between 1973 and 1990. Twenty years ago, American workers were the best compensated in the world. Today, American workers rank thirteenth among industrialized nations in terms of compensation and benefits. In 1973, the average American worker earned $445 a week; twenty years later, that same worker was making $373 a week. And they are working harder for less money. U.S. workers put in about 200 more hours per year than West European workers, who typically obtain four- to five-week vacations, often legally mandated.

Americans at the lower end of the wage scale are now the lowest paid workers in the industrialized world. Eighteen percent of American workers with full-time jobs are paid so little that their wages do not enable them to live above the poverty level.

The majority of new jobs created in America today pay only $6.00 or $7.00 an hour, offer no health or retirement benefits, and no time off for sick leave or vacation. One-third of the nation's work force is now "contingent" labor, without any job security.

But enough statistics. The simple fact is that today's economy, which works very well for the super-rich, is not meeting the needs of ordinary Americans.

Reversing these obscene and terrifying trends is not as hard as the experts make out. The solution involves, among other things, talking about taxes. Have you ever wondered why the first words out of any Republican's mouth are always, "No new taxes"? The reason is that a progressive tax policy is the most efficient and powerful way to ensure that wealth is distributed more fairly. The Republicans and many Democrats are not in favor of an equitable distribution of wealth, though of course they never say outright that they favor inequality. They just repeat their mantra, "No new taxes."

To begin reversing the growing inequality in the distribution of wealth, we can rescind the tax breaks given to the rich over the last twenty years. From 1971 to 1981, the combined Social Security and income tax bills of median-income families shot up 329 percent, while the combined tax bills of individuals and families with income of more than $1 million fell 34 percent. Reagan, with the support of a Democratic Congress, cut the top federal tax rate for the richest Americans from 70 percent to 28 percent. Meanwhile, Carter and Reagan substantially raised the regressive Social Security tax for working Americans. From 1977 to 1990, the social security tax was raised nine times—an increase of 31 percent. In 1953, corporations contributed 33 percent of all tax dollars. Today, they contribute less than 10 percent. During the 1980s, some multibillion dollar corporations did not pay one penny in taxes.

As Citizens for Tax Justice has indicated, nine out of ten Americans would have paid *less* in federal taxes in 1992 if Congress had done nothing to "reform" the tax system since 1977. Yet, incredibly, the government would have brought in almost $70 billion *more* a year—a substantial portion of the federal deficit.

What is needed today is a reversal of the policy direction of the last twenty years and the development of a truly progressive tax system in the United States. At a time when this country is seeing a proliferation of millionaires and billionaires, the rich must start paying their fair share of taxes. To give President Clinton credit, his first budget in 1993 did precisely that. It raised taxes on the wealthy and lowered taxes for the working poor by increasing the earned income tax credit. But that was only a small step forward—one which he does not seem likely to repeat.

We need to establish a more progressive income tax. The more you earn, the more you pay. Not only is that a fair principle, but greater progressivity would lessen the inequities in income that currently afflict us. There is no reason that those who earn over $200,000 a year should not pay a significantly larger percentage of their income in taxes than they currently do. Of course, the greed of the wealthy knows no bounds. They and many of their conservative mouthpieces are even trying to sell the nation on a flat tax, allowing a billionaire to pay at the same rate as a mother of two earning $5.50 an hour in her service-sector job. That is precisely the *wrong* direction to take. We need to reaffirm the just principle that those who benefit the most economically from our society should pay the most to sustain it.

It is also time, high time, to establish a tax on wealth similar to those that exist in most European countries. Simply stated, a wealth tax would require the very wealthiest Americans, people worth millions of dollars, to pay taxes on their accumulated wealth, rather than enabling them to get ever richer without giving anything back to the society which makes their wealth possible. A tax on wealth could raise tens of billions of dollars a year.

We can also reverse the inequitable distribution of wealth by closing loopholes in corporate taxes. If we eliminated tax breaks for corporations, corporate subsidies, and other forms of corporate welfare, we could save $125 billion a year. Those savings could be applied to health care, education, social services—and to balancing the budget. By slashing special breaks for corporations, we could help working families immensely—and ordinary Americans would not have to pay a cent more in taxes.

Why don't the great majority of Americans elect a government that will look out for their interests and fight for a fairer distribution of wealth? We can only answer that question if we look the unpleasant truth straight in the eye. And the truth is that the fabric of American democracy is currently extremely fragile, and that the U.S. government as currently constituted does not represent the interests of ordinary citizens.

Although the corporate media doesn't discuss it too often, the facts are quite clear. In the presidential election of 1996, less than half of all eligible voters cast their ballots. Two years earlier, when the Gingrich-dominated Congress was elected, only 38 percent of Americans voted. This compares with over 70 percent participation in most other major industrialized countries. In South Africa, millions of black citizens waited patiently in line, some for as long as three days, to exercise their right to vote for the first time. Overall voter turnout figures tell only part of the story. Voting among the poor is almost nonexistent. Among different age groups, the young vote in lower numbers than any other group. Public cynicism about the democratic process has never been greater, and individual belief in the possibility of democratic change has never been more threatened.

What does this tell us about the health of democracy? Today, America is in danger of becoming an oligarchy.

An oligarchy is a form of government in which a small group of people hold power. It seems clear that a smaller and smaller group of citizens are determining our nation's future. The poor are disenfranchised, not by law, but in fact. The young think that voting has little to do with them or their prospects. Ordinary citizens have decided that the political process is likely to fail them, and so they vote in ever smaller numbers.

In recent elections, the concept of "one person, one vote" has been supplanted by the influence of big money. The more money you have, the more power you have. Some citizens participate by contributing hundreds of thousands of dollars to the politicians and parties of their choice. Most citizens contribute no money and do not vote. To paraphrase Orwell, some citizens are clearly a lot more equal than others.

It is in the interest of those who have great wealth and immense corporate power to weaken democracy. The less power the people have, the fewer checks there are on those who already control the American economy and its resources. The greater the belief that participation in the political process doesn't really make a difference, the more likely it is that people will give up hope that we can ever attain a just society and a decent standard of living.

Make no mistake about it: the wealthy and their political representatives are working hard to keep people away from the voting booths. They have vigorously opposed legislation that would make it easier for people to vote. They have corrupted campaign financing, so that citizens have lost faith in the political process. They have turned negative campaigning into a high art, with the result that huge numbers of voters demonstrate their disgust with gutter politics by refusing to vote on election day. They have begun the process of dismantling social programs so that citizens increasingly feel that government cannot and will not do anything to meet their needs.

What can we do to revitalize democracy? How can we bring tens of millions of Americans back into the political process?

SOME SIMPLE STEPS TO REINVIGORATING DEMOCRACY

Revitalizing the electoral process is, in some ways, a simple matter. If the goal is to get more people to vote—and that certainly should be one of our goals—then it is high time we establish automatic voter registration for every American who is eighteen or older. Given the growth of technology through the "information highway," a social security card or driver's license should be all that is required for voting. Same-day registration, allowing every American to register up until election day, would substantially increase voter turnout.

Similarly, we must make it more convenient for people to vote. We can open the polls, as is done in other nations, over a two- or three-day period—including at least one weekend day—so that working Americans will have more time to vote. Oregon has shown us another possible route: in that state, voting can be done by mail over a period of up to four weeks, and as a consequence voter turnout has risen.

But we need to do more than just increasing voter turnout. We must do a much better job in educating our citizens about the political process. It is time for our schools to offer young people an education for democracy. If our school curricula took the rights and duties of citizens as seriously as they do varsity football, home economics, and even study hall, young people would be far more likely to participate in the democratic process, and be better informed.

"But what about the damaging effect of money on the nation's elections?" I can hear you saying. And you are absolutely right: we will not reinvigorate democracy until we have thoroughgoing campaign finance reform. Not only do campaign finances currently pervert the political process by buying influence, but the existence of huge donations and the access they buy convinces many Americans—not erroneously—that voting is less important than money in determining national policy.

Given the fact that we have huge states like California and small states like Vermont, campaign finance reform on the national level can get a bit complicated, but some elements of *real* reform are clear. Most importantly, we must limit the amount of money that candidates can spend on an election. If less money were required to run successfully, the impact of big contributors would be reduced. And if there were reasonable campaign spending limits, it would no longer be possible to "buy" an election. Make no mistake: in the current situation, the candidate with the largest war chest will almost always be the victor.

How can we limit campaign spending? There are several alternatives. What we need, immediately, is a national debate about which path is the best to follow. We could provide public funding for campaigns, thereby setting limits on the amount of money that a candidate can spend. Or, as the Democrats proposed several years ago, we could provide matching public funds for every contribution of under, say, $200 a candidate receives. That way, huge donations that would no longer dominate campaign financing and the impact of ordinary citizens would be doubled. Or we could make free television time available, in sizable quantity, to every candidate. Television advertising is, after all, the largest expense in a campaign and the motor that drives the cost of campaigns higher and higher. We could, and should, restrict bundled contributions, "soft money," enormous individual donations garnered at $10,000-a-plate dinners, and "uncoordinated" independent expenditure advertising—all ways of allowing monied interests to buy influence by circumventing efforts to limit campaign spending.

Whatever course we take, we need to address these key requirements: capping the amount of money that can be spent, providing public funding, limiting private funding, encouraging small donations, and making television time available cheaply or at no cost. Our goal should be to get over 80 percent of our fellow citizens to vote, to ensure that votes and not money determine which direction our leaders take, and to increase dramatically our efforts to ensure that those who vote are well informed.

THE CORPORATE MASS MEDIA: AMERICA'S UNTOLD STORY

A knowledgeable and informed electorate is essential to a working democracy. We fall far short of that ideal. A principal source of the crisis in American democracy is the oligopoly—a handful of megacorporations—controlling the media, which ostensibly informs Americans about what is happening and what our political choices are. To say the least, the media is doing an horrendous job of providing Americans with what they need to know in order to be active participants in a vital democracy.

Americans get about 85 percent of their news from television.

Almost all of that comes through six major television networks. NBC is owned by General Electric, CBS by Westinghouse, ABC by Disney, and Fox by Rupert Murdoch, the right-wing billionaire. CNN was recently bought by Time-Warner, the world's largest entertainment conglomerate. "Public" television is also increasingly controlled by a wide variety of corporate interests.

The problem with television is not just what is reported but, more importantly, what is *not* reported. It's no accident that we get thousands of hours of discussion about the O. J. Simpson trial and almost no discussion about the growing gap between rich and poor or our regressive tax system. Why is it that there is massive coverage of airplane crashes, but almost no coverage of corporate disinvestment in the United States?

There are any number of business and Wall Street shows. But despite the fact that 15 million Americans are trade unionists, there isn't one national television program exclusively devoted to discussing the goals and problems of the trade union movement, and the needs of American workers. In fact, most Americans have never seen even one prime-time television show on the positive role that trade unions have played in protecting the lives of working Americans. And while extreme right wingers are regular guests on various talk shows, almost no progressive voices are heard on prime-time TV.

The most important "story" of the last twenty years has been the precipitous decline in the standard of living of America's working families. Television, which provides instantaneous coverage of earthquakes thousands of miles away, seems to have "missed" this issue.

The conflict of interest in corporate ownership of our major television networks is enormous. Let's take a brief look at General Electric, the nation's largest corporation, which owns the NBC television network.

General Electric makes billions of dollars producing weapons. So it is keenly interested in defense spending and questions of foreign policy. Additionally, General Electric has shipped thousands of American jobs overseas to take advantage of cheap labor. So it is keenly interested in NAFTA, GATT, MFN with China, and other issues shaping the trade policy of the United States. In the early 1980s, General Electric got away with paying absolutely nothing in federal taxes—and would like to be in the same position again. So it is keenly interested in federal tax policy. General Electric, with a long reputation as an anti-union corporation, constantly battles with workers. So it is keenly interested in federal labor policy.

General Electric contributed $100,000 to a PAC controlled by presidential candidate Bob Dole. In the past, it has contributed heavily to both political parties. So it is keenly interested in the effort to prevent campaign finance reform. General Electric invests billions of dollars in financial institutions. So it is keenly interested in banking and insurance regulations. General Electric has invested billions of dollars in the electronic media. So it is keenly interested in communications legislation. And these are just a few of the areas in which General Electric has a stake.

Is it possible that the enormous financial interests of the General Electric corporation influence the news and programming of NBC? Frankly, you'd have to be very naive to believe otherwise. But of course, it's not just General Electric. Recently, Disney bought ABC, Westinghouse bought CBS, and Time-Warner bought CNN. The *New York Times* bought the *Boston Globe*. Gannett Corporation buys every newspaper in sight. Rupert Murdoch owns Fox Broadcasting—and *TV Guide*, Twentieth Century–Fox, Harper-Collins publishers, and 150 newspapers and magazines in various countries.

Today, one of the greatest crises in American society is that the ownership of the media is concentrated in fewer and fewer hands. Those hands are, as a result, more powerful than ever before. Needless to say, there is not a lot of discussion in the corporate media of this issue. Just how concentrated is media ownership? Ben Bagdikian has written a very important book called *The Media Monopoly* in which he relates that:

- Eighty percent of the daily newspapers in this country were independently owned at the close of World War II. Today, 80 percent of daily newspapers are owned by corporate chains. Just eleven companies control more than half the nation's daily newspaper circulation.
- Ninety-eight percent of the daily newspapers in America have a monopoly as the only paper in town.
- Although there are more than 11,000 magazines published in the United States, today just two corporations control more than half of all magazine revenues.
- Although there are 11,000 local cable television systems, only seven companies have a majority of the 60 million cable TV subscribers.
- Three companies own more than half the television business. Four companies own more than half the movie business. Five companies rake in more than half of all book revenues.

Limiting this concentration of power over the media, which allows a few giant corporations to determine much of what we learn, presents a very difficult dilemma—and I do not have all the solutions. While we want to address forthrightly the problem of corporate control of the media, we do not want to tread on two of our most precious freedoms: freedom of speech and freedom of the press. But there are reforms we can make which do not impinge on these freedoms.

THREE POSITIVE STEPS WE CAN TAKE TO DEVELOP
A FREER AND MORE RESPONSIVE MEDIA

The first step we should take is vigorous antitrust prosecution. In the early years of this century, when the railroads had a stranglehold over the crop sales of midwestern farmers, Congress passed legislation to bust the trusts and limit their monopoly. There is an equally pressing—perhaps even more pressing—reason for us to pass media antitrust legislation today: the current monopoly over thought and expression is clearly a serious danger to our fragile democracy.

A second step would be to provide significantly greater funding for public radio and public television. Greater funding would wean public broadcasting from its dependence on corporate advertising, which it euphemistically calls "underwriting." And greater funding would allow public radio and television stations to proliferate. With more stations, public broadcasting could accommodate an even greater diversity of public needs.

Third, the Federal Communications Commission should reestablish two principles that formerly served this country well: the public service requirement and the fairness doctrine. Every television and radio station should once again be required to devote a meaningful percentage of its programming to public service broadcasting. The public, after all, owns the airwaves through which signals are broadcast, and the rights-of-way in which cables are strung. And every television and radio station should once again have to follow the fairness doctrine: those with opposing views should have the right to respond to viewpoints expressed on the station.

Will these initiatives—antitrust prosecutions, public funding for public broadcasting, and a strong FCC role—reverse the current monopolization of those "industries" which inform us as to what is happening, what the world looks like, and how we can change that world? Unhappily, I doubt it. The mass media is too lucrative and too important in maintaining the dominance of monied interests to be reined in that easily. But these initiatives would be important first steps toward curbing corporate control and moving toward a society in which information flows more freely.

Let's suppose for a moment that we could open up the media to a much greater diversity of opinion and ideas, establish a more vibrant and well-informed democracy, and move toward a fairer distribution of wealth. Would the great work of building the America we dream of be accomplished?

Hell, no. The work would only have begun.

Let me put the progressive agenda as plainly as I can. Not until there is good, decent-paying work for every American can we be satisfied that the nation's promise is being fulfilled.

DOWNSIZING, JOB FLIGHT, AND THE WAR ON WORKERS: THE RACE TO THE BOTTOM

I am old enough to remember the presidency of Lyndon Johnson, when the government fought a "war on poverty." In recent years that war has been transformed by representatives of both major parties into a war on the poor. More important yet, but less reported, is that in the years since Ronald Reagan was elected president, corporate America has waged war against this nation's workers.

We live in an era of "downsizing." Well-paid workers are laid off in huge numbers, while the executives who axe their jobs earn enormous bonuses. Those workers are often replaced by what is called "contingent" labor. Every day over 35 million Americans go to work as temporary or contract labor. That's one out of every three workers. As an indication of what kind of society we are becoming, two out of every three jobs created in the private sector during the 1980s were temporary, not permanent. In fact, the ranks of contingent workers are growing so rapidly that some estimate they will outstrip permanent full-time workers within the next ten years. Manpower, Inc., is now the largest private sector company in the United States, employing some 600,000 workers.

The consequences of downsizing and hiring temps are devastating for American workers. So is another major strategy used to boost corporate profits: reducing labor costs by shipping American jobs beyond our nation's borders. In today's global economy, the major American export is our jobs. Why pay American workers a living wage when in Mexico workers can be hired for a dollar an hour? In China the hourly wage is as low as twenty cents.

We can see the consequences of this war on workers. As the number of contingent workers has grown and millions of jobs have been shipped overseas, the number of full-time employees at the Fortune 500 companies has plunged dramatically, from 19 percent of all American workers twenty years ago to less than 10 percent today. Between 1979 and 1994, just ten of the most prominent Fortune 500 companies (including Ford, AT&T, General Electric, and ITT) eliminated more than one million decent-paying manufacturing jobs at the very same time that many of them were expanding their investments and creating jobs in China, Mexico, and other low-wage countries.

The greatest job growth has been in the service sector, which pays poorly and often provides no benefits. More than three out of every four jobs created in the 1980s were in the low-paying retail trade and service industries.

People are desperate for jobs, but all too often decent-paying jobs are not available. People work longer hours for less. Many people work two, even three jobs to keep afloat. The bond between employer and worker—do good work and your job will be safe—has eroded. Without economic security, the American dream is crumbling.

Let me be blunt. The government must accept responsibility for helping to create an economy that provides work for and ensures the economic well being of all its citizens.

WHAT WE NEED TO REBUILD THE MIDDLE CLASS AND REDUCE POVERTY: DECENT-PAYING JOBS

I know it is not fashionable to speak of what government is supposed to do for people. We live in an era of "tough love," of the survival of the fittest, when each of us is supposed to do everything for ourselves. Today, a national industrial policy is considered an anachronism by the apologists for corporate America, even though those same apologists never have any quarrel with massive government efforts to assist "free-market capitalism" or establish "free trade" as our industrial policy. We don't hear the major corporations hollering about "government intervention" when the Federal Reserve Board makes decisions which lead to increased unemployment. While there is a rush to cut welfare for the poor, corporate welfare is vigorously defended by the wealthiest people in America. We seem to have socialism for the rich and rugged individualism for the poor.

Frankly, much of our economic policy is a disgrace, designed to benefit the wealthy few at the expense of the average worker. We have government "payoffs for layoffs" in the defense industry, tax breaks for downsizing, and trade policies like NAFTA, GATT, and MFN with China which make it easy for corporations to ship jobs overseas.

It is time we developed an economic program that works for ordinary people, and that rebuilds and expands the middle class. There is no reason why, in the richest nation in the world, every American should not have a job that sustains a decent living. There is much that government can do to make this happen.

First, government can once again level the playing field between capital and labor. Trade unions in the United States are the main reason we have an eight-hour day, a five-day work week, employer-provided health benefits and pension plans, and occupational safety and child labor legislation. Unions led the effort for Medicare, Medicaid, affordable housing, and many other programs enjoyed today by millions of Americans. Strong unions were the reason why, twenty years ago, American workers led the world in terms of wages and benefits. And not coincidentally, today American workers rank thirteenth in the world in terms of wages and benefits.

In 1954, almost one of every three employees belonged to a labor union. Today, less than one in six workers is unionized. This stunning drop in union membership is no historical accident. For decades the federal government, through labor legislation and the National Labor Relations Board, acted as an umpire to maintain a level playing field between workers and management. But President Reagan's union-busting posture in the air traffic controllers' strike, and a generation of NLRB members hostile to the rights and needs of working people, have given one advantage after another to management. The possibility of workers "winning" a strike is almost unthinkable today: unions are struggling just to preserve past gains. Almost everywhere, corporations are in control and unions on the defensive, if not in actual retreat.

We need to pass labor legislation that ensures equity in contract negotiations between workers and management. Developing fair labor legislation is not hard to do—legislation to achieve the same purpose was passed during the New Deal. Such legislation would ban the permanent replacement of striking workers. It would allow unions to be certified by simple card check: if a majority of employees in a bargaining unit join a union, the union automatically represents them. It would mandate compulsory arbitration of first contracts if a stalemate between labor and management occurred, since refusing to negotiate in good faith is one of management's main tactics. It would repeal prohibitions against strikes and secondary boycotts.

Real labor law reform would also strengthen and expand the enforcement powers of the National Labor Relations Board. All of these provisions sound technical, but their impact would be enormous. They would once again establish "rules" giving workers the opportunity to fight their own battles—for decent wages, for fringe benefits, for safe working conditions—without being fired or stalemated or isolated.

But providing fair opportunities for the trade union movement is not enough. The government must protect the lowest paid workers, men and women who in most instances are not unionized. For working people, the new global economy is all too often a race to the bottom. The wage in China or Guatemala or Poland is increasingly the wage against which American workers must compete.

In the face of this problem, the least we can do is raise the minimum wage to a *living* wage. Last year, the president and Congress took a step in this direction. But it was not enough. The minimum wage should be set at a rate sufficient to support a family of three above the poverty line. In a country where CEOs earn

170 times what the average factory worker earns—where CEO pay has increased 514 percent in twenty-four years, while workers' pay failed to keep up with inflation—we can do no less.

What about the hemorrhage of jobs abroad? Can we do anything about the disastrous effects of the global economy on American workers? According to the experts, no. But the experts echo the message their employers want us to hear.

We need to address the issue of trade forthrightly and understand that our current trade policy is an unmitigated disaster. Our current record-breaking merchandise trade deficit of $112 billion is costing us over 2 million decent-paying jobs. President Clinton, like Bush and Reagan before him, is supporting a trade policy that protects the interests and profits of multinational corporations, while compromising the interests of American workers. NAFTA, GATT, and Most Favored Nation status with China must be repealed, and a new trade policy developed.

Let's look at some of the components of a sensible trade policy. First, we must recognize that trade is not an end in itself. The function of American trade policy must be to improve the standard of living of the American people. America's trade policy must be radically changed, by committing ourselves to a "fair" rather than "free" trade policy. This means developing and supporting legislation that safeguards American manufacturing jobs and cuts our enormous balance of payments deficit. Companies should be encouraged to invest *here*, in the United States. Currently, this is not the case. There are all sorts of incentives, ranging from direct payments of subsidies to tax breaks to tax loopholes, which encourage corporations to ship American jobs beyond our borders. It is time to tighten our tax laws, eliminate corporate welfare, and penalize corporations that eliminate American workers so that they can replace them with low-paid workers overseas.

It is important that we use our leverage as the world's largest and most lucrative market to protect American jobs. Reagan, Bush, and Clinton have all supported policies that opened our markets wide to foreign products, asking far too little in exchange. At the same time, we must explore new economic models here at home. We need to develop more worker-owned businesses. We must move from agribusiness to sustainable agriculture, not only for the sake of our economy but also for our environment. We must once again insist that it is at least as important for businesses to meet human needs as it is for them to augment their bottom line.

But reforming the private sector is not enough. The government has a very large role to play in rebuilding our physical and social infrastructure, and when it accepts that role, it will create millions of new jobs at the same time.

LET'S REBUILD AMERICA: GOVERNMENT HAS AN IMPORTANT ROLE TO PLAY

Let's face it, under heavy pressure from Republicans and conservative Democrats, the nation has not paid attention to the things government is *supposed* to do. No private company can safeguard the quality of our drinking water. No multinational corporation can provide us with decent roads and inexpensive mass transportation. No amount of charity will house all the homeless, feed all the hungry, or protect the personal safety of all Americans. The government has a very large role to play in making the world we inhabit livable and safe.

Rebuilding our physical infrastructure means repairing our aging roads and bridges, cleaning up toxic waste dumps, constructing sewage treatment facilities, restoring our schools and libraries and equipping them with computers so that all Americans can enter the information age. It means building affordable housing so millions do not have to pay exorbitant rents to live with peeling lead paint and substandard plumbing in crime-infested areas. It means establishing fast, reasonably priced mass transportation in and between our cities.

Rebuilding our social infrastructure is also necessary. It is high time we put more cops on the beat, had more trained teachers in the schools and more nurses in our health care clinics. High-quality and affordable day care should be available in every community. We need more inspectors to monitor the quality of our meat, the potential dangers of our pharmaceuticals, the safety of our airplanes. We require more affordable nursing homes for the elderly and job training for young men and women, together with retraining for workers who have lost their jobs.

CAN WE DO ALL OF THIS AND MOVE TOWARD A BALANCED BUDGET?

Won't all of this cost money? Yes. Isn't it foolish to spend money rebuilding our infrastructure when we have a huge national debt? No. Because there is one final way to build and expand the middle class: we must make radical changes in our national priorities.

If we cut military spending and corporate welfare, we would have more than enough money to meet America's needs. This nation currently spends $260 billion a year on defense, even though the Cold War is over. (We are spending $100 billion to defend Western Europe and Japan against nonexistent enemies.) And this $260 billion does not count the $30 billion spent annually on intelligence or the $20 billion in defense-related expenditures hidden away in our federal spending on energy.

Combine a sizeable chunk of that $310 billion we spend on defense-related matters with the $125 billion we spend each year on corporate welfare, and there is adequate money to rebuild our infrastructure and meet the pressing needs of Americans. (We can do this and still have the strongest military in the world.) And this is before we increase revenues by instituting a more progressive income tax that requires the wealthy to pay their fair share, and before we establish a wealth tax on millionaires.

We do not have to cut back on nutrition programs for poor children, Medicare, Medicaid, Social Security, and other vitally needed programs to balance the budget. We can move toward a balanced budged and significantly increase funding in a wide range of areas which will improve life for the American people and, in the process, create millions of decent-paying jobs. We can do it if we have the courage to put the people's interests before corporate interests, and to make fundamental changes in our national priorities.

In rebuilding America, we need to concentrate in particular on two issues that both the president and Congress have failed to address adequately: health care and education.

HEALTH CARE FOR ALL THROUGH A SINGLE-PAYER SYSTEM

The United States is the only industrialized nation, besides South Africa, that does not have a national health care system. In every other developed nation, health care is a right and not a privilege.

After Clinton's failure to reform our health care system, we ended up with a cumbersome, profit-driven, consumer-unfriendly, inefficient health care delivery system dominated by insurance companies. And I mean *dominated*.

Managed care pretends to be efficient. That is because it cuts back on health care for many of us, and rations it for the rest. It is a sign of how bad things have become that the last Congress had to pass legislation allowing a mother to stay in the hospital for at least twenty-four hours after giving birth. The insurance companies had decided that if drive-by banking worked, then it seemed a reasonable bet that drive-by deliveries would work, too.

But in their well-publicized initiatives to reduce costs, not one single insurance company has proposed reducing their profits from "managing" health care. The solution to our health care crisis—80 million uninsured or underinsured—is not difficult to find. We need a single-payer system administered at the state level. Currently, we spend one-quarter of all medical expenses on paperwork and bureaucracy. By eliminating most of the paperwork involved in health care, single-payer systems produce remarkable savings. In the United States, those savings would be enough to insure every single American. We not only would all be covered, we could go back to having freedom of choice in picking our doctors. And this would cost no more than the nation is currently spending on medical care.

Universal medical care would improve the quality of life for tens of millions of Americans. It would also be a major step toward reaffirming that through the development of a rational, nonprofit, cost-effective health care system, government in a democratic society can meet the basic needs of its people.

THE COMING CRISIS IN EDUCATION

Conservatives are smart. They know that all across America there is discontent with our educational system. Rather than improve our schools and expand educational opportunities, however, they plan to exploit that discontent to dismantle democracy still further. The vehicle for this dismantling is known as "the voucher system."

The right wants to provide every parent with a voucher—a sort of publicly funded check, allowing them to purchase the education of their choice. Wealthy parents can use the money to reduce their tuition costs at prep schools. Religious parents can send their children to parochial schools—under this scheme, the separation of church and state will be abandoned. Meanwhile, the public schools will get correspondingly less funding. And the public schools, of course, will be where poor and working-class children will be educated. Their educational horizons will contract and their alienation from the American mainstream will widen.

No longer will society have a stake in seeing that every young person learns about American history, about our traditions of dissent and tolerance. Our most democratic institution—the one place in the nation where rich and poor, white and black, native-born and immigrant came together in a mutual enterprise—will cease to exist.

More ominous yet, once the direct link between government and public education is eliminated, it will be very easy to cut back significantly on support for education. Certainly, if the right wing can push cutbacks in welfare that will add another million children to the poverty rolls and cutbacks in Medicaid that will deny health insurance to millions of low-income kids, there is no reason to believe that major cuts in government support for public education will be far behind.

These are real dangers. But once again, there are things we can do to stop them coming to pass. We need to reaffirm our support for quality public education and the right of all children to get the best education possible. We can increase federal funding to improve the quality of our public schools. At the same time, we would be relieving some of the burden of the regressive property tax from the shoulders of the nation's working people and the middle class. Much of the anger at public education today stems from the fact that it is largely funded through very regressive taxes.

We can insist that it is the right of every young person—and every adult—to pursue an advanced education by ensuring that adequate funding is available for scholarships, college loans, and work study. We can provide new funds to expand Head Start programs. If we provide funding for day care centers, we can guarantee a solid base of early education to every child while at the same time really supporting the hard-pressed American family. We can transform President Clinton's embattled and experimental Teach for America program into a massive domestic Peace Corps that would transform every classroom in the nation.

TOWARD A PROGRESSIVE AND DEMOCRATIC FUTURE

What I have outlined here is a basic program for rebuilding American society. But there is much more to be done.

First, we have to rid the country of any vestige of racism, sexism, and homophobia. I am convinced that providing decent jobs for all and a better education for the young will be the linchpins of that effort. Too often liberals believe that being "against" prejudice is all that is required to bring about a more just and equitable society. Not true. Only when every man and woman has a *place* in American society—and this means, I believe, a decent-paying job—will we begin to eradicate the hatreds that are based on jealousy and insecurity. And only when every American is economically secure enough to stand up to insults of any sort will all Americans be free of the power of prejudice to define them.

We must be vigilant about protecting our environment. Economically, it makes no sense to degrade our soil, air, and water in the interest of quick profits, only to spend billions ten years from now to remedy the mess we've made. The enormous cost of cleaning up existing toxic waste sites reveals that pollution is only cost-deferment.

In health terms, environmental degradation makes us far sicker than we would otherwise be, and reduces the quality of everyday life. Effective health care begins with prevention, and preserving a liveable environment is one of the best medical investments we can make.

It is not as if acting as careful stewards of our environment is inefficient, as corporations so often claim. Safeguarding the environment creates new industries, new jobs, and new opportunities for workers to make a decent living. And it ensures that future generations will not have to bear the cost—in money, in illness—of our folly.

There is much more that this country needs. We should have a foreign policy guided by the principles of freedom and justice. We should maintain a firm commitment to a woman's right to equality in all areas of life. We need to face up to the root causes of crime and drug addiction, and the escalating circulation of guns. We should support the arts, rebuild communities, and honor our veterans. We must give our children hope and our elders the respect they have earned.

I am convinced that if we can muster the courage to work together, we can do what needs to be done. Building a progressive future requires building a progressive movement. And that means that in every community in America citizens must stand up and say, "We believe in economic justice for all. We will no longer accept a situation in which the wealthy and powerful have undue influence. We are going to change this nation, and we are going to start by doing what needs to be done from the grassroots on up."

It is time, in other words, for you to begin doing in your community what many of us have begun doing in Vermont: take a stand, organize, and use the political process to build democracy all over again.

If Americans—young and old, black and white, male and female, Hispanic and Asian, straight and gay, veteran and pacifist, worker and student and retiree—join together in a progressive politics at the grassroots level, it will surely spread outward and eventually reshape the United States into the greatest society that has ever existed.

As we move toward a progressive and democratic future, I am sustained by the hope that one day, when millions of Americans are actively involved in the political process and are standing up for their rights and those of their children, a majority of the members of Congress will then represent the interests of ordinary people, and not the rich. When that day comes, we will no longer be outsiders in the House.

That House, and this country, will then belong to all of us. And that's the way it should be.